AMERICAN IMPERIALISM

BAAS Paperbacks

Published titles

African American Visual Arts
Celeste-Marie Bernier
The American Short Story since 1950
Kasia Boddy
American Imperialism: The Territorial Expansion of the United States, 1783–2013
Adam Burns
The Cultures of the American New West
Neil Campbell
The Open Door Era: United States Foreign Policy in the Twentieth Century
Michael Patrick Cullinane and Alex Goodall
Gender, Ethnicity and Sexuality in Contemporary American Film
Jude Davies and Carol R. Smith
The United States and World War II: The Awakening Giant
Martin Folly
The Sixties in America: History, Politics and Protest
M. J. Heale
Religion, Culture and Politics in the Twentieth-Century United States
Mark Hulsether
The Civil War in American Culture
Will Kaufman
The United States and European Reconstruction, 1945–1960
John Killick
American Exceptionalism
Deborah L. Madsen
American Autobiography
Rachael McLennan
The American Landscape
Stephen F. Mills
Slavery and Servitude in North America, 1607–1800
Kenneth Morgan

The Civil Rights Movement
Mark Newman
The Twenties in America: Politics and History
Niall Palmer
American Theatre
Theresa Saxon
The Vietnam War in History, Literature and Film
Mark Taylor
Contemporary Native American Literature
Rebecca Tillett
Jazz in American Culture
Peter Townsend
The New Deal
Fiona Venn
Animation and America
Paul Wells
Political Scandals in the USA
Robert Williams

Forthcoming titles

The American Photo-Text, 1930–1960
Caroline Blinder
The Beats: Authorship, Legacies
Robert A. Lee
American Detective Fiction
Ruth Hawthorn
Black Nationalism in American History: From the Nineteenth Century to the Million Man March
Mark Newman
Staging Transatlantic Relations, 1930–1960
Theresa Saxon
American Poetry since 1900
Nick Selby
The US Graphic Novel
Paul Williams

edinburghuniversitypress.com/series/baas

American Imperialism

The Territorial Expansion of the
United States, 1783–2013

ADAM BURNS

EDINBURGH
University Press

Edinburgh University Press is one of the leading university presses in the UK. We publish academic books and journals in our selected subject areas across the humanities and social sciences, combining cutting-edge scholarship with high editorial and production values to produce academic works of lasting importance. For more information visit our website: edinburghuniversitypress.com

© Adam Burns, 2017

Edinburgh University Press Ltd
The Tun – Holyrood Road, 12(2f) Jackson's Entry, Edinburgh EH8 8PJ

Typeset in 10/12 Adobe Sabon by
IDSUK (DataConnection) Ltd

A CIP record for this book is available from the British Library

ISBN 978 1 4744 0213 2 (hardback)
ISBN 978 1 4744 0215 6 (webready PDF)
ISBN 978 1 4744 0214 9 (paperback)
ISBN 978 1 4744 0216 3 (epub)

The right of Adam Burns to be identified as the author of this work has been asserted in accordance with the Copyright, Designs and Patents Act 1988, and the Copyright and Related Rights Regulations 2003 (SI No. 2498).

Contents

	Figures	vi
	Acknowledgements	viii
	Introduction: Defining an Empire	1
1	Atlantic to Pacific (1783–1893)	8
2	Heading Northwards (1812–1903)	30
3	Leaving the Continent (1817–90)	50
4	A Two-Ocean Empire (1890–98)	70
5	Spanish Plunder (1898–1917)	92
6	An Empire among Equals (1899–1917)	113
7	Occupation over Annexation (1912–73)	136
8	Continuing Imperialism (1940–2013)	159
	Conclusion	180
	Bibliography	182
	Index	209

Figures

Many thanks to the Perry-Castañeda Library Map Collection, University of Texas Libraries (https://www.lib.utexas.edu/maps/), from which all of the following public domain maps were taken. The images have been cropped and re-coloured from the originals.

Fig. 1.1 Map of Colonial North America (1989), from *American Military History*, United States Army Center of Military History, available at: http://www.lib.utexas.edu/maps/historical/colonial_1689-1783.jpg (accessed 31 August 2016)

Fig. 1.2 Westward Expansion, 1815–1845 (1989), from *American Military History*, United States Army Center of Military History, available at: http://www.lib.utexas.edu/maps/historical/west_expansion_1815-1845.jpg (accessed 31 August 2016)

Fig. 1.3 Admission of States and Territorial Acquisition (n.d.), US Bureau of the Census, available at: http://www.lib.utexas.edu/maps/united_states/territory.jpg (accessed 31 August 2016)

Fig. 3.1 Central America and the Caribbean (Reference Map) (2013), CIA, available at: http://www.lib.utexas.edu/maps/americas/central_america_ref_2013.pdf (accessed 31 August 2016)

Fig. 4.1 US and Outlying Areas, 1970 (1970), from *The National Atlas of the United States of America*, A. C. Gerlach (ed.), Washington, DC: US Department of the Interior, Geological Survey, available at: http://www.lib.utexas.edu/maps/united_states/us_terr_1970.jpg (accessed 31 August 2016)

Fig. 5.1 Philippines (Small Map) (2015), CIA, available at: http://www.lib.utexas.edu/maps/cia15/philippines_sm_2015.gif (accessed 31 August 2016)

FIGURES   vii

Fig. 6.1 American Samoa (Small Map) (2015), CIA, available at: http://www.lib.utexas.edu/maps/cia15/american_samoa_sm_2015.gif (accessed 31 August 2016)

Fig. 6.2 Panama (Small Map) (2015), CIA, available at: http://www.lib.utexas.edu/maps/cia15/panama_sm_2015.gif (accessed 31 August 2016)

Fig. 6.3 US Virgin Islands (Small Map) (2015), CIA, available at: http://www.lib.utexas.edu/maps/cia15/virgin_islands_sm_2015.gif (accessed 31 August 2016)

Fig. 8.1 Northern Mariana Islands (Small Map) (2015), CIA, available at: http://www.lib.utexas.edu/maps/cia15/northern_mariana_islands_sm_2015.gif (accessed 31 August 2016)

Fig. 8.2 Arctic Region (Political) (2012), CIA, available at: http://www.lib.utexas.edu/maps/islands_oceans_poles/arctic_region_pol_2012.pdf (accessed 31 August 2016)

Acknowledgements

As with any extended writing project, I was keen to have as many people pass judgement on my work as possible before letting it out into the public domain. Special thanks must firstly go to the wonderful American historians at the University of Edinburgh who so generously gave up their time to read draft chapters and provide invaluable feedback: Frank Cogliano, Fabian Hilfrich, Rhodri Jeffreys-Jones and Robert Mason. I would also like to thank Julie Burns, Charles Conquest and Brian Greenwood for reading my draft chapters to ensure the volume worked as a whole. I am most grateful to the libraries of the University of Leicester and University of Bristol, whose online and printed materials have proved vital in making this book possible. Finally, I would like to express my gratitude to the tireless series editors Emily West and Martin Halliwell, the reviewers of my initial proposal, and Michelle Houston and Adela Rauchova at EUP, without whom this book would have likely remained unwritten.

Introduction:
Defining an Empire

'American imperialism' is a term that is often used by both proponents and critics of US foreign relations around the world today.[1] However, a universally accepted definition of the term does not exist, and this volume does not seek to attempt the arduous or ill-fated task of providing one. Although the historiography of the term is discussed synoptically later, it is useful to provide a working definition. Historian Paul MacDonald critiques 'narrow' definitions of empire – those that focus on 'political sovereignty' that is overt, explicit and durable – and points to the fact that even when one excludes informal or diffuse modes of political power, it is often difficult to ascertain whether one state has assumed political sovereignty over another.[2] Into this latter category, MacDonald puts more difficult-to-place examples such as protectorates, military occupations, and foreign base agreements.[3] This book takes the very broadest approach to the narrowest definition of 'American imperialism', including the overt, explicit and durable assertions of political sovereignty alongside the more difficult-to-place examples.

Whether or not one deems it a useful term, the United States has certainly been imperialist in the past. Almost all historians would accept that the United States had an 'imperialist moment' at the end of the nineteenth century when, in the wake of the Spanish-American War of 1898, it annexed far-flung territories but withheld full admission to the union. However, agreement beyond this is difficult to find. Some trace US imperialism all the way back to the earliest continental expansion, the subjugation of Native Americans and the ideology of Manifest Destiny which spoke of a divinely mandated mission for the United States in expanding from the Atlantic to the Pacific.[4] Others trace it forward to the present day, including the proliferation of US military bases overseas and

I

the United States' still unequal relationship with many of its insular possessions where, for example, Puerto Ricans can help choose the Democratic and Republican candidates for the US presidency, but not actually vote for the president.[5]

This exploration of US territorial expansion, ranging from its earliest days to the present day, aims to allow readers to form their own opinions about the story of American imperialism. Here, the relatively uncontested examples of US imperialism, such as that seen in the Philippines between 1898 and 1946, are brought together alongside less commonly identified cases, such as the US occupation of Japan after the Second World War, and cases of unrealised imperial ambition, such as in Liberia and Canada. This volume additionally seeks to balance the coverage of US imperialism between places more widely written about, such as Cuba, and those instances that rarely merit more than a line or two in general volumes, for example the US Virgin Islands or American Samoa. Finally, the following chapters spend a relatively equal amount of time on the period before 1898, the Spanish-American War period itself, and the years that followed, in contrast to other volumes that often focus on only one or two of these periods without seeking to explore the whole span of US imperial history.[6]

This volume does not seek to include within its exploration of 'American imperialism' what most scholars would deem 'informal imperialism', be it economic domination, cultural hegemony or other varieties that do not require some assertion of formal political sovereignty or, at the very least, military occupation. This is not to say that other definitions of American imperialism are not valid, but they are beyond the remit of this study. What is explored here is the history of the United States as a nation that has been an empire from the start. It spent decades expanding this empire, first in North America and then overseas, and even in the present maintains a strategic territorial presence across the globe.

The literature on American imperialism, especially when one accepts the full variety of its definitions and forms, is vast and has grown exponentially in the last few decades. As Alyosha Goldstein noted in a recent edited collection on the topic, since 9/11, 'debates and discussions on U.S. empire have become ubiquitous throughout scholarly and popular forums'.[7] The resulting literature on the US and its projection of imperial power almost always includes a historiographical section that provides an overview of certain key volumes, by or against which the authors define themselves.⁸ What follows here is a short overview of the most important shifts in the historiography over the last century.

Most overviews of this topic begin with *A Diplomatic History of the United States*, the 1936 work of historian Samuel Flagg Bemis, which is the paradigmatic 'traditionalist' interpretation of American imperialism. Bemis's so-called 'aberration thesis' suggested that the imperial moment which followed the Spanish-American War of 1898 was both accidental and all-but-unique in US history, an idea promulgated by scholars such as Julius Pratt and Ernest May in subsequent years.⁹ The first major revisionist turn came with the New Left (Wisconsin) school of the 1950s and early 1960s, including historians such as William Appleman Williams and Walter LaFeber, who saw 1898 not as an aberration, but as the culmination of the economic development of the United States in the nineteenth century.¹⁰ The revisionists brought US imperialism to the forefront of academic interest and controversy but, although they expanded the roots of US imperialism to well before 1898, they approached American imperialism as something broadly informal and economic in nature, with the inevitable exception of the 1898 period.¹¹

In the early 1980s, historians such as Richard Drinnon and Walter Williams examined the similarities between the conquest of the American West and the imperialism of 1898 and beyond, looking in particular at ethnicity and parallels in the subjugation of native peoples.¹² Indeed, where it is easy to see Native American relations with the US and its citizens as domestic history, as scholarship since the late 1980s has increasingly noted, it should perhaps be considered more accurately as part of US foreign relations since 'these relations took place in an international arena devoid of a superior authority'.¹³ In more recent decades, an acceptance that the roots of US imperialism lie in the Revolutionary era has grown. A good example of such an approach is Walter Nugent's *Habits of Empire* (2008), which aims to give a continuous history of American imperialism from the end of the Revolutionary War to more recent times. Nugent's work spends the vast majority of its time on the period prior to 1898, arguing that tying together this initial phase of US imperialism with later phases was his primary goal.¹⁴ At the other end of the chronological spectrum, historian Niall Ferguson, in his 2005 paperback *Colossus: The Rise and Fall of the American Empire*, calls the United States in the period of the early twenty-first century an 'empire in denial', but an empire nonetheless. One of Ferguson's main aims is to present the United States as a nation that is, and always has been, an empire.[15] Unlike Nugent, Ferguson focuses mostly on the post-1898 period, and usefully ties examples explored here (including the occupations of Germany and Japan) to the post-9/11 interventions in the Middle East. These authors, along with the many other scholars cited here, continued to fuel and expand the debate over American imperialism among both academic and popular readerships up to the present day.

This book analyses a broad range of such specialist secondary literature to provide a clear sense of the disputes that exist to this day regarding the course of American imperial history. In addition to this, it draws upon a variety of primary source material to add depth and colour to its evaluation, such as political speeches and contemporaneous journals and newspapers. Newspapers were crucial in disseminating both pro- and anti-imperialist messages across the United States and, as such, are sources used here to help illustrate the arguments that punctuate debates over American imperialism. For example, in the late 1890s, powerful editors such as William Randolph Hearst and Joseph Pulitzer used their New York-based newspapers to call for intervention in the ongoing Spanish-Cuban conflict, if largely to increase newspaper circulation.[16] During this same period, hundreds of anti-imperialist politicians and private US citizens used newspapers, pamphlets and magazines to spread their views to a more general audience.[17] Combined, this mix of engagement with secondary and primary materials helps to emphasise the variety and complexity that continue to make the history of American imperialism such an intriguing subject.[18]

The following chapters are organised in a broadly chronological manner, with each chapter divided into thematic subsections, most of which are geographical in nature. In these subsections, where appropriate, the tale of US imperialism is explored beyond the broader chronological boundaries of the chapter as a whole. The overall aim is to provide an accessible introduction to American imperialism, narrowly defined, but broadly exemplified. In doing so, this volume seeks to bring back together what are too often dealt with as the separate parts of the history of American imperialism.

Chapters 1 and 2 explore the continental expansion of the United States, taking the annexation of former European imperial territories and/or Native American lands to be the earliest form of

US empire-building. Chapter 3 considers the same time period as these early chapters, but serves to illuminate some frequently overlooked early signs of imperial interest overseas. The colonisation of Liberia and US designs on Cuba, for example, provide interesting precedents for the discussions and debates over imperialism that would re-emerge in the 1890s. The emphasis on overseas imperialism continues into Chapters 4 and 5, which focus on the era widely regarded as the least contentious period of 'American imperialism': the series of annexations of overseas island territories that took place before and after the Spanish-American War of 1898. Chapter 4 additionally explores the debates of the era, from the motivations for the war itself, through disagreements over the subsequent annexations of the former Spanish overseas possessions, to the rise and decline of the American anti-imperialist movement.

Chapter 6 considers annexations that took place in the years following the Spanish-American War but were not a direct result of it. These later annexations show that formal imperialism did not end with the Spanish-American War, and illuminate the rising importance of 'preclusive imperialism', the idea that the US should annex territories at least partially to keep them out of enemy hands. Chapter 7 deals with medium-to-long term 'occupation' of territories rather than annexation. Though the long-term Caribbean occupations of the early twentieth century are frequently discussed alongside the post-1898 annexations, the medium-to-long term occupations of Germany and Japan after the Second World War are not. However, this book sees the evolution towards occupations (rather than annexations) from the early 1900s to the mid-century as the precursor of post-1950s foreign policy. Shorter-term and often less direct 'occupations' have been more commonplace since the Second World War, but there are many important parallels with earlier forms of direct imperial rule. The occupations of Germany and Japan provided a far more planned and overt assertion of sovereignty than later occupations, and were a template for US interventions such as that in Iraq from 2003. Chapter 8 concludes the book by looking at examples of how a more formal imperialist drive still endures into the twenty-first century. From overseas bases to claims over the Arctic, the United States has not entirely drawn back from the formal imperialism it followed in the previous centuries.

Notes

1. To clarify, this volume explores the imperialism of the United States. The term 'American imperialism' is used in the title simply because it is what many academics, as well as worldwide media, continue to use to refer to the United States' imperialist policies (see discussion by Immerman, *Empire for Liberty*, p. 3). Though, generally speaking, this volume uses the term United States (or US) throughout, where possible, in places the lack of a malleable adjectival description for the US has required the use of the term 'American', but its imprecision as a descriptor is duly noted.
2. MacDonald, 'Those who forget historiography', p. 50.
3. Ibid.; Immerwahr, 'Greater United States', p. 390, suggests that bases and other such small outposts 'act as staging grounds for . . . economic, military and cultural interventions' and – as US imperial territories – should not be underestimated. His lecture gives a fantastic overview of US imperialism along the lines of that explored here – linking early continental expansion to the annexations of 1898 and present-day US base culture.
4. Nugent, *Habits of Empire*; Drinnon, *Facing West*; Williams, 'US Indian Policy', pp. 810–31. The term 'Manifest Destiny' was coined by journalist John O'Sullivan in 1845.
5. Ferguson, *Colossus*; Immerwahr, 'Greater United States', pp. 373–91.
6. For example, Nugent's *Habits of Empire* focuses on the pre-twentieth-century US empire, while Ferguson's *Colossus* focuses on the post-1898 empire (for discussion see below).
7. Goldstein, 'Genealogy of US Colonial Present', p. 11.
8. For just two relatively recent overview introductions, see: Goldstein, 'Genealogy of US Colonial Present', pp. 1–32, and McCoy et al., 'On the Tropic of Cancer', pp. 3–33.
9. Morgan, *Into New Territory*, p. 8.
10. The 'Wisconsin School' is so-called because many of its most famous proponents taught or studied at the University of Wisconsin. See particularly Williams, *Tragedy of American Diplomacy*, and LaFeber, *The New Empire*. They mainly represented thinkers from the New Left in US politics, critical of US foreign policy in the period and thus drawn to re-evaluate the nature of American imperialism. For exceptional coverage of the Wisconsin School, see: Morgan, *Into New Territory*.
11. Mommsen, *Theories of Imperialism*, pp. 93–4.
12. Drinnon, *Facing West*; Williams, 'US Indian Policy', pp. 810–31.
13. DeLay, 'Indian Polities', p. 298.
14. Nugent, *Habits of Empire*, p. xiv.
15. Ferguson, *Colossus*, pp. 2–6.

16. Fellow, *American Media History*, p. 162. Though, as Fellow notes, very few today would argue that the war would not have happened without their editorial intervention.
17. Morgan, *Into New Territory*, p. 40.
18. The bibliography provides a list of online resources that will enable readers to further explore these sources.

CHAPTER I

Atlantic to Pacific (1783–1893)

This volume traces United States imperialism back to the year 1783, the first occasion when the newly recognised nation of the United States enhanced its territorial boundaries following the end of the Revolutionary War (1775–83) with the signing of the Treaty of Paris. In addition to the British there were, of course, many other settlers residing across the rest of the North American continent in the eighteenth century, including settlers of the very oldest variety, Native Americans. Over the course of the next century the United States came into contact, and often conflict, with all of these rival settlers in the course of building what would become their new empire. The westward expansion of the United States in this period was truly remarkable and, in just over a century, the US grew from a small group of Atlantic coastal colonies to a transcontinental empire able to rival the far older imperial powers of Europe.

Expansion from the Atlantic

The first clear calls for territorial expansion in the thirteen colonies can be traced back to the end of the French and Indian War (a satellite conflict in the Seven Years' War), the last major conflict in North America prior to the Revolutionary War. At this stage, of course, the thirteen colonies were still part of the British Empire. After defeating its French and Spanish rivals in North America, the 1763 Treaty of Paris saw Britain take control of French Canada (New France), Spanish Florida and the eastern half of French Louisiana (referred to here as Appalachia). Following the end of hostilities, King George III issued a proclamation that the new territory to the west of the established colonies, mainly consisting of Appalachia, was 'out of bounds' to any would-be settlers from the existing British colonies bound by the Atlantic coast in the east. The population of the thirteen colonies duly added this restriction to their growing

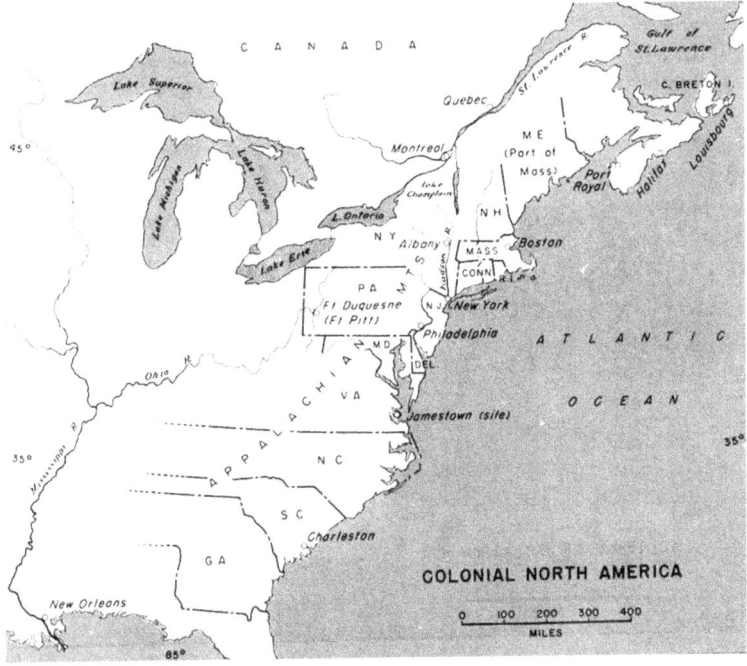

Figure 1.1 Map of Colonial North America

list of grievances, which was gradually accruing in the years prior to the United States' Declaration of Independence in 1776. Although those who wished to settle the western frontier generally ignored the king's proclamation, it was nevertheless seen as undue meddling in the affairs of the colonists. Expansion – like representation and taxation – became a fundamental concern for those seeking independence and for the early republic itself.

The idea of the United States as an 'empire' was there from the very beginning. Thomas Jefferson, the author of the Declaration of Independence and one of the most influential founding fathers, harboured ideas of his new nation as a republican 'Empire of Liberty' that would spread across the continent. Jefferson did not want to recreate the sort of empire the Americans had just overthrown to gain their independence, but it was an empire he sought nonetheless.[1] Historian Richard Immerman draws attention to a change in phrasing by Jefferson some years later when referring to empire – from an

'Empire *of* Liberty' to an 'Empire *for* Liberty'. Immerman sees this change as marking a 'commitment to a more aggressive, proactive extension of that sphere of liberty – and hence a greater American empire'. Indeed, Immerman sees the use of the word 'empire' by George Washington and his contemporaries as not simply a synonym for 'state' but as something that signalled further ambitions beyond consolidation of what already existed.[2] The very founders of the United States had made clear their vision for this new nation. It was to be a transcontinental empire.

With such imperial visions in mind it is unsurprising that, even before the Revolutionary War had ended, the Continental Congress had passed the following resolution on 'federal lands' in October 1780:

> The unappropriated lands that may be ceded or relinquished to the United States ... shall be disposed of for the common benefit of the United States, and be settled and formed into distinct republican States, which shall become members of the Federal Union, and have the same rights of sovereignty, freedom and independence as the other States.[3]

Many historians suggest that, at least up until 1898, this was broadly speaking the regular course of events in American expansion: and, for what eventually comprised the contiguous forty-eight states, this was largely the case.[4]

The 1783 Treaty of Paris, which saw Britain officially recognise that its thirteen American colonies were lost, also set out the United States' territorial gains in its second article.[5] So large was the amount of land conceded to the United States in 1783 that Charles Gravier, comte de Vergennes, the French foreign minister and wartime ally of the United States, was somewhat disappointed. Gravier had hoped to keep the United States dependent on France and was ready to support Spanish claims to the wider Appalachian region.[6] As early as 1783, even the allies of the United States were aware that the new nation had real potential to grow significantly in power if its territorial expansion was left unchecked.

In the summer of 1787 the Northwest Ordinance took over from the 1780 resolution, providing new rules for the territories that were not part of the original thirteen colonies and how they might become fully-fledged states. As one group of historians puts it, by organising the first 'territory' of the United States (the Northwest Territory), the Confederation Congress 'bridged the gap between wilderness and statehood by providing a system of limited self-government, the essence of which has been repeated for all continental and most insular possessions of the United States'.[7] In effect, the ordinance, in line with the gradual cessation of wide-ranging claims by the thirteen original states, led to the pattern that would see a number of new territories admitted to the union later acquiring separate statehood, rather than simply expanding the existing states into the frontier territories.[8]

One state that did not fully fall into this organised model was the 'Vermont Republic'. Here, Vermonter Ethan Allen and his 'Green Mountain Boys' took the opportunity afforded by the Revolutionary War to try and assert the state (then the New Hampshire Grants) as independent of both Britain and the two states that laid claim to the territory at the time (New Hampshire and New York).[9] Not recognised by the revolutionary authorities, Allen and his followers instead made an offer to place Vermont back into the British Empire as 'a separate government under the crown'.[10] However, the State of New York and the US Congress later moved to accept the claims of Vermonters to statehood and they were admitted as the fourteenth state, the first *new* state of the union, in 1791. Many other new states (formed from the territories ceded by the original thirteen states) entered the union in the following years but few declared themselves independent republics before seeking admission.[11] In the mid-nineteenth century, two far larger states notably followed the lead of Vermont by joining the United States as self-proclaimed independent republics, though by this time the new states came from lands situated far beyond the boundaries the Treaty of Paris had fixed for the US.[12]

The first territory ceded to the United States by Great Britain after the Revolutionary War had been conducted in line with the well-established tradition of the 'spoils of war' – a transferral of imperial possessions from one empire to another under duress. However, the Louisiana Purchase of 1803, which roughly doubled the size of the young nation, was to be the first example of the United States buying territory from another empire. The French had been allies of the Thirteen Colonies during the Revolutionary War and during this time had signed a treaty of perpetual alliance. Their common bond in 1778 was a mutual distaste for the British Empire, rather than a shared love of democracy – France at the time being ruled by the absolutist Bourbon monarchy. However, this in itself does not help explain why, just twenty years after the Revolutionary War ended, the French decided to sell what was left of their North American mainland possessions to the United States.

If anything, the turn of events in France in the intervening years made the 1803 sale of Louisiana to the United States even more unlikely. France itself had undergone, and was still undergoing, radical change at home following its own Revolutionary Wars (1798–1802). Just a few years before the sale of Louisiana, the French had signed the Treaty of San Ildefonso with Spain, which saw them retake control of it for the first time since 1762. Furthermore, the treaty was not effectively enacted or made public until 1802, the year before the sale, and – technically – it did not allow France to sell the territory.[13] Many saw Napoleon Bonaparte, now the sole consul and effective dictator of the French Republic, as keen to re-impose French imperial power in North America, hence the retrocession from Spain. Having just re-established French power in North America, it seemed unlikely that a man as ambitious as Napoleon would relinquish it so soon afterwards.

The US did not harbour any great expectations for immediate concessions from the French. Indeed, even the most vocal expansionist US frontiersmen only really hoped for control of the port of New Orleans and navigation rights on the Mississippi.[14] Yet, for only $15 million, Napoleon went several steps further than anybody anticipated and sold the entirety of French Louisiana to the United States. Napoleon's volte-face on extending French influence in North America might have been down to any number of compelling reasons. The worsening situation in the profitable French colony of St Domingue (Haiti) and increasing French interest in India are two imperial explanations for the sale. Closer to home, one might question the wisdom of sending troops to low-value colonies in the Americas when the situation in France and its relations with its European neighbours were so volatile. In addition, the sale would avoid the territory falling into the hands of the British and prevent a UK-US alliance (similar to the reasoning behind ceding the territory to Spain back in 1762).[15] As Ian Tyrell puts it, without the Napoleonic Wars the Louisiana Purchase would have been 'neither possible nor necessary'.[16] It is fair to say that the sale was first and foremost a result of imperial overstretch and represented a rationalisation of French possessions overseas so that Napoleon could concentrate on his European empire. The Louisiana Purchase was at least understandable, if not foreseeable.

Historian Francis Cogliano describes Thomas Jefferson, the US president in 1803, as the 'father of the first American empire'.[17] For Jefferson, the very success of the American republic was bound to that of the 'Empire of Liberty' via the acquisition of land and securing free trade. Nevertheless, the acquisition of the Louisiana Purchase territory raised important questions about the role of imperial expansion: for example, was such acquisition even within the government's power – especially considering Jefferson's strict constructionist views of the Constitution? Jefferson himself certainly doubted for a time whether his government had the power to acquire the territory without a constitutional amendment.[18] This question was only answered twenty-five years later by Chief Justice John Marshall, when he equated the government's war- and treaty-making powers with its ability to acquire territory 'by conquest or treaty'.[19] In spite of this retrospective clarification, many anti-imperialists over the subsequent two centuries continued to raise the question of constitutionality when it came to imperial expansion.[20]

Though the political predispositions of monarchical and revolutionary France proved decisive in both the establishment of the United States and the nation's rapid expansion, Spain, in contrast, was a somewhat reluctant and powerless bystander. Although the Spanish had ceded control of Louisiana to France by 1802, Spain did nothing when the French ignored the treaty obligations that barred transferring sovereignty to a third power. After the Louisiana Purchase, the United States was unquestionably a regional power to be reckoned with, and Spain now stood in the way of the United States' inexorable growth towards the two Floridas.

The history of the Floridas was as complex and ever-changing as much of the rest of North America in the eighteenth century. Following the French and Indian War, Great Britain had seized control of the French and Spanish territories to the south and west of the thirteen colonies and created the territories of East Florida (the formerly Spanish peninsula), and West Florida (the formerly French 'panhandle'). After the Revolutionary War the Spanish had regained control of the Floridas but, almost from the start, the US regarded the nominally Spanish-controlled Floridas both with suspicion and potential.

The first signs of US manoeuvrings near Florida pre-dated the Louisiana Purchase, and came with the Treaty of San Lorenzo (1795–6), also known as Pinckney's Treaty, after the US special envoy to Spain, Thomas Pinckney. Though partly down to the volatile situation in Europe, this treaty was mainly Spain's cautious response to the negotiations between the US and Great Britain that had ended in the pro-British Jay's Treaty (1794–5).[21] Prior to Jay's Treaty, Spain had been keen to restrict US influence and trade in its territories. Yet, with Pinckney's Treaty, Spain changed direction markedly, allowing the United States to use the Mississippi and access the port of New Orleans. In addition, Spain accepted the 31st Parallel as the border between the United States and Spanish Florida. The signing of Pinckney's Treaty was a significant turning point in the expansion of the United States. It resulted in improved suppression of Native Americans in the region; an end to murmurings of cession in the Kentucky region, and thus increased national unity; and a period of growth and consolidation for the early republic.[22] In the long run, though, it acted as a precursor to further US expansionism.

In 1802 Thomas Jefferson tried to purchase West Florida (along with New Orleans) for the United States, but the more appealing Louisiana Purchase soon overshadowed his initiative.[23] However, after the Louisiana Purchase in 1803, the United States became increasingly concerned about instability in West Florida, and began to fear that it might fall into the hands of a power more dangerous than Spain. Some argued that the Louisiana Purchase had included West Florida within its boundaries, and – not coincidentally – many living on the United States' southern frontier coveted more land.[24] In addition to these factors, West Florida remained a troublesome refuge for escaped slaves and a launching platform for Native American attacks upon southern US states.

William C. Davis argues that Presidents Jefferson and Madison merely 'allowed' Spain to administer West Florida after 1803 until an opportunity arose to strike. He regards Madison's eventual annexation of the territory as 'passive expansionism'.[25] On 23 September 1810 an exceptionally short rebellion was staged in Baton Rouge, West Florida, and the Republic of West Florida was born. Support in West Florida itself for US annexation came more after the revolution of 1810 than before it, as its majority of Anglo-American inhabitants by the early 1800s were only superficially loyal to Spain as long as it provided stability and cheap land.²⁶ Four days later President Madison issued a proclamation that, as disturbances in West Florida had not been controlled by the Spanish authorities, 'a failure of the United States to take the said territory into its possession may lead to events ultimately contravening the views of both parties, whilst in the meantime the tranquillity and security of our adjoining territories are endangered'.²⁷ By 10 December 1810 the US had annexed the bulk of West Florida without either war or payment.

East Florida proved a little trickier to annex than its western neighbour and contained fewer 'revolutionary' US settlers than the western province. An 1811 resolution by the US Congress set out its objections to any transfer of sovereignty of East Florida to a third party and expressed approval for its future annexation if Spain were to agree. This 'No Transfer Resolution' was aimed at denying Britain the option of annexing the territory in the run-up to the War of 1812.²⁸ The US regarded East Florida, like the west before it, as a safe haven for undesirables. The chief aggravator in the period leading up to the annexation of East Florida proved to be the Seminole tribe who, along with many escaped slaves, sided with Great Britain in the War of 1812 and conducted cross-border raids into the United States. In 1812 a band of renegade settler-revolutionaries attempted to stage a West Florida-style rebellion that might result in annexation. Although Madison officially rejected such calls, he only mildly rebuked the rebels' actions and even sought assurances from Spain that they would not be prosecuted.²⁹

Between 1817 and 1818 President Monroe authorised General Andrew Jackson to cross the border into East Florida in what is now called the First Seminole War. Jackson, however, exceeded his mandate and launched what was effectively a full-scale invasion of the Spanish territory. Spain was in a terrible negotiating position – despite the illegality of Jackson's actions – as its attention was torn, particularly by its South American possessions, where revolutions against Spanish rule were widespread. President Monroe adopted the line that Spain needed either to control its territory fully or pass over this responsibility to the United States. Spanish foreign minister Don Luis de Onís had very few options if he were to avoid war with the United States. Therefore, after lengthy negotiations, both Secretary of State John Quincy Adams and Onís signed the Transcontinental Treaty (1819), or Adams-Onís Treaty, which came into force in 1821.³⁰ This treaty not only ceded the rest of Florida to the United States but also settled the full border between New Spain (the rest of Spain's North American land empire) and the United States.[31] In return the United States rescinded its claims on Texas and, although the US did not pay for Florida as such, it did accept liability for US claims against Spain up to the amount of $5 million.[32] With extension into the Floridas, the United States had shown that post-1783 expansion would not simply be explained away as 'accidental imperialism', but that it was willing to apply force and pressure – where necessary – to achieve its ends.

Expansion in the South-west

The Transcontinental Treaty with Spain, ratified by the US Senate on 22 February 1821, had only limited efficacy, and within three decades the United States had moved its border much further south and west. Only six months after the ratification of the Transcontinental Treaty, the Treaty of Córdoba of 24 August 1821 saw Spain relinquish control of New Spain and established the newly independent Mexican Empire (Mexican Republic from 1824). From this point onwards the United States had an independent Mexico to deal with, rather than Spain, if it was to further its imperial ambitions. At first the Mexican authorities encouraged the gradual infiltration of settlers from the United States into the Texas region of northern Mexico, where the population increased rapidly, but this policy was later reversed when Mexico barred US immigration in 1830.[33]

Mexico became increasingly wary of potential US designs on the region, and an 1826 uprising in Texas, coupled with attempts by Presidents John Quincy Adams and Andrew Jackson to purchase Texas for $1 million and $5 million respectively, did little to assuage Mexican doubts.[34] Great Britain also began to worry about the future of Texas, largely due to its financial links with Mexico and an ongoing campaign to promote the abolition of slavery in the region, particularly after the institution had been abolished in most of the British Empire in 1833.[35] In October 1835, during a period in which the new Mexican leader/dictator Antonio López de Santa Anna tried to reassert Mexican control in the region, US settlers in Texas resisted violently at what became known as the Battle of Gonzales. In the months that followed, Texas declared itself an independent republic and war between Texas and Mexico, including the famous Battle of the Alamo in April 1836, continued

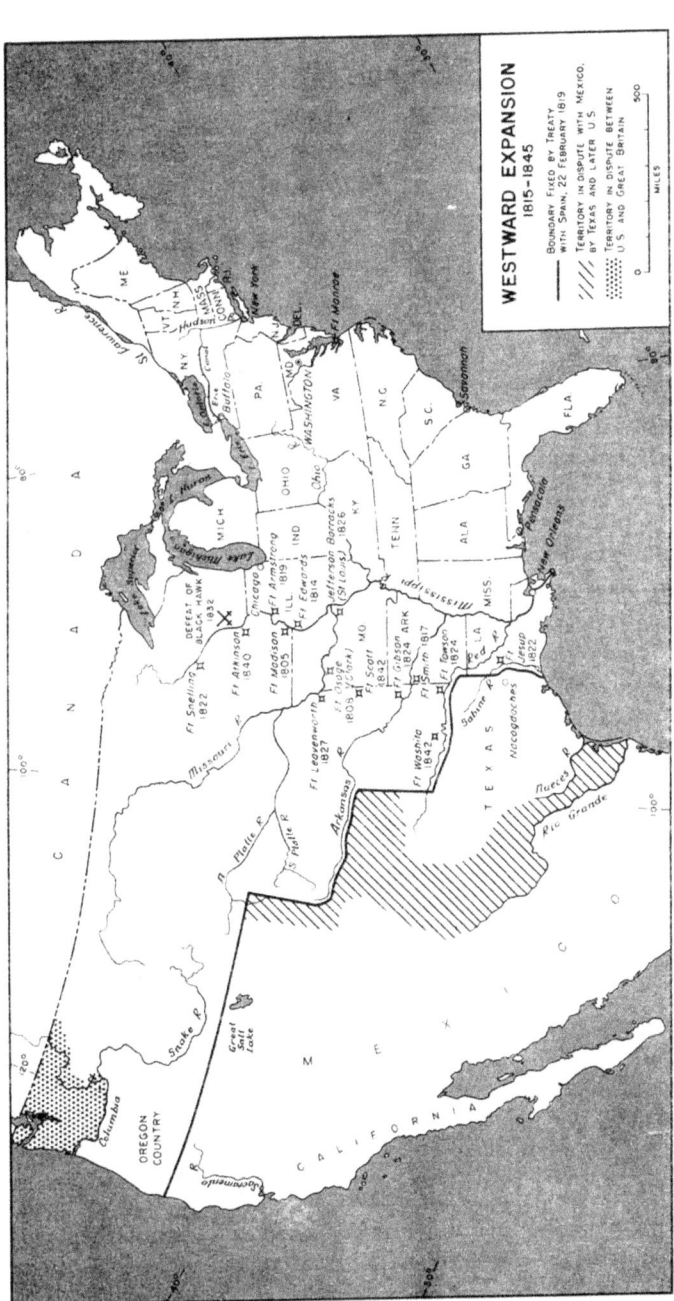

Figure 1.2 Westward Expansion, 1815–1845

until May 1836 when Mexico conceded defeat. However, the US did not annex Texas rapidly, as the bulk of West Florida had been incorporated in 1810. In fact, annexation was more than a decade in the making.

In 1835 President Andrew Jackson – the man who spearheaded the annexation of Florida and attempted to buy Texas in 1829 – rejected the overtures of the new Texan president Sam Houston. The primary issue dividing the northern abolitionists and southern slaveholders of the United States was the extension of slavery into new territories. The predominantly southern US settlers in Mexican-owned Texas began to outnumber the existing *Tejano* population by the 1830s, and with them they had reimported the institution of slavery (which the Mexicans had abolished in 1829). The burning question that therefore remained was whether the Republic of Texas would be annexed as a slave or free state (or even states). Added to these issues, recognition of Texan independence – and even more so the annexation of the republic – could well have led to prolonged conflict with Mexico.[36] Jackson opted for a diplomatic line and delayed official recognition of Texas until 3 March 1837, the day before his successor Martin Van Buren was sworn in as US president.

Britain and France welcomed the Republic of Texas as an independent state, seeing this as preferable to US annexation and further incursion on the Caribbean shoreline, as well as providing a useful new trading partner. Van Buren went no further than Jackson in simply recognising Texan independence, but John Tyler – the Whig who came to the presidency after William Henry Harrison's untimely death – promoted annexation far more fulsomely, especially after his own party had disowned him.[37] Tyler signed a treaty of annexation in 1844, which was then debated by the US Senate with both Democrats and Whigs divided over its merits. Proponents of annexation pointed to the old Jeffersonian argument of the necessity for large territorial expanses to achieve a true farming republic, as well as stressing the commercial, communication and trading benefits. Nevertheless the issues of slavery and war with Mexico remained equally pressing – and the Whig Party in Congress (if not their president) opposed immediate annexation.[38] The issue also led to the Democratic Party selecting the pro-annexation James K. Polk as their presidential nominee in 1844 ahead of the anti-annexationist Martin Van Buren.[39]

Texas provided the first real instance of the United States' desire to expand its territory having a substantial impact on both domestic political parties. President Tyler lacked the two-thirds votes in the Senate necessary to ratify his treaty, so instead he secured it by means of a joint resolution of Congress, requiring only a simple majority in both the House and the Senate, which passed in March 1845 and came into effect in December 1845. The resolution stated that: 'Congress doth consent that the territory properly included within, and rightfully belonging to the Republic of Texas, may be erected into a new State, to be called the State of Texas.'[40]

The annexation of Texas and its consequences in the later 1840s were part of a grander movement called 'Manifest Destiny'. This phrase, coined by John L. O'Sullivan in 1845, would propound a belief in the inexorable nature of the growth of federal democracy across the Western Hemisphere. Frederick Merk deems the term 'novel and right for a mood', summing up a feeling of God-ordained right to expand over a non-defined area that many regarded as extending from the Atlantic to the Pacific, if not over the entire Americas. He goes on to note that, to most Americans in the 1840s, this meant that any peoples keen to apply for admission to the union were welcome, though some, such as the Mexicans, might require a period of tutelage before they were allowed in.[41] Albert Weinberg suggests that many factors encouraged expansion through Manifest Destiny: 'metaphysical dogmas of a providential mission and quasi-scientific "laws" of national development, conceptions of national right and ideals of social duty, legal rationalisations and appeals to "the higher law", aims of extending freedom and designs of extending benevolent absolutism'.[42] A creed that served the United States well beyond expansion into Texas, Manifest Destiny had long-lasting implications for the development of US imperialism.

Although Texas had been annexed on 29 December 1845 without recourse to war with Mexico, war was not long in coming. Just as some in the US had argued that Texas lay within the bounds of the Louisiana Purchase of 1803, so the boundaries of earlier treaties and nations were once again disputed as regarded the extent of Texas. The United States argued that the border between Texas and Mexico was formed by the Rio Grande River, whereas the Mexicans claimed that it was the Nueces River that truly marked the border. President Polk sent John Slidell to negotiate with the Mexicans over the border issue with a mandate to discuss further territorial concessions by Mexico for a variety of prices: from $5 million for New Mexico, up to $25 million for the territory extending to the Pacific Coast.[43] When Slidell's diplomacy failed, Polk sent General Zachary Taylor to the Rio Grande to claim the territory the US felt was Texan already, and by May 1846 the United States was at war with Mexico. Many historians have blamed Polk's aggressive actions for starting the Mexican-American War, seeing Slidell's mission as designed to engineer a diplomatic rejection that would allow for war. However, Ward McAfee makes a compelling case that the president had little choice other than to act as he did, and that, though his actions were antagonistic, Polk had high expectations of the mission's success.[44]

In June 1846 the ongoing tension precipitated a revolt in Mexico's Alta Californian province, where fearful US settlers in the area seized the Mexican outpost of Sonoma and declared independence in the so-called 'Bear Flag Revolt'.[45] Later, led by the explorer John Frémont, the rebels marched upon San Francisco and claimed the region for the US, though US troops were not far behind.[46] The parallels with Texas seem relatively clear, but as John Pinheiro notes, the big difference was that the Californian rebellion received support from the US and the 'republic' lasted little over a week, whereas Texas existed for an entire decade.[47] Following the fall of Mexico City to US forces in September 1847 the war reached its effective conclusion by the end of that year, but negotiating a treaty still proved a distant prospect. A number of factors stalled Mexican negotiations, from pride and political instability in Mexico, to the political situation in the United States. From the US point of view, many were frustrated by the failure of diplomacy to date, and Polk was pushed to assume a tougher line with Mexico.[48] Nicholas Trist, a diplomat whom Polk had attempted to recall on 6 October 1847, signed a peace treaty almost four months after he had been recalled. On 2 February 1848 the two countries finally agreed to the Treaty of Guadalupe Hidalgo, by which the United States gained control of Alta (Upper) California and New Mexico, along with establishing the Rio Grande as the border between Texas and Mexico. In addition to dealing with several financial issues, including $15 million in compensation for lands lost by Mexico, the treaty also guaranteed the property and rights of Mexicans who now lived in US territory. Indeed, unless they wished to return to Mexico or keep their Mexican citizenship, the residents

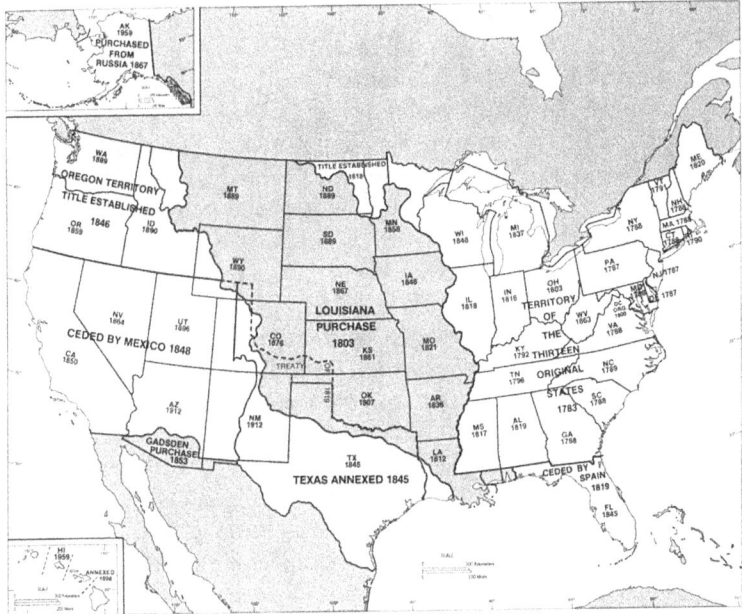

Figure 1.3 Admission of States and Territorial Acquisition

of conquered territories automatically gained US citizenship once civil government was established.[49] One final suggestion of expansion came in April 1848, when President Polk asked Congress to intervene to support an uprising in the Yucatán province of Mexico, but when the rising was quelled, Polk withdrew his request.[50] Though the treaty signalled the end of the war, it was far from an end to the United States' imperialist intentions.

With the Treaty of Guadalupe Hidalgo, the United States obtained a vast portion of territory that connected the newly annexed Texas to the Pacific Ocean. Though Texas had been largely settled as a 'slave state', the new areas of former Mexican territory had not been and their future as 'slave' or 'free' was critical in terms of whether or not they would be able to gain statehood in the short term. The southern states were keen to hark back to the Missouri Compromise of 1820, designed to settle the expansion of slavery into the Louisiana Purchase territories, which had settled a northern limit for slavery (after the admission of Missouri) as the Parallel 36°30' (N). Though the compromise line only applied to these earlier territories, much of California and New Mexico lay below this invisible boundary as well, leading slavery advocates to call for the line to be extended to the Pacific. Meanwhile, those in the antislavery camp, such as Pennsylvania Congressman David Wilmot, suggested that slavery should simply be prohibited throughout the lands ceded to the US after the Mexican War.

A solution to this divisive issue came not with President Polk, nor ultimately with his successor Zachary Taylor, but with Millard Fillmore, the Whig who came to office when Taylor died unexpectedly in office. Fillmore agreed to yet another 'compromise' on the issue of slavery – simply known as the Compromise of 1850, which eventually passed through a divided Congress as a number of separate measures. One of these saw California, with its population increasing at an astronomical pace following the 'Gold Rush' of 1849, permitted to join the union as a free state in 1850, bypassing an extended territorial phase. The Compromise of 1850 also saw what remained of the Mexican cession divided into two territories: Utah and New Mexico, both far larger than their present-day state namesakes. In these territories the issue of slavery was to be settled by popular sovereignty. With this, and a final settlement of the Texan border with New Mexico, the shape of the southern US border was almost complete.

The last section of territory in this region did not declare itself a republic, nor was it conquered through warfare; instead it took the form of a negotiated purchase. In 1853 President Franklin Pierce sent James Gadsten as an emissary to Mexico to negotiate the purchase of a strip of land to the south of New Mexico territory. Initially Gadsten asked for a fairly substantial tranche of land but, after negotiations, he scaled back his demands to a (still impressive) 30,000 square miles of northern Mexico, in return for $10 million. The Gadsten Purchase arose as a result of both outstanding border tensions and policing issues left ambiguous by the Treaty of Guadalupe Hidalgo.[51] Of particular note in putting pressure on the US to make the purchase were those advocating a southern railroad route to California that would ideally pass through territory within Gadsten's revised purchase boundary. The Gadsten Purchase was the final piece in what now comprises the southern border of the continental United States.

Linking the Coasts

Although European powers had divided the North American continent among themselves by the time of US independence, much of the land they claimed was sparsely, if at all, settled by Europeans. Despite this, European imperialism did result in Native American populations decreasing dramatically, particularly due to the introduction of new diseases from Eurasia to which they had no natural immunity. Disease would only account for part of the death toll, however, and as Jill Lepore shows, even the early Puritan settlers of New England were no strangers to the violent subjugation of Native peoples that would follow over the coming centuries.[52] In the years that followed the settlement of North America, Native Americans proved to be both feared enemies and valuable allies, but most of all they proved to be in the way of imperial expansion: be it British, French, Spanish, or that of the United States.

Throughout early US history, the nation had always had a western frontier. Yet by 1890, according to Frederick Jackson Turner's famous essay 'The Significance of the Frontier in American History', the western frontier as a defined, unsettled area had ceased to exist. Although Turner declared the frontier closed, he perpetuated a commonly held notion that the United States had spent the previous century claiming 'an area of free land'. Of course Turner knew that hundreds of Native American tribes resided in this 'free land', but in his eyes the Native population did not really matter in the grand scheme of things, except in so far as they presented a challenge against which hardy frontiersmen might prove their mettle and forge a distinctly 'American' character.[53] Largely omitted from the earlier sections of this chapter, the United States' clashes with Native Americans are the last, and perhaps most important, dimension of American imperial expansion on the continent.

The first president, George Washington, believed that the objective of the federal government was to move the Native American population west of the Mississippi River.[54] Similarly, Thomas Jefferson had designs on removing Native Americans in existing territories as 'a prelude to expansion' – advocating what Ian Tyrell terms an 'ethnic homeland' by either assimilation or extermination.[55] By expecting the Native American population to conveniently 'disappear' in one way or another, the US was able to see continental imperialism as only subjugating the 'other' temporarily and in a limited way, but in reality, as Jeffrey Ostler notes, the United States was 'committed to a system of colonial rule'.[56] The US presented the Native Americans with a choice about giving up their land, but it was generally a choice of 'how' rather than 'if'. Yet as Pekka Hämäläinen notes, the confrontation between the US and Native Americans should not simply be presented as one of vanquisher and victim. The Comanche people of the south-west, for example, had forged their own empire in the early nineteenth century, and were powerful actors in their own right.[57] Yet this clash of empires was far from being an equal one, and there was only one likely winner in the long term.

For new western states to emerge, white settlement of the vast expanses brought under US control by the Louisiana Purchase was required. Leading figures in the region, such as the governor of Indiana Territory, William Henry Harrison, were keen to settle these lands by whatever means necessary. In the controversial Treaty of Fort Wayne (1809) Harrison dubiously negotiated a huge land sale, provoking the violent reaction of Shawnee leader Tecumseh and others wishing to protect Native American lands and customs, leading to one of the rarer features of this period, an attempt to bring rival tribes together to fight the United States.[58] From the point of view of the United States, the Natives were not only undesirable as savage interlopers, but as allies for the British traders on the frontier who were rightly suspected of supplying weapons to, and encouraging, the Natives in the run-up to the War of 1812. Following the final defeat of Tecumseh and his allies at the Battle of the Thames in 1813, the government again helped to encourage US settlement by offering land bounties for soldiers who had fought in the conflict. Native Americans would once again be moved out and white settlers moved in.

The Lewis and Clark expedition of the nineteenth century's first decade drew settlers further and further to the South and West.[59] However, the so-called 'Five Civilized Tribes' of the modern-day states of Florida (Seminoles), Georgia (Cherokee), Alabama (Creek) and Mississippi (Chicksaw and Choctaw) remained a partially 'civilised' and 'Christianised' nuisance to would-be settlers.[60] The Creek War (during the War of 1812) saw the future president General Andrew Jackson defeat an uprising in Alabama and Georgia, gaining him a national reputation and yet further land concessions from Native Americans. Jackson continued to bolster this reputation in the First Seminole War later that decade. For Michael Hunt, Jackson represented one who 'had imbibed a heady frontier brew of land hunger and Indian hating' and used military campaigns and treaties to shatter Native American power in the region in the 1810s, a policy he perfected during his presidency in the 1830s.[61] It was as US president that Jackson's infamous policy towards Native Americans saw all five tribes forcibly emigrate to a huge reservation in the west, now comprising most of modern-day Oklahoma. Jackson became known by Native peoples as 'Sharp Knife' and, with his belief that the two races could not live peaceably alongside one another, he decided that Native Americans should be moved beyond a 'permanent Indian frontier' west of the Mississippi River (a boundary soon moved further westwards).[62] The Cherokees' horrendous march westwards in the late 1830s became known simply as the 'Trail of Tears'.

Alongside the expansionism that followed the Mexican-American War came an almost evangelical prophesying of the United States' 'Manifest Destiny' to settle North America from the Atlantic to the Pacific, as ordained by the Almighty himself. It became a doctrine for expansionism, and its civilising, Christianising tone helped to justify the necessity of Native American removal. Although, the Civil War created a small hiatus in the realisation of Manifest Destiny, it was, in its narrowest designs, achieved by the end of the century. Fresh from defeating the Confederacy in the Civil War (1861–5), the 're-United' States set about a new phase of Native American dispersal and destruction. With pioneers, settlers and military encroachment came a steep decline in the buffalo population of the United States, with dire consequences for the Native peoples that relied on the buffalo for clothing, food and fuel, among other things. With the growth of transcontinental railroads came more settlers, and calls to obtain the raw materials and minerals that lay within the territories remaining under Native American control in the West. US soldiers often massacred Native peoples who were not willing to sign away their lands and instead stood their ground.[63] Nevertheless, historian Robert Wooster rightly warns against painting US military actions against Native Americans too one-dimensionally as a war of extermination, as this serves to underestimate the variety and complexity of these imperial encounters.[64] The 1860s and 1870s saw a series of small-scale wars between the veteran Civil War soldiers of the United States and several scattered bands of Native American tribesmen. Of these, the most notable and mythologised event was the Battle of Little Bighorn, the site of George Custer's famous 'last stand' against the Sioux in 1876. However, such victories as this proved pyrrhic in the long run, and US troops redoubled their efforts to avenge Custer's martyrdom. By the 1880s most armed resistance was over and the US sectioned off remaining Native Americans into reservations.

Despite the widespread formation of reservations by the 1880s, the US government's desire to satiate land-hungry settlers saw yet further developments. Along with humanitarian impulses to assimilate Native Americans, this land hunger led the government to pass the General Allotment Act (Dawes Act) in 1887. The act, which broke down reservations into smaller individualised plots, aimed to recreate Native Americans as republican farmers. The act also foregrounded a renewed attempt to Americanise, or culturally assimilate, Native Americans through measures such as government boarding schools, where students would be taught in English and learn about the superiority of the US political system. It also had the useful side-effect of providing even more land for speculators. The US took the best of the lands, and redistributed the worst to Native Americans. By the time of the Wounded Knee Massacre of 1890, which represented the symbolic end of Native American armed resistance to US conquest, the United States had subdued the continent's original settlers and subsumed them – but more importantly their lands – almost entirely into their own empire. In the same year an Organic Act created Oklahoma Territory and, that same decade, the 1898 Curtis Act applied the system created by the Dawes Act to the so-called 'Five Civilized Tribes' in their new home territories. The native peoples put up some resistance to this effective incorporation within the United States, and even made a last-ditch attempt to have half of Oklahoma admitted as the majority-Native State of Sequoya, but to no avail.[65] In 1907 (Oklahoma) and 1912 (New Mexico and Arizona) the final three states of the contiguous United States were admitted to the union, and it could be said that Manifest Destiny had been accomplished.

Historian Walter L. Williams accurately identifies the anomalous status of Native American peoples as one of the clearest signs of US imperialism in action. Native Americans, he argues, were classified by an 1831 Supreme Court decision as 'domestic dependent nations', and effectively 'wards' of the United States, or even 'colonial subjects'.⁶⁶ It seems surprising now that when Williams wrote this piece in 1980, so few had noted the striking resemblance between the way Native Americans were seen and treated and how Europeans ran some of their overseas colonies. There is little to distinguish such actions from the contiguous empires of Russia or the Ottomans. Little, that is, but speed, for in only a single century the United States had transformed itself from a small band of sparsely populated settlements on the east coast to a vast transcontinental empire.

Notes

1. Onuf, *Jefferson's Empire*, p. 1.
2. Immerman, *Empire for Liberty*, pp. 5–8.
3. Reproduced in Morison et al., *Growth of the American Republic*, p. 230.
4. Mid-twentieth-century US historians such as Samuel Flagg Bemis and Ernest May, as noted in the introduction, subscribed to what became known as the 'aberration thesis' – that an 'imperial moment' around 1898 was uncharacteristic of US history as a whole.
5. Article II (of the ten in the treaty) began by stating that 'all disputes which might arise in future on the subject of the boundaries of the said United States may be prevented, it is hereby agreed and declared, that the following are and shall be their boundaries', before going on to list these boundaries in detail (see: Treaty of Paris, 1783, *Avalon Project*). The Mississippi River formed a new western border with Spanish (western) Louisiana, but some 'expanded' northern and southern borders remained less well defined and are explored in more depth later. The French ceded the western half of Louisiana to Spain secretly in the Treaty of Fontainebleau (1762), to avoid losing it to the British.
6. Jones, *Limits of Liberty*, p. 56.
7. Morison et al., *Growth of the American Republic*, pp. 232–3.
8. The original states ceded frontier lands to the federal government in the 1780s and 90s, creating the first territories from which new states would be formed.
9. See especially: Bellesiles, 'Legal Structures on the Frontier', pp. 895–915.
10. Bennett, *A Few Lawless Vagabonds*, pp. 171–2.
11. Maine, for example, had been part of Massachusetts for many years before becoming a state in its own right in 1820.
12. The other two, explored later in this chapter, were Texas (1845) and California (1850).

13. See: Lawson and Seidman, *Constitution of Empire*, pp. 19–20.
14. Bush, *The Louisiana Purchase*, p. 75.
15. Elman, 'Extending Offensive Realism', p. 572.
16. Tyrell, *Transnational History*, p. 15.
17. Cogliano, *Emperor of Liberty*, pp. 5–6.
18. For in-depth coverage of this issue, see: Lawson and Seidman, *Constitution of Empire*.
19. Ibid. p. 21.
20. In subsequent debates, questions were often raised about the extent to which the US Constitution needed to be applied to newly annexed territories, particularly after 1898.
21. Jay's Treaty sought to settle outstanding differences between the US and Britain that had remained after the 1783 Treaty of Paris.
22. Young, 'The future of the Arctic', p. 526, pp. 534–5.
23. Wood, *Empire of Liberty*, pp. 368–9.
24. Rodriguez, 'West Florida', p. 350.
25. Davis, 'Republic of Florida'.
26. McMichael, *Americans in Spanish West Florida*, p. 4.
27. Madison, 'Proclamation 16'.
28. Weeks, *John Quincy Adams*, p. 28.
29. Sonneborn, *Acquisition of Florida*, p. 40.
30. See: Weeks, *John Quincy Adams*.
31. As explored later in this chapter and in Chapter 2.
32. For an excellent review of the legality of presidential actions in both East and West Florida, see: Currie, 'Rumors of Wars', pp. 1–40.
33. Martin, *A Nation of Immigrants*, p. 89.
34. Riccards, *Ferocious Engine of Democracy*, p. 141.
35. Barker, 'Annexation of Texas', p. 50.
36. Freehling, *The Road to Disunion*, pp. 367–8.
37. Tyler, a member of a small faction of states'-rights Whigs, effectively broke with his party and continually frustrated their actions. See: Howe, *Political Culture*, p. 142.
38. See: Morrison, 'Westward the Curse of Empire', pp. 221–49.
39. See: Morrison, 'Martin Van Buren', pp. 695–724.
40. 'Joint Resolution of the Congress of the US', *Avalon Project*.
41. Merk, *Manifest Destiny*, p. 24. The idea of prolonged tutelage for certain ethnicities was a substantive theme in the 1898 annexations.
42. Weinberg, *Manifest Destiny*, p. 2.
43. Griswold del Castillo, *Treaty of Guadalupe Hidalgo*, p. 13.
44. McAfee, 'Reconsideration of the Origins of the Mexican-American War', pp. 49–65. McAfee sees historians such as Glenn Price and Charles Sellers as presenting a picture of Polk as determined to fight a war of conquest.

45. The flag (still the state flag today) bears the image of a grizzly bear and the words 'California Republic'.
46. Schwenkbeck, 'Bear Flag Revolt', p. 128.
47. Pinheiro, *Manifest Ambition*, p. 119.
48. Singletary, *The Mexican War*, pp. 158–9.
49. Weber, *Foreigners in Their Native Land*, pp. 140–60. For historical interpretation of the treaty see: Griswold del Castillo, *Treaty of Guadalupe Hidalgo*, Chapter 7.
50. LaFeber, *American Age*, pp. 121–2.
51. Ortega, 'Gadsten Purchase', p. 361.
52. Lepore, *Name of War*.
53. Turner, 'The Significance of the Frontier in American History', pp. 1–3.
54. Churchill, *A Little Matter of Genocide*, p. 209.
55. Tyrell, *Transnational History*, p. 16.
56. Ostler, *The Plains Sioux*, pp. 13–17.
57. Hämäläinen, *Comanche Empire*, pp. 141–2.
58. Owens, *Mr. Jefferson's Hammer*, p. 208.
59. The Lewis and Clark expedition (1804–6) was commissioned by President Thomas Jefferson to explore and map the newly purchased Louisiana territory and to find a navigable water route across the continent all the way to the Pacific Ocean.
60. The term 'Five Civilized Tribes' is certainly problematic, but was commonly used at the time as a seemingly positive one, suggesting that these particular peoples had adopted customs more similar to those of the United States.
61. Hunt, *Ideology and US Foreign Policy*, p. 54.
62. Brown, *Bury My Heart at Wounded Knee*, pp. 5–8.
63. Perhaps the most notable massacre was at Sand Creek, Colorado in 1864.
64. Wooster, *Military and US Indian Policy*, p. 4. Wooster argues that a number of other factors, such as divergences between the War and Interior Departments, personal and political disputes, and misconceptions about Native Americas, all allowed for a variety of types of clashes to occur across a vast geographical span. Yet he concedes that though the means differed, the subjugation, removal and acculturation remained constant.
65. Kidwell, *Chocktaws in Oklahoma*, pp. 187–8.
66. Williams, 'US Indian Policy', pp. 811–12.

CHAPTER 2

Heading Northwards (1812–1903)

When the United States broke away from the British Crown in the Revolutionary War, one unintended effect was the creation of a separate nation to the north. This was not what some in the United States had envisaged. For example, prior to the Revolutionary War, Thomas Jefferson expounded a belief that the Canadians would join the union. Yet, by the end of the war, the Canadian colonies were firmly under British control.[1] Throughout the following century and more, the United States continued to look northwards as well as westwards as its empire grew and – whether expanding into Oregon Country or Russian Alaska – Britain continued to complicate and frustrate this particular direction in the course of US imperialism.

Canada

Although the British possessions located above the thirteen colonies were not united formally until 1867, the relationship between Canada, or British North America as it was more formally called, and the United States was of fundamental importance to both nations in their formative years. More importantly, though, the reluctance of Canada to succumb to the attractions of their southern neighbour and leave the British Empire to join the one being forged by the United States intrigued and infuriated Americans for more than a century.

The United States, from its very beginnings, envisaged a future that included the British provinces to its north. Indeed, Article XI of the Articles of Confederation (which served as the first constitution of the early United States), stated clearly that the question of Canadian incorporation remained open:

> Canada acceding to this confederation, and joining in the measures of the United States, shall be admitted into, and entitled to

all the advantages of this Union; but no other colony shall be admitted into the same, unless such admission be agreed to by nine States.[2]

British North America seemed a natural region for US expansion and annexation, yet even in the formative years of the United States its northern neighbour came to appear increasingly dissimilar as time passed.

British North America was formed from a diverse admixture of peoples, much like its southern republican neighbour. However, the most sizeable group of non-British settlers was its French-speaking population, which saw more danger to its cultural heritage as a tiny minority within the new United States than as a substantial section of the population in British North America. This significant group helped to secure a sense of 'separateness' for British North America, but it was far from being the only such group. The failure of the United States to bring the northern British colonies along with them in the revolution led to around 40,000 loyalists emigrating north, along with roughly 4,000 African and Native Americans. These later immigrant groups added further weight to a sense of difference that already existed between the two North American neighbours. Between 1791 and 1812 a further 65,000 followed them, though recent scholarship has questioned how 'loyal' some of these 'late loyalists' really were, suggesting instead that they were simply tempted by cheaper land and lower taxes.[3] Nevertheless, these influxes not only helped boost the relatively sparse population of British North America, but also – in the main – pushed its populace further towards favouring a continued union with the British crown.

The newly independent United States, unsurprisingly, did not immediately assume friendly relations with its former imperial master, and as the years progressed after the Treaty of Paris relations between the two began to sour once more. Some of this was no doubt due to the fact that the United States was a relatively small coastal nation surrounded by potential enemies in the shape of Britain, France and Spain. It was an accepted fact that Britain dominated the Atlantic, and therefore even the coast itself was a hostile border of sorts. Additionally, the actions of France and Britain during the turn of the century helped heighten fears of a future military engagement. France, an invaluable ally in the struggle for independence, became a trickier ally after the fall of Louis XVI. Indeed, by 1798 the United States and France were engaged in an undeclared 'quasi' naval war (due partially to French seizures of US ships), which lasted until 1800. However, this conflict was less significant than the war that resulted from continued friction with Great Britain. The ever-changing situation in France after the French Revolution saw the French almost continually at war with Britain after 1793. By 1803, with Napoleon firmly in charge, the French removed themselves from the North American equation by selling the entirety of their Louisiana territory to the US, leaving Britain as an even more important neighbour.[4] Tellingly, Thomas Jefferson wrote to James Madison in 1809 that, after the Louisiana Purchase, he expected the US would eventually acquire East and West Florida, Cuba and British North America, the latter of which was certainly in American minds as the War of 1812 approached.[5]

Both France and Britain had proved difficult but indispensable trading partners, and the warring European nations had attempted to embargo trade with their respective enemy, creating a host of problems for the neutral US. Despite attempts to withdraw from European trade, by 1810 the United States lifted its own counter-embargo and it was Britain – controller of the seas – that proved the more stubborn resistor of US neutrality. After 1810 the British continued to seize and search US ships, impress American sailors into the British navy, and block US trade with the French. By June of 1812, President Madison was convinced that war was the only solution, and asked for Congressional consent to fight the 'Second War of Independence'.

Historian Donald Hickey attributes Madison's decision to move for war to a number of motives, including: maritime issues; the ambitions of the US west; issues with Native Americans in the West; removing the British threat permanently; and uniting the nation against the Federalist Party. However, Hickey also notes that this was not only the second and last time that the US went to war with Great Britain, but also the second and last time that the US tried to 'conquer Canada'.[6] More recently, Richard Maass has argued that expansionism – or 'land hunger' – was not a genuine motive for the War of 1812, but that the war was the result of an unsuccessful bluff to gain concessions from the British. He suggests that, although Madison saw the material value of Canada, the key development of the War of 1812 was to reveal the US leadership's 'widespread rejection of the desirability of [Canadian annexation]'.[7] The observation that the war might have made the US leadership less desirous of annexing British North America is compelling, but calls for annexation were not always led from the top. Between the War of 1812 and the American Civil War, although most talk of annexation was sparked by rebellious Canadians, supporters in the US were always readily found among the populace in the states along the US-British North American border.

Although the War of 1812 led to some notable events in US history, such as the British burning the White House in 1814, in terms of territorial gain the war was of little consequence.[8] In 1814 peace negotiations began in Europe, culminating in the signing of the Treaty of Ghent on Christmas Eve. The treaty largely reset affairs to the pre-war status quo, and returned any lands still under enemy occupation. Although the war might not have altered the geopolitical landscape dramatically, it did reveal how the very existence of British North America still seemed a somewhat transient one in the eyes of many North Americans. Indeed, as Shaun McLaughlin's recent work shows, there was yet another fluttering of interest in annexation during the late 1830s, in what has been dubbed 'The Patriot War'.[9] Although not a real 'war' as such, a series of rebellions in Lower Canada (modern Quebec) and Upper Canada (modern Ontario), arising during late 1837, led to a protracted insurgency by Canadian rebels who fled to the United States and found much popular support for their cause there.

Led by Scots-Canadian William Lyon Mackenzie, the rebels went so far as to proclaim the 'Republic of Canada' from their base on Navy Island in the Niagara River on the British North American border with the United States. Unofficial US support for the rebels caused a major incident between the Americans and British, when in 1837 the Royal Navy chased down an American-based supply ship, the SS *Caroline*, in US waters. In 1838, the regrouped rebels formed 'Hunter's Lodges' of US-based Canadians and American sympathisers intent on raiding the British North American border: the foremost of the resulting skirmishes being the Battle of the Windmill in November 1838. By the end of the year, most of the rebels had been rounded up and transported to British Australia as a result. A further small 'conflict' of sorts arose at the same time between local militias in New Brunswick and Maine in what was nicknamed the 'Aroostook War'. At stake here was the US-British North America border between this north-eastern province and state, raising the very real possibility of a third military conflict between Britain and the US. Although there had been no casualties by the time a diplomatic solution was reached in March 1839, there had been a serious level of escalation, with the US Congress and President Van Buren authorising financial and military support for Maine.[10] Following the Patriot and Aroostook Wars, issues of cross-border resentment continued to be put to the respective diplomats to resolve, and in 1842 Britain and the US signed the Webster-Ashburton Treaty. This aimed to resolve most of the remaining boundary disputes, many of which were still hangovers from the Treaty of Paris (relating to both the east and west of the United States), but failed to resolve the dispute over the Oregon border.

The final significant incident in US-Canadian relations prior to the American Civil War involved the founding of the Annexation Association in 1849, which sought the political union of the two states. The association comprised primarily two distinct groups with quite different motivations. The first group was made up of British businessmen in Quebec who were disappointed with British economic policies in the province. The second group, led by Louis-Joseph Papineau, consisted of French-Canadian nationalists who preferred US democratic institutions to those in Quebec. In 1854, a reciprocity treaty between the US and British North America led to the eventual collapse of the Annexation Association, largely because many annexationists believed that reciprocity would ultimately lead to the annexation of British North America anyway.[11]

Although for a number of years the United States turned its eyes inwards both before and during its Civil War (1861–5), for Canada a fear remained that a victorious Union in the Civil War might turn its attention northwards and attempt to build upon its successes. Some in the US resented Canada as a refuge for draft-dodgers and shelter for Confederates who were able to conduct fruitless, but nonetheless frustrating, raids on the Union states during the war.[12] US Secretary of State William Seward, the architect of the Alaska Purchase, was one of the arch-annexationists of the nineteenth century. For him, as with Alaska, British North America offered an obvious space for expansion. Following the Civil War, the victorious Unionists had a large and battle-hardened army, and political capital could still be gained from the offer of more land in the Canadian north, as well as from anti-British Irish-American voters. In July 1866, shortly after the lapse of the Reciprocity Treaty, Republican Congressman Nathaniel Banks introduced an 'Annexation Bill' in the US House of Representatives proposing the admission of the British North American provinces into the US. The *New York Times*, in an editorial commenting on the bill, noted that it seemed inappropriate to allow the Canadian provinces to join the union unhindered while the southern, formerly Confederate, states were forced to undergo military occupation and various conditions in order to 're-join' the Union. It remarked sarcastically: 'Would it not be more in keeping with Congressional action to annex their [Canadian] territory by force, legislate for them without their consent, govern them by military law, forbid them representation, and teach them in general how they must bear and behave themselves upon all matters?—after learning which their case may be considered.'[13]

A couple of years later, Secretary of State Hamilton Fish suggested that Britain resolve American claims for damages inflicted by the British-built ship, the *Alabama* – used by the Confederacy during the American Civil War – by ceding Canada to the United States. The administrations of Presidents Andrew Johnson and Ulysses Grant, however, preferred a more gradualist approach to annexation than Secretaries of State Seward and Fish, and Canadian malcontents of the period tended to favour secession ahead of annexation.[14] Between 1866 and 1871 the United States half-heartedly made moves to put down a number of Fenian raids led by US-based Irish nationalists who aimed to invade parts of Canada in order to press the British to accept Irish calls for self-government. Not without a renewed sense of danger from its southern neighbour, on 1 July 1867, the new confederation of Canada was formed, the first of the British Empire's self-governing dominions. Following this, in 1871 delegates signed the Washington Treaty, which finally settled a number of post-Civil War claims including the *Alabama* damages.[15] Thereafter, the only significant issues between Canada and the United States that remained unresolved centred on the Alaska boundary (discussed later) and the perennial question of fishing rights off the North Atlantic coast.[16]

The 1880s and the early 1890s saw perhaps the final murmur of 'annexation-ism', with those on either side of the border setting out ideas for union. In an 1883 article for the *North American Review* entitled 'A Canadian View of Annexation', Prosper Bender suggested that it was 'one of those important dormant issues never wholly out of sight'.[17] Bender also set out the case for why the US and Canada would both benefit from formal union: 'Consider the vitalizing, fructifying effects of the great waves of American capital and population which might be directed over that "Great Lone Land"!'.[18] An edition of *Harper's Weekly* in 1886 featured a cartoon about the potential annexation of Nova Scotia to the United States in order to bring an end to the century-long dispute over fishing rights.[19] Lastly, the British-born historian Goldwin Smith wrote *Canada and the Canadian Question* in 1891, where he set out that for innumerable reasons, 'Canada' was an untenable conglomeration of ethnicities and geographies, and that its inevitable destiny was to become part of an expanded United States.[20] Despite such sentiments, the nineteenth century witnessed a gradual ebbing of annexationist sentiments on both sides of the border, even if the issue has risen again at various points over the last century or so.[21] In reality, it was in the wake of the American Revolution that the likelihood of the United States annexing Canada was at its height, and what in that period some imagined a likelihood given time, now seems a relatively remote prospect for US imperial expansion in the near future.

Oregon

In the early years of the United States, Oregon Country, as it became known, was a very distant place from an East Coast perspective, although its coast had been explored as early as 1792 by the US Captain Robert Gray. In 1803, with Napoleon's hasty sale of Louisiana to the US and the doubling of US territory, Oregon became that much closer. That same year, Thomas Jefferson instructed explorer Merriweather Lewis to 'explore the Missouri river, & such principal stream of it, as, by it's [sic] course & communication with the water of the Pacific Ocean, may offer the most direct & practicable water communication across this continent, for the purposes of commerce'.[22] The resulting Lewis and Clark expedition that took place between 1804 and 1806 led to a successful, if not entirely practical, navigation of a route to the Pacific via the Rocky Mountains, the first US attempt to form an 'Oregon Trail'. Connecting the eastern United States to the Pacific, before the Mexican-American War of the 1840s at least, made more rapid progress at the northern end of US frontiers than the southern.

The United States was not the only nation with a claim to Oregon Country, an area comprising a vaguely defined landmass running from Spain's northern California Province in the south to Russia's Alaskan possessions in the north, and spanning the Rocky Mountains along the way to the Pacific Ocean. In spite of these northern and southern neighbours, though, the main claimants to the area were the United States and Great Britain.[23] It was these two nations that agreed the Treaty, or Convention, of 1818 in order to try and resolve the issue of sovereignty over Oregon Country. The accepted maximum north-south extent of Oregon Country was the area between 54° 40' (N) and 42° (N), and both Britain and the US had some prior claim to this territory. The British claim came mainly in the form of fur traders such as the substantial Hudson's Bay Company (HBC) and its fierce rivals the North West Company of Montreal (NWC). The Americans also had ambitions in the region's fur trade, through John Jacob Astor's mission to set up his Pacific Fur Company around 'Fort Astoria' in Oregon Country between 1810 and 1813. Astor's venture ended in failure during the War of 1812, when the British temporarily took control of Oregon Country and the NWC purchased Astor's Oregon assets. After signing the Treaty of Ghent in 1814, Britain relinquished its sole possession of Oregon Country, but the HBC continued to run Fort Astoria as 'Fort George' for a number of years afterwards.[24]

Despite the vast expanse of the territory under contest, the real heart of the debate was the land that lay between the 49th Parallel, the border already agreed up to the Rocky Mountains, and the land south of the parallel but still north of the Columbia River. The British sought to claim the river border ahead of the 49th Parallel, but the Americans desired access to the Puget Sound, which such a British claim would deny. The resulting compromise delayed any permanent settlement and began a ten-year 'joint occupancy' of Oregon Country with free movement for either side. However, it soon became clear that the British had the best commercial side of the deal, because the NWC had already purchased Astor's company. In 1821 the British government, tired of the ongoing conflict between the HBC and NWC, forced a merger of the two companies, and the now-expanded HBC had an effective monopoly over Oregon Country for the next two decades. The initial ten-year agreement was also extended indefinitely in 1827.[25]

By the 1830s settlers had started to move into the east of Oregon Country from the United States, beginning with Methodist missionaries led by Jason Lee, who in 1834 settled the Willamette Valley.[26] In response, somewhat later, the Hudson's Bay Company also decided to try and initiate settlement in the region to bolster its claims. James Sinclair, a Scots-Métis HBC worker, led the HBC contingent from Britain's Red River Colony (now Manitoba) in late 1841. Sinclair's belated 'counter-colonisation' attempts led one contemporary missionary to comment, 'Thus we see Oregon fast filling up', but according to historian Will Bagley the HBC aimed to settle in far less fertile soil than the Americans.[27] Indeed, in 1843, a 'Great Migration' from the US to Oregon Country began with around 250 wagons carrying 900 people headed to Oregon from Platte City, Missouri.[28] That same year, US settlers established their own provisional government in the region, a system that would last effectively until 1848.[29]

In 1844, Democratic presidential nominee James K. Polk stood on his party's platform to annex Texas and the whole of Oregon to the United States:

> Resolved, That our title to the whole of the Territory of Oregon is clear and unquestionable; that no portion of the same ought to be ceded to England or any other power, and that the reoccupation of Oregon and the re-annexation of Texas at the earliest practicable period are great American measures, which this Convention recommends to the cordial support of the Democracy of the Union.[30]

This platform is indicative of the burgeoning confidence of the US in their claims to the region by 1844. From 1844–5 the numbers surging into Oregon Country from the United States continued to rise steeply, leading some in the US to call for the furthest possible claims, leading to a popular slogan: '54° 40' or fight'. With the increased US settlement, and the relocation of the western headquarters of the HBC from Fort Vancouver on the Columbia River to Fort Victoria on Vancouver Island, the tide had begun to turn decisively against the British. Polk, who had been elected as an out-and-out expansionist, was then faced with the task of fulfilling his rhetoric – a call for the most extreme northern American claim in Oregon Country. The British prime minister, Sir Robert Peel, felt that national honour was now at stake in the Oregon situation, leading him to note that the British had 'as much right under the existing [1818] treaty to occupy and to fortify as the Americans have', and Peel even considered dispatching an increased military presence to the region. Such bellicose talk demonstrated to President Polk that Britain was willing to take decisive measures to stop the most extreme US claims.[31] However, a third US-British war was not to be, and at least part of the reason for this was that US attention was more firmly focused on the Texan-Mexican situation, which had been the focus of political debate for almost a decade. Polk had overseen the admission of Texas to the union in December 1845, and with the real possibility of war with Mexico looming, Britain felt that it might gain something from a president looking for a compromise in order to remove the potential for another war in the north.

The acquisition of both Oregon and Texas constituted part of the run-up to the US Civil War, regarding the admission of new 'slave' and 'free' states and how this would alter the balance of power in the US Congress. The potential annexation of slaveholding Texas would be balanced by the addition of a 'free' Oregon, but an enormous '54° 40″ Oregon might also scare the slaveholding South. Here US imperialism was checked not by ambition and desire, but by fear on the part of politicians of the potential public backlash when it came to the extension of slavery to newly acquired territories and states. In addition, there was the danger that the US might end up fighting two wars on different fronts at the same time: one with the British and Canadians, and another with Mexico. By early 1846, the British press became critical of what they saw as the unwillingness of the United States to submit the matter of Oregon to arbitration. For example, the *Morning Herald* asked:

> Why had America refused to submit the question to arbitration? Is it because their title is beyond dispute? Nay, what was made the pretext for Mr. [Caleb] Cushing's turgid threepenny balderdash, which he dignified by the name of a Lecture on Oregon? Why, 'because there was a general impression in the public mind that Great Britain had as good or better title to Oregon than America.' This was the excuse for Mr. Cushing's catchpenny publication, and yet we are now coolly told that the American title is of so fine a character that it cannot be submitted to the arbitration of Governments or individuals, however impartial.[32]

The Examiner, a British intellectual journal, reported that even John Quincy Adams, who had been secretary of state and US president during earlier negotiations over Oregon Country, had re-entered the debate. Adams' novel reasoning behind US claims in 1846 seemed to be based on biblical passages from Genesis – 'go forth and multiply etc.' – much to the cynical amusement of the editors:

> The abrogation of all titles or claims derived from charter, from treaty or from common understanding is certainly bold and new ground for even an American statesman to take. The replacing them by a claim derived from Genesis is newer still. But what is most new, most original, and most ludicrous is the assumption, that the grant conveyed by the Deity in the three verses of Genesis was exclusively made to the people of the United States![33]

Despite some tension, both sides were ultimately willing to compromise, and a final solution was reached in the Oregon Treaty of 1846 wherein the 49th Parallel was extended to the Pacific Coast, with the exception of Vancouver Island, the entirety of which would remain British. US imperial ambitions in the south-west had trumped their interests in pursuing the maximum extent of Oregon Country.

In 1848, Oregon was formally organised into a US incorporated territory; however, its boundary with the British colony of Vancouver Island (established in 1849) remained somewhat unclear, and a handful of small islands held the key to continued international tension. Unfortunately, the Oregon Treaty of 1846 proved a little too vague in its description of the nautical boundary between the US and Vancouver Island. The treaty suggested that the border would go through the 'main channel' between the mainland and Vancouver Island, but, as geography would have it, there were two main channels: the Haro Strait, claimed by the US, and the Rosario Strait, claimed by the British. The choice of strait would determine whether the San Juan Islands would lie within British or American waters. Thus began the last significant chapter in the Oregon boundary dispute.[34]

The matter of the Oregon boundary first came to the notice of US and British governments when the HBC established a sheep farm on San Juan Island in 1853. US customs officials demanded that duty be paid on the 1,300 sheep and, when the HBC refused, the officials confiscated some of the sheep and the US State Department advised waiting for formal settlement. Three years later, negotiations slowly began to resolve the boundary issue.[35] However, when an American citizen, Lyman Cutlar, shot an HBC-owned pig that had been ruining his crops, the whole debate over sovereignty was reignited. Britain responded by threatening to arrest Cutlar and evict other US citizens, and in response Oregon landed a sixty-four-man unit on the island. Vancouver Island's governor then continued the escalation of events by dispatching three ships – HMS *Tribune*, *Satellite* and *Plumper* – along with, initially, forty-six Royal Marines and fifteen Royal Engineers. When President Buchanan became aware of the escalating tensions, he sent General Winfield Scott to the island. Scott negotiated a joint military occupation of the island that lasted for twelve years, with a British garrison in the north and an American one in the south. In 1871, following the Treaty of Washington between Britain and the US, the two nations agreed to neutral arbitration by the German Kaiser, Wilhelm I. Wilhelm's commission took nearly a year to decide in favour of US claims and the Haro Strait became the agreed boundary, with Britain removing its last forces from the islands in late 1872.[36] The San Juan Island incident, often referred to as the 'Pig War', brought an effective end to Oregon/Washington-Canadian boundary disputes, but by this stage the grander imperial ambitions of the US in Oregon had long been tempered.

A full-scale war between the US and Britain over Oregon had perhaps only really been likely in the mid-1840s. However, the combined considerations of growing domestic unrest over the issue of slavery's expansion into the territories and the potential of having to fight two imperialist wars simultaneously had deterred even the pro-expansionist President Polk. By 1872 the old Oregon Country had been divided between Britain and Canada decisively. The northern section became the merged colonies of Vancouver Island and British Columbia, joining Canada under the latter name in 1871. The southern portion created the Territory of Washington and the State of Oregon, though some of the remaining land was ceded to Nebraska and Idaho territories during the Civil War years. Only one final part of the Canadian border had yet to be ascertained, and that was its western border with Alaska.

Alaska

The final episode in the United States' northern expansion during the nineteenth century is also the best known: the acquisition of Russia's North American possessions. Russian claims had a long heritage, from the early naval exploration of Mikhail Gvozdev (1732) and Vitus Bering (1741), to the 'right of occupation' established by Russian entrepreneurs in the eighteenth century. Lydia Black suggests that in contrast to the 'unbridled exploitation' of literary and political portrayals of the 'Russian period' in Alaskan history, the actual number of Russians was insignificant, rarely exceeding 500 in total. Indeed, she notes that Russians settling in Alaska seemed more desirous of stability and trading links with Native Alaskans than the sort of military confrontation with which the US met the Plains Indians in the nineteenth century.[37] However, one could argue that the Russian-Native Alaskan relationship was born of necessity more than enlightenment. To look to a parallel a couple of centuries before, the small population of French in North America had forged close relationships with native peoples in order to survive in relatively hostile natural environments and see off competition from European trading competitors. For the still-tiny population of Russians in nineteenth-century Alaska, this situation would have seemed all too familiar.

Russian settlement in Alaska dated back to 1784, when Grigori Shelekhov settled in Three Saints Bay on Kodiak Island during the reign of Catherine the Great. Shelekhov and his associate Ivan Golikov set up what became the Russian-American Company (RAC), a chartered company of the Russian Empire, not unlike the successful British Hudson's Bay Company (HBC). The RAC had a trading monopoly, initially granted in 1799 with a twenty-year renewal, with the expectation that the company would bear the costs and responsibility of managing the territory. This represented a turn to western European methods of governance accelerated under Peter the Great.[38] But despite this large monopoly, the RAC was never a great commercial success and the colony never became self-sufficient, often being forced to expand south to the borders of what was then Spanish California. The RAC also failed to effectively prohibit its competitors from trading with Alaskan Natives and therefore increasingly came into conflict with the HBC and the North West Company (NWC) of British North America. By the 1840s the commercial questionability of the RAC, coupled with the unpopularity of the company among Natives, led Russia to consider the long-term viability of the Alaskan enterprise.[39]

The obvious competitors for Russian Alaska were its two nearest neighbours: British North America and the United States. In the Convention of 1825, Britain established, though not entirely definitively (see discussion of the Alaska Boundary Dispute below), its borders with Russia in North America. Indeed, it was Britain who in one way appeared to have the most likely desire to extend influence into Alaska, as the HBC had leased substantial swathes of RAC territory in the form of the 1838 'Stikine Lease'. However, as Ian Jackson argues, given the dubious profitability of the region during the HBC lease years, the British had seen only dim prospects for the region, and by the 1860s the Americans might have been the only credible buyers.[40]

Twists and turns of European diplomacy also altered the course of the Alaskan situation. The Crimean War (1853–6), fought between Russia and an alliance of the British, French and Ottomans, played an important role in the eventual sale of Alaska in 1867. During the war, the RAC and HBC agreed a truce, with an assurance that Britain would not invade Alaska. This decision was made largely for the British to maintain US goodwill during the conflict. In the aftermath of the British allied victory in the Crimean War, the Russians turned their attentions to consolidating their interests in China, annexing the Amur-Ussuri region in the years after the war.[41] The enormous debts accrued during the defeat in the Crimea also saw Russia focus on more profitable trade with the newly 'opened' nation of Japan and seek to offload the expense of naval patrols needed to maintain the monopoly in Alaska. In 1860 the Russian government decided to alter the RAC lease and remove its monopoly, a deal the RAC declined, leaving Russia with little option but to sell the territory.[42]

In 1853, the Governor General of eastern Siberia noted that the US and not Britain were the likely future masters of Alaska, stating that Russia 'ought to be convinced that the United States are bound to spread over the whole of North America'.[43] The eventual US purchase of Alaska is, however, usually presented as the work of the arch-expansionist William Seward, the US secretary of state from 1861–9. As well as positioning Seward clearly as the instigator of the purchase, many Americans at the time saw the Alaska Purchase as 'Seward's folly', and suggested cynically that it might be used as a national icebox, a polar bear garden, or a place for

Seward to retire.[44] However, historian Richard Welch Jr. argues that the purchase was 'not as unpopular as the traditional interpretation holds', and that this can be seen in the Senate's necessary two-thirds support for the measure. He suggests that the myth of public displeasure at the purchase is largely due to general ignorance about Alaska, and that when one looks at contemporaneous newspapers, they indicate either general support for or indifference to Seward's scheme.[45]

The negotiations for the purchase of Alaska resumed after the US Civil War, with Seward seeing it as a good location for naval bases vital to expansion in the Pacific region. Russia's representative, Edouard de Stoeckl, was instructed to accept not less than $5 million for the territory, and within two weeks had struck a seemingly decent deal for $7.2 million. The US Senate, whose attention was elsewhere in the aftermath of the Civil War (with the policy of Reconstruction of the South, and the attempt to impeach President Johnson), passed the treaty by seventy-three votes to two. The House of Representatives acted more slowly, but, once the impeachment attempt had failed, voted the appropriations needed to complete the purchase. On 28 July 1867 they approved the payment of the $7.2 million to Russia. Some allege the House vote was the subject of bribery; for example, Donna Dickerson argues that Stoeckl was indeed given the means to get the measure more positive attention, at least in the press.[46] Regardless of whether or not this was a 'crooked' deal – though the process was certainly not wholly transparent – by the end of the year the purchase was complete.

In British North America, the US purchase of Alaska, coupled with other factors such as the prevailing economic climate, led western Canada to look more favourably at the prospect of US annexation.[47] As the *New York Times* reported on 22 September 1867:

> the secret aim and desire of English statesmen has been, of recent years – and is now – to give both the Atlantic and the Pacific Provinces the chance of cutting loose from their leading strings. . . . They are an isolated dependency without any of the life-giving subsidies which the Atlantic Provinces have been able to rely upon. And in this condition they are as ripe for annexation to the United States as it is well possible to conceive. The purchase by our Government of the territory of Alaska, instead of inspiring the British Columbians with any feeling of

alarm, has rather given them some share of political courage, and has stimulated their hopes for release, sooner or later, from the bondage of an unnatural Colonial connection.

Although such reportage sounds like wishful thinking, it did tie into the long-held view in the United States that Canada would ultimately be incorporated into the American Empire. After all, this report came only a year after the United States had introduced a bill calling for the annexation of Canada. Such sentiments arose once more during the final major episode in the Alaska tale – the dispute over the Alaska boundary with Canada at the start of the twentieth century – when once again the United States sought to expand its imperial reach in the north of the continent.

After the completion of the Alaska Purchase, the US government showed little genuine interest in Alaskan affairs, with the small exception of an Organic Act in 1884 which allowed for the gradual establishment of an administration for the 'District' of Alaska. However, this all changed after the discovery of gold in the Canadian Klondike territory in the mid-1890s, when Alaskan ports such as Skagway became important gateways to a surge of prospectors in a northern gold rush. More discoveries followed in Nome (1898) and Fairbanks (1902) in Alaska itself, and both the British and the Americans became keen to claim the maximum extent of the Pacific coastal ports to which they felt they were entitled.

The Anglo-Russian Convention of 1825 had granted only a relatively vague boundary concerning the Alaska 'panhandle' that trails down the Pacific coast of Canada. A joint commission set up between 1898 and 1899 also failed to come to an agreement, as Canada was determined to control the heads of key fjords on the Pacific Coast. In 1903 the US and Britain assembled an international tribunal consisting of three Americans, two Canadians and Lord Alverstone, the Lord Chief Justice of England.[48] In the official report of proceedings, what becomes abundantly clear is that it was Alverstone who stopped deadlock in the affair. With the three Americans and two Canadians maintaining a fairly partisan stance, Alverstone sided more often than not with the Americans. The result was a victory for the US, who maintained control of the entrances to key fjords and left only two of four islands at the mouth of the Portland Canal as Canadian gains. So frustrated were the Canadian contingent, they refused to sign the final award and wrote minority opinions in protest.[49]

The result of the Alaska boundary dispute was met very differently on either side of the 49th Parallel. In the US it was seen as a victory for President Theodore Roosevelt's arbitrators, while in Canada the Prime Minister, Wilfred Laurier, saw it as making British diplomacy 'odious to the Canadian people'. Traditionally, Canada had tended to portray the deal as a British 'sell-out' or a result of Theodore Roosevelt's bullying.[50] Yet David Haglund and Tudor Onea suggest that the deal was actually an example of Roosevelt acting rather honourably, and Britain striking a decent bargain.[51] These years were a high point in Anglo-American relations, and with the increasingly aggressive Japanese and German empires drifting into America's Pacific concerns by this stage, neither Britain or the United States had much to gain from pushing too hard. The Canadians, however, did not see things this way at all, and US papers such as the *Washington Post* in October 1903 reported from Vancouver that:

> There is much talk of annexation and of Canada becoming independent, business men generally being much dissatisfied at what they denounce as British disregard of Canadian interests to please the United States. . . . It is a matter of comment that loudest among the discontented are Englishmen residing here. Many of them say that Canada will never achieve her greatest possibilities until she becomes a part of the United States.[52]

What is clear once more is a call from a rebellious populace seeking annexation by their American neighbour, a theme that recurs in a number of instances explored in this volume. But the United States, as discussed earlier in this chapter, had predicted the inevitability of expansion of the American 'Empire of Liberty' into Canada for over a century, to no avail.

Alaska was a 'slow burner' in terms of US imperial interest. Initially seen by Seward's critics as an unnecessary expenditure, it proved over the years to be a canny investment. Not only did the US take territory that might otherwise have been seized by British North America but, in the very long view, the Cold War might have been even chillier if it had remained in Russian hands until the twentieth century. Canada lost out in the Alaska debate, but as historians like Jackson have noted, perhaps in 1867 (if not in 1903) there was little apparent commercial benefit to the annexation of Alaska from the point of view of Canada's leading economic force in the West, the Hudson's Bay Company.

Purchased in 1867, Alaska did not acquire formal territorial status until 1912, and it was only the gold rushes of the 1890s that led the United States to give any serious thought to its future. The Second World War provided the second major period of focus on Alaska, when the territory became renowned for its prime strategic value. As Steven Haycox and Mary C. Mangusso put it, WW2 changed Alaska 'even more drastically than the gold rushes'.[53] On 3 January 1959 President Eisenhower, the former Supreme Commander of Allied Forces during the war, oversaw the admission of Alaska as the 49th State of the Union, after a decade of debate over the suitability for full statehood of the first non-contiguous state.

Overall, the expansion of the United States to the north was achieved through negotiations with Britain and Russia, but notably *not* Canada. Though the War of 1812 might be given as an exception to this rule, it is certainly possible to see that conflict more as one of US frustration at British interference in its affairs than as a war for expansionism. After all, if the War of 1812 is ascribed expansionist motives, it signally failed to achieve its aims. Success was far more evident when the US exerted diplomatic pressure on Britain, encouraged emigration to Oregon, and took fortuitous advantage of the disinterest of others in Alaska. Ultimately, territory in each case explored in this chapter passed bloodlessly from the hands of a European empire into those of an increasingly formidable American one.

Notes

1. Thompson and Randall, *Canada and the United States*, p. 14.
2. 'Articles of Confederation: March 1, 1781', *Avalon Project*.
3. Thompson and Randall, *Canada and the United States*, pp. 11–17. For a more recent take see: Taylor, *Civil War of 1812*. This is certainly the most credible explanation, especially given that some 'late loyalists' moved North harbouring hopes of spreading republican ideals upon their arrival.
4. See Chapter 1.
5. Lawson and Seidman, *Constitution of Empire*, p. 2.
6. Hickey, *The War of 1812*, p. 3.

7. Maass, 'Difficult to Relinquish', 72, pp. 96–7.
8. The war itself has been explored by many historians, and will not be the focus of attention here. For good recent studies see: Borneman, *1812* and Drez, *The War of 1812*.
9. See: McLaughlin, *The Patriot War*.
10. See: Campbell, *Aroostook War*.
11. Monet, 'Annexation Association'.
12. Herring, *From Colony to Superpower*, pp. 253–4.
13. 'Article 7', *New York Times*, p. 4.
14. Pletcher, *The Diplomacy of Involvement*, p. 53.
15. Among the representatives at the treaty discussions was the first prime minister of Canada, Sir John A. Macdonald.
16. This debate, dating back to a provision in the Treaty of Paris (1783) that allowed for both Britain and the US to fish off of the Newfoundland coast, continued into the twentieth century, when the matter was settled by the Permanent Court of Arbitration at The Hague in 1910.
17. Bender, 'Canadian View of Annexation', p. 326.
18. Bender, 'Annexation of Canada', p. 49.
19. Kennedy, 'On this Day'.
20. Smith, *Canada and the Canadian Question*.
21. This idea still occasionally arises in the Canadian press, a recent example being when Peter Zeihan's book, *Accidental Superpower*, suggested oil-rich Alberta might be better off joining the United States.
22. Mackin, *Americans and their Land*, p. 158.
23. Spain renounced its claims to the territory in the Adams-Onís Treaty of 1819 (see Chapter 1), and the Russian Empire gave up its claims in separate treaties with the USA (1824) and Great Britain (1825).
24. Emmerich, *John Jacob Astor*.
25. Ibid.
26. Dodd, 'Oregon Country', p. 265.
27. Bagley, *So Rugged and Mountainous*, p. 114.
28. Dohnal, *Columbia River Gorge*, p. 21.
29. Dodd, 'Oregon Country', p. 265.
30. '1844 Democratic Party Platform', *American Presidency Project*.
31. Black, *Fighting for America*, p. 235.
32. 'The London Papers', *The Observer*, p. 6.
33. 'Quincy Adams Upon Genesis', *The Examiner*, p. 162.
34. After 1853 the border was technically now with Washington Territory, as it was separated from Oregon Territory to its south.
35. Ruttan, 'The Pig War'.
36. Vouri, 'The Pig War'; for detailed coverage, see: Vouri, *The Pig War*.
37. Black, *Russians in Alaska*, p. xiii.
38. Vinkovetsky, *Russian America*, p. 9, pp. 66–7.

39. Dickerson, *Reconstruction Era*, pp. 183–4.
40. Jackson, 'Stikine Territory Lease', pp. 289–306.
41. Goldfrank, *Origins of the Crimean War*, pp. 294–5.
42. Dickerson, *Reconstruction Era*, p. 184.
43. Jackson, 'Stikine Territory Lease', p. 291.
44. Hinckley, 'American Botany Bay', pp. 1–2.
45. Welch, 'American Public Opinion', p. 102.
46. Dickerson, *Reconstruction Era*, pp. 184–5.
47. Neunherz, 'Hemmed In', pp. 118–33.
48. The three Americans were: Secretary of War Elihu Root and Senator Henry Cabot Lodge of Massachusetts (both Republicans), along with the Democratic Senator for Washington State, George Turner. The two Canadians were the lawyers Sir Louis-Amable Jetté and Allen B. Aylesworth.
49. 'The Alaska Boundary Case', *UN Office of Legal Affairs*.
50. McCulloch, 'Theodore Roosevelt and Canada', pp. 293–313, suggests that Canada had only agreed to join the second British war against the Boers in South Africa (1899–1902) in order to gain firmer British support on the Alaskan issue.
51. Haglund and Onea, 'Victory without Triumph', p. 21.
52. 'Bitter in Canada', *Washington Post*, p. 1.
53. Haycox and Mangusso, *Alaska Anthology*, p. xxv.

CHAPTER 3

Leaving the Continent (1817–90)

Although the United States' annexations around the time of the Spanish-American War – including Hawaii, Cuba and the Philippines – are the best-known examples of the nation extending its imperial reach overseas, there were precedents for US interest beyond the mainland well before this period. In Liberia, for example, the United States created a pseudo-colonial enterprise of its own when it began relocating African Americans to West Africa. Additionally, the US also expanded its reach tentatively into the Pacific Ocean when searching for raw materials, but in these instances colonisation was not even under consideration. Finally, the island of Cuba remained a draw for US attention throughout the nineteenth century and, as was the case with Canada, the US saw this Caribbean island as likely to fall under its control given time.

Liberia

The United States' first imperialist venture outside of its own hemisphere came with its early-nineteenth-century involvement in West Africa. Although there were early attempts to resettle African Americans in Yorubaland, in what later became Nigeria, the first successful scheme developed in what came to be called Liberia, 'the land of freedom'.[1] The move was not driven directly by the US government, but instead by the American Colonization Society (ACS). Its aims sounded similar to those of many European colonial powers of the day, despite the United States' history of critiquing Old World colonialism dating back to the time of the American Revolution. The ACS played a similar role to that of chartered companies in the British Empire. A chartered company often served as a vital precursor to formal British annexation in later years, like, for example, the British East India Company. The British gave such chartered companies permission to carry out the duties that would usually be overseen by the imperial power itself: governing, protecting and profiting from its sphere of influence. Like the British, the US planned on taking similar 'benefits' to the 'dark continent' in line with the famous explorer David Livingstone's three 'C's: Christianity, commerce and civilisation. However, where US plans differed from those of most European ventures was that the colony was not initially intended to be ruled by a white elite, or settled by whites, but instead to provide a homeland for the unwanted free blacks and formerly enslaved of the United States.

The idea of establishing a colony for unwanted populations was not exclusive to the US in this period. Indeed, as a starting venture for US overseas imperialism, this seemed comparable only to one pre-existing venture: the unusual corner of the British Empire that was Sierra Leone. A chartered company, the Sierra Leone Company, had established the Sierra Leone colony and relocated free blacks from Nova Scotia in British North America there. Some years later the British government took formal control of the coastal settlement, annexing the interior as a formal protectorate when the 'Scramble for Africa' began in the 1880s. Indeed, so similar was the British colony in Sierra Leone that Thomas Jefferson even considered sending the surfeit free black population of the United States there instead.[2] One of the reasons such a plan never came to fruition was that the British feared an influx of freedom-loving African Americans might in turn radicalise the blacks of Sierra Leone.[3] The United States, therefore, appeared to be on a similar course.

Formed in 1817, the American Colonization Society aimed to establish a homeland in Africa where former slaves in the United States could be 'repatriated'. Abolitionists within the United States were among some of the scheme's earliest adherents, believing that the ACS could one day eliminate slavery in North America, by offering a solution to the potential 'negro problem' that the abolition of slavery would leave. US churches also supported the venture, as historian Charles Foster argues: 'So much benevolence in a single package proved irresistible to the churches which almost unanimously endorsed the Colonization Society though their ecclesiastical bodies.'[4] The resettlement seemed to provide a dual function. Firstly, it would give the free blacks the opportunity to spread their Christianised and 'civilised' ways to the inhabitants in their vicinity. Additionally, it would help the

United States maintain an orderly society back home without the chaos that many southern slaveholders predicted if abolition were ever to occur. Indicative of these ideals was one of the scheme's founders, Presbyterian minister Robert Finley of New Jersey. Finley believed that while in an ethnically diverse society, blacks could never be equal, and therefore resettlement in Africa was a fine solution for both white and black Americans alike. So compelling was the scheme that in 1819 the US Congress went so far as to appropriate $100,000 for the ACS. By 1822 the ACS had established its first settlement in Monrovia, on Cape Mesurado, taking its name from US president James Monroe.

In 1824 Liberia gained its first constitution, which broadly outlined US plans for the territory's future. The colony was set for staggered moves towards eventual self-government, during which it would be stewarded and tutored by the ACS. Similar promises of self-government followed by a potential (distant) independence were given to many subsequent US overseas colonies and, in this respect, Foster sees the Liberian Constitution as setting a precedent for subsequent US imperial endeavours. From the start, the US promised Liberia strong black representation in its own government, unlike the British colony in neighbouring Sierra Leone. The ACS agent was the only white man in the administration and he controlled the judiciary, minor officials, and a standing army of fifteen.[5] If Liberia was to be the start of an overseas US empire, seemingly its government would be one quite different to the many British models in the region.

Building upon its early successes, the ACS continued to purchase further lands and expand its foothold in West Africa. As an ACS pamphlet of 1831 detailed:

> The first purchased territory presents the form of a tongue of land, twelve miles in extent. In 1825, Mr. Ashmun purchased of the natives an extensive and fertile tract of country, extending nine miles on the coast, from Montserado [Mesurado] to the Saint Paul's, and indefinitely in the interior. . . . To the original territory additions have been made, as the growing want of the colony, actual, or anticipated, required. The country thus obtained, embraces large tracts of fertile land, capable of yielding all the rich and varied products of the tropics; possessing great commercial advantages . . .[6]

With the ACS expanding its holdings, while also attempting to generate a viable economy, the varied settlements were soon incorporated into what was named the Commonwealth of Liberia. As with any such overseas territorial foothold, this burgeoning activity meant that the new colony caused some tension in the region with its neighbouring imperial outposts. In this case, the main 'local' rivals were the French Côte d'Ivoire and British Sierra Leone. Indeed, by the 1840s some of those involved in British African affairs felt that if Britain was to abandon its Gold Coast (later Ghana) colony, then the United States might well seek to take control there as well.[7]

The British were not alone in foreseeing an imperial future for America's African offshoot. In 1839, the president of Vermont's Colonization Society, Elijah Paine, noted that: 'if the Federal Government should Colonize the whole Western and Southern coast of Africa, (which is not already occupied by Great Britain,) merely for the purpose of commerce with that country, I think they would discover statesman-like talents, which they have rarely heretofore discovered'.[8] He went on to argue that, though naysayers might raise the issue of whether such action would be constitutional, in the longer run this might prove a good value investment, through creating an economy to fund the transportation of all African Americans back across the Atlantic. Thus, though Liberia might well have been founded and utilised almost solely for the disposal of an unwanted population, the US was not without voices that anticipated a greater imperial role in the future.

The international status of Liberia was the subject of some curiosity, not least from the British, keen to expand their trading influences in the region. As one commentator put it, the US intervened in Liberia 'so frequently between the natives and the colonists, patching up difficulties and settling disputes, that it was commonly understood that the settlements were under the protection of the United States ... to all intents and purposes a *de facto* colony of the United States'.[9] As late as 1843, the US secretary of state responded to a British query over Liberia's status that it was 'an object of peculiar interest' and that the US would be 'very unwilling to see it despoiled of its [Liberia's] territory rightfully acquired'.[10] However, independence was, at that point, not long in coming. The ACS severed its official connections with the running of the colony in 1846, and Liberia declared its independence following a convention in 1847 that resulted in a new constitution.

The US was remarkably slow to formally recognise the new Republic of Liberia. Britain was the first nation to recognise the sovereignty of the new Liberian government, but the United States waited until the midst of the Civil War in 1862 to concede the republican status of what had been close to becoming its first overseas colony.[11] A key reason for this was that not everybody in the United States would have taken kindly to recognising a black-run nation.[12] However, even after Liberian independence, the ACS was not finished with its proto-imperial mission. When President Lincoln issued the Emancipation Proclamation in 1863, he might have all but ended slavery in the US, but he had not eradicated what many in the divided nation regarded as the 'problem' of the nation's (free) black population.

Historians Phillip Magness and Sebastian Page have recently revealed that Lincoln was discussing the idea of a colony in British Honduras in the 1860s.[13] Indeed, in his preliminary Emancipation Proclamation of September 1862, Lincoln stated that: 'the effort to colonize persons of African descent, with their consent, upon this continent, or elsewhere, with the previously obtained consent of the Governments existing there, will be continued'.[14] However, as Eric Foner has recently observed, after issuing the final proclamation in 1863, Lincoln ceased talking publicly of colonisation, due perhaps to a recognition that such statements had failed to persuade African Americans or reconcile his more northerly US critics to the idea of emancipation. In the following months Lincoln gradually abandoned the idea of colonisation, though he remained concerned as to what exactly would happen to formerly enslaved people after the war.[15] In the war's aftermath, the ACS issued an outline for continued efforts to colonise black Americans in Liberia, garnering support from a number of prominent white southerners, and issuing a new pamphlet entitled *Information about Going to Liberia*. Civil War General John W. Phelps explained the ongoing 'negro problem' thus: 'Every sensible nego [sic] must see that it is a great deal easier for him to Christianize and nationalize Africa than it is to Africanize the United States. So long as he remains here he will be a negro and we shall be Saxons.' However, by the end of the 1860s the fortunes of the ACS had waned significantly, as most black and white citizens of the United States did not desire such resettlement.[16]

For the Liberians themselves, the legacy of pseudo-US imperial rule was a mixed blessing. Those who had emigrated to the settlement – the Americo-Liberians – controlled the nation of Liberia from 1847 well into the late twentieth century. The connection to the United States, however, meant that by the turn of the century Liberia was the only fully independent country in Africa along with Abyssinia (which was later annexed by Mussolini in the 1930s). The US continued to support the Liberian government against indigenous/tribal uprisings and European threats to their territorial integrity. In the case of Liberia, the United States had carried out all the groundwork for imperial expansion, but ultimately chose to reject formal annexation. Unlike expansion into Texas and Oregon, colonisation was not to be the chosen method of US imperial expansion overseas.

The Guano Islands

Although the US-led expansion in Liberia never resulted in formal annexation or the formation of a protectorate, it did adhere to the nature of much 'creeping' imperialism by Europeans during the nineteenth century via the 'chartered company' route. Trading interests commonly provided the precursors for protectorates and then formal annexation, and they did so in the case of the so-called 'guano islands'. Many standard texts on US expansionism tend to dismiss or footnote the guano islands entirely, and move on instead to the 1890s when the more obvious examples of US imperial expansion occurred outwith the North American continent.[17] However, where the idea of Liberia as the first example of US overseas imperialism is not wholly satisfactory, the guano islands provide a far more solid specimen of early US imperialism overseas.[18]

As Jimmy Skaggs outlines at the start of his volume *The Great Guano Rush*, guano – as a commodity – became fiercely sought after in the early nineteenth century, with 'a veritable global rush' seeking the valuable bird droppings that had proved to be a miraculous fertiliser rich with many key soil nutrients, such as phosphates.[19] In this period, the primary source of guano were islands (most notably the Chinchas) claimed by Peru, a nation that had somewhat cornered the market in this increasingly valuable material. This placed the Peruvians in a position to raise the price accordingly. But it was really only in the mid-nineteenth century that the United States and its European imperial rivals began to look beyond its Peruvian suppliers to the thousands of tiny, and usually uninhabited, islands that peppered the Pacific Ocean. Here, they reasoned, there was plentiful guano without the increasingly burdensome levies charged by Peru for access to theirs.

On 4 August 1852, the *New York Tribune* reported on the growing speculation about the potential for claiming 'guano islands':

> While the English merchants and politicians have been discussing the question of their right to carry away this fertilizing material from these islands, a shrewd Yankee merchant of this city, Mr. A. G. Benson, with his associates, has solved the problem in the usual go-a-head manner of his nation. Having satisfied himself by sufficient inquiry that the guano was good, was inexhaustible, and was accessible, he also satisfied himself fully under the law of nations it belonged to the whole world, and the rest of mankind if they chose to take it away. ... Mr. Benson has had a correspondence with the Government at Washington, and he has not probably gone so deeply into the matter without proper assurances from that quarter that he shall be protected.[20]

This extract brings to the fore a number of the issues that arose over the sudden commercial exploration and exploitation of these Pacific islands. Firstly, that the primary, and often only, motivation behind the territorial expansion was the guano itself. The scattered rocks of the Pacific were not desired for their intrinsic value, natural beauty, or even, in the main, their strategic value. The simple fact was that the US coveted the islands because birds had defecated upon them. However, although in so many ways different from the Liberian venture discussed above, the guano islands were also claimed by chartered companies, the first and foremost of which was the American Guano Company. In the years that followed, there arose a number of rival companies spurred on by the success of the early ventures, such as the US Guano Company, the Phoenix Guano Company and the Pacific Guano Company.

As guano fever grew, so did the potential for disputes. For example, in 1854, both US and British traders laid out their claims to Aves Island, an island later claimed by Venezuela, and it was this episode that saw the first proposed bill that might have extended US 'sovereignty' over a guano island. However, the bill that finally passed the US Senate in 1856 dropped the word 'sovereignty' for the word 'appertaining', a term with no real legal definition.[21] Indeed, 'appertaining' as a legal term proved a conveniently malleable one, later clarified by Attorney General Jeremiah Black, who eventually suggested that 'actual continuous, exclusive possession' was required.[22] On 18 August 1856, President Franklin Pierce signed the finalised act that stated:

> when any citizen or citizens of the United States may have discovered, or shall hereafter discover, a deposit of guano on any island, rock, or key not within the lawful jurisdiction of any other government, and not occupied by the citizens of any other government, and shall take peaceable possession thereof, and occupy the same, said island, rock, or key may, at the discretion of the President of the United States, be considered as appertaining to the United States . . . [23]

The fourth section of the act noted that the US would not be bound to retain any guano islands after the guano's removal, but – as the fifth section stressed – the US president was authorised to deploy the armed forces to protect the discoverers of any US guano finds. The Guano Island Act (GIA) conferred upon the United States the 'mantle of empire' and both the passage of the act and the possessions acquired as a result of it began the passage of official overseas imperialism for the United States. Indeed, Dan O'Connell suggests that, when it came to uninhabited island possessions, the 'pervasive mood' in the United States appeared to be an 'enthusiastic zeal for these noncontiguous territories'.[24]

Following the passage of the act, US forays into overseas imperialism brought it into further contests with its rivals. US claims over Navassa Island in the Caribbean, for example, are still contested by Haiti. Claims over the Johnston Islands brought the US into a dispute with the Kingdom of Hawaii when, following US claims in 1859, Hawaii asserted its own right to the islands, albeit in a somewhat lacklustre way.[25] In 1898, the *Washington Post* reported on an incident at Clipperton Island, 1,500 miles off of the Pacific coast of Mexico, where 'the American flag was hauled down and the Mexican flag substituted' when guano hunters overstepped the boundaries of the 'unclaimed' clause of the GIA.[26] However, for the most part, the initial theory that the US claimed the guano islands simply for the guano appeared true, at least until the 1930s, when the increasingly tense international situation made the US government reconsider their utility.

During the New Deal era, President Franklin Roosevelt's administration oversaw a renewed affirmation of US rights over the guano islands, many of which had long been exhausted of their precious deposits. As Japan began its relentless attempt to subdue China in the mid-1930s, the United States became aware that the empire of the rising sun was becoming a far more immediate threat in the Pacific. In June 1938, the US Congress formally reasserted all 'possessory rights' over the guano islands. The US reclaimed the '"etceteras" of the Pacific' and, in order to show effective occupation of the islands, began to strategically settle small groups of Hawaiians on the islands for the furtherance of their claims. As a 1941 article in the *American Journal of International Law* noted, in the years immediately prior to US entry to World War Two, 'certain small uninhabited islands in the Pacific Ocean have assumed sudden importance for the British Empire and the United States'.[27] With US possessions after 1898 stretching all the way to the South China Sea, the military and strategic importance of the guano islands as existing and/or potential Pacific bases became far clearer.

One notable strategic island group that rose to particular prominence was Midway Atoll. First claimed in a formal ceremony in August 1867, Midway was placed under the control of the US Navy Department. Like Wake Island (which was not claimed by the US until 1899), Midway was one of only two tiny US Pacific possessions occupied for reasons other than guano.[28] Midway served primarily as a key coaling port for US ships on the way to Asia, and only grew in importance as the century came to an end. In the early twentieth century it became a stopover for the trans-Pacific telegraph cable. A 1904 article in the *New York Times*, entitled 'Lonely Midway Islands', painted a vignette of Sand Island, the most significant in the Midway Atoll, and its fourteen inhabitants, who felt that 'ever since the cable came here we have considered ourselves our country's outpost'. The two Chinese settlers among this group were described as 'the only China pebbles allowed on the beach' and, as to the sole woman inhabitant of the island, 'No Queen ever received more homage or more ready and willing obedience'.[29] However, by 1935, the same newspaper was heralding the opening of a new airport on Sand Island, as it somewhat inaccurately reported: 'This tiny dot on the map . . . has now become the newest colony under the Stars and Stripes and is the world's first mid-ocean airbase.'[30] By 1941 a naval station was opened in the atoll, and the military base on Midway was attacked along with its Hawaiian neighbours at Pearl Harbor that December. Indeed, the atoll is probably the best known of the US's tiny Pacific possessions because of the 1942 naval battle near it, which saw a decisive shift in the Pacific war in favour of the Allies.

In the present day the United States lays claim to nine tiny overseas 'insular areas': Palmyra Atoll, Navassa Island, Johnston Atoll, Baker Island, Howland Island, Jarvis Island, Kingman Reef, Midway Atoll and Wake Atoll.[31] Aside from Navassa, which lies in the Caribbean, the rest of the islands, the bulk of which were guano islands, lie in the Pacific. With the exclusion of Palmyra Atoll, which was once part of Hawaiian territory, the other eight islands or island groups are all classified as US unincorporated and unorganised territories.[32] At different times legislation has been introduced, but not carried through, that would have seen sections of these islands placed under the jurisdiction of either the state of Hawaii, or American Samoa.[33] However, these nine small island groups illustrate the earliest assertion of formal US territorial possession upon distant territory. Of course, much more of the Pacific was to come under US control at the end of the nineteenth century, but by that time the debate about the value and nature of US imperialism had moved on markedly.

Early Cuban Intrigue

Unlike Liberia and the tiny Pacific guano islands, Cuba, only ninety miles from the coast of Florida, had always been a prime candidate for US overseas expansion (though, to a lesser extent, interest elsewhere in the Caribbean was also evident in the mid-nineteenth century, as will be shown in Chapter 7). In the first decade of the nineteenth century, Thomas Jefferson wrote to James Madison that Napoleon Bonaparte might consider ceding Cuba to the Americans, if only to stop them aiding Mexico and its neighbours.[34] Far better this, thought Jefferson, than a possible cession to the British, which would leave the US vulnerable in its soft underbelly.[35] However, from the 1820s to the late 1840s, the 'dominant feature' of US Cuban policy was to guarantee Spanish sovereignty over Cuba in order to keep out the more powerful and threatening empires of Britain and France. This support for Spain, however, was to be maintained only until the inevitable day when Cuba drifted into American hands.[36] Indeed, John Quincy Adams regarded Cuba as a 'natural appendage' of the United States: a 'ripe fruit' that would slowly gravitate towards the USA – a metaphor later commentators continued to use.[37] In 1823, Adams became the first secretary of state to argue that 'the annexation of Cuba to our federal republic will be indispensable to the continuance and integrity of the Union itself', but that this annexation would likely come via a Cuban revolution rather than US force alone.[38]

Between the sixteenth century and 1898, Cuba remained, almost unbrokenly, a Spanish colony. When Spain lost control of most of its vast mainland American possessions in the early 1800s, the island remained the jewel in what was left of its considerably diminished empire. One of the reasons Cuba had not followed its American republican neighbours was the continuing support for slavery on the island, particularly among the Criollos (the second tier of Spanish imperial society on the island, below the pure-Spanish Peninsulares). In the 1820s and 1830s the Criollos, keen to maintain the existing societal structure, began to desire annexation by the United States. In addition, following various slave revolts in the 1840s, many Criollos felt the US could provide them with more stability than Spain.[39] By the mid-1840s, therefore, the US was faced with two paths: either allow an unthreatening Spain to continue in control of Cuba rather than the potential alternatives of Britain or France, or try and do a better job of governing Cuba itself.

The Mexican War of 1846–8 really advanced the Cuban debate within the United States. As the US began to take control of swathes of formerly Spanish territory on the continent, many looked to Cuba as another route for territorial expansion. However, such expansion would prove as divisive politically in the US as its continental expansion did. For US southerners, the fact that the island was well established as a slave territory was a positive factor. When the war ended, the bulk of the new territories acquired under the Treaty of

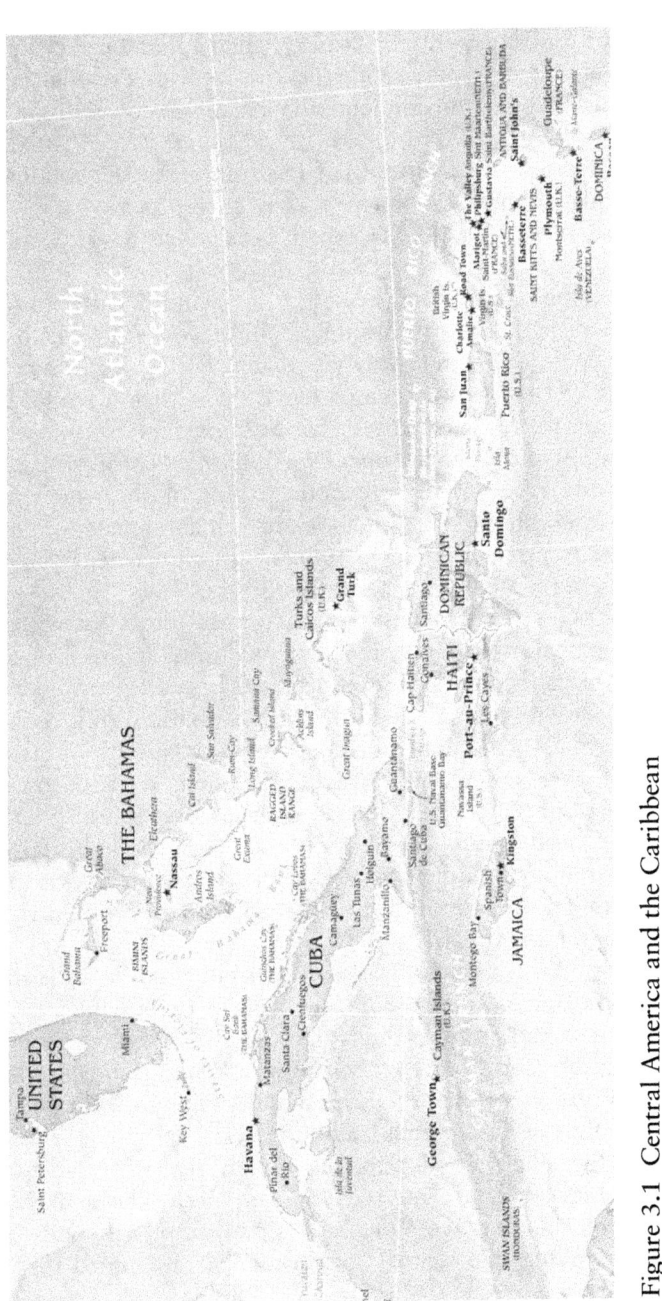

Figure 3.1 Central America and the Caribbean

Guadalupe-Hidalgo were not fertile ground for the expansion of slavery. As a result, some southerners pushed for the annexation of Cuba as a route to maintaining the 'balance' between slave and free states once achieved by the Missouri Compromise of 1820, but unsettled by the vast acquisitions of 1848. To northern abolitionists Cuba's annexation was anathema for just such reasons.

Adding these ideas to the expansionist doctrine of Manifest Destiny so prevalent in the 1840s, the government's traditional policy of supporting Spanish rule on the island in order to keep out the British and French disintegrated. Indeed, the *Jeffersonian Republican* noted in June of 1848 that if Polk's successor were to be former Democratic senator Lewis Cass, then it would be a vote for Cass and Cuba, foreseeing an immediate future where both 'Oregon and Cuba are ours by conquest'.[40] During this same period, Moses Beach, the influential editor of the widely read *New York Sun*, popularised the idea of Cuban annexation in his paper's editorials and John O'Sullivan, the journalist who had coined the term 'Manifest Destiny', unsuccessfully tried to press Secretary of State Buchanan to take action. However, with the help of Democratic senator Stephen Douglas, O'Sullivan took the annexation plan to Polk himself, and convinced the president to take the idea to cabinet. Indeed, the information Polk received from the likes of O'Sullivan, especially regarding the potential for an uprising (see below), caused the president to move towards obtaining Cuba.[41] Polk decided against forceful annexation, instead favouring purchase of the island. The eventual offer was for $100 million, an offer that was firmly rejected by the Spanish, whose foreign minister informed the US that they would rather see it 'sunk in the ocean'.[42]

Much of the attention on Cuba and its potential for annexation centred upon the idea of a popular revolt in Cuba, which the US could then seize as an opportunity to invade.[43] The figurehead of the planned insurrection was Narciso López, a Venezuelan who sought to seize Cuba away from the Spanish and maintain slavery on the island. In the eyes of covetous US southerners López was the perfect man for the job. He aimed to lead a filibuster (an unsanctioned army aiming to overthrow the government) to oust the Spanish, but neither Polk nor his two Whig successors accepted López's idea. Notwithstanding this lack of support, López attempted to carry out his plans in 1849 and the US stopped him. His efforts were nicknamed 'buffalo hunts' by the US press and, as Tom Chaffin notes, were 'seldom covert'.[44] López tried once more in 1850, when there was again no popular rising in support of his efforts, and one final time in 1851, when he was finally captured by the Spanish and executed. However, his exertions had elicited some sympathy in the US South, resulting in riots against Spain in both New Orleans and Mobile.[45] With this in mind, it is unsurprising that the US government had used a number of tactics to try and suppress López, ranging from criminal indictments to use of the US navy.[46] The Whigs were the anti-expansionist party of the era, having warned against the dangers of the Mexican-American War, and they were particularly determined to stop forceful acquisitions of territory and maintain existing neutrality laws.[47] The antics of López and the temptation of Cuba might have engendered some support in the US South, but it would clearly have needed a Democratic president to bring about its annexation. The cause of US imperial expansion into Cuba was awaiting a sympathetic ear in the White House.

With the election of Democrat Franklin Pierce in 1852, the expansionists had a president who was firmly on their side, along with an even more fervent secretary of state in the guise of William Marcy. Pierce's appointee as Minister to Spain, Pierre Soulé, was also an expansionist, his 'primary goal' being the acquisition of Cuba.[48] Relations with Spain deteriorated quickly under Pierce's administration, partially due to resentment at the increasing commercial interests of the US in the island, and reached a dangerous brink at the end of Pierce's first year in office. In February 1854, Cuba seized the US cotton-carrying vessel *Black Warrior* on the grounds that it had violated harbour regulations, and US southerners soon called for war. Pierce considered military action, but first instructed Soulé to seek reparations from Spain. Soulé took this a step further than his remit allowed, telling Spain that it must respond within forty-eight hours and that the Cuban officials responsible should be dismissed – demands which Spain matter-of-factly ignored.[49] However, the *Black Warrior* affair was not the last failure of US diplomacy that had Soulé at its heart.

A more well-known incident in this era was that of the doomed Ostend Manifesto in April 1854. Marcy had authorised Soulé to offer up to $130 million to Spain for Cuba and, if this failed, to 'direct your efforts to the next desirable object', being Cuban liberation from Spain and any other European influence. The result of Marcy's instructions, and his other suggestion to meet with the US ministers to Britain and France (ultimately in Ostend in Belgium, and Aix-la-Chapelle in Prussia), were some of the worst-kept 'secret meetings' in US history, causing a contemporary to note that the US had 'planned a burglary of great proportions and published a prospectus in advance'.[50] The 'manifesto' stated that Cuba was essential to the security of the United States and that, if Spain would not sell the island, the US was within its rights to 'wrest' the island from Spain: 'immediate acquisition by our government is of paramount importance'.[51] The results of these discussions met with fierce criticism from the New York press, who branded the negotiations 'atrocious' and 'buccaneering'.[52] However, had Soulé and the manifesto been successful, he 'would have been reckoned by his contemporaries as one of the shrewdest and boldest American ministers of his time, one who understood the secret of dealing with Spain'.[53] Nevertheless, the Ostend Manifesto's aims were not achieved, and the diplomatic and domestic upheaval caused by its widely reported goals did not provide a fillip for Pierce's administration as it approached the 1854 midterms.

Pierce's administration might have considered war with Cuba over the *Black Warrior* affair, and the purchase of the island in the Ostend Manifesto, but the president also gave the go-ahead to filibustering efforts, particularly one led by John Quitman, the former pro-slavery governor of Mississippi. Correspondence suggests that Senator Stephen Douglas had assured Quitman the president would not stand in his way were he to launch a filibustering campaign against Cuba – though he should keep its preparation low-key.[54] However, whatever indications of tacit support Pierce gave, his actions suggest he later changed his mind on this issue, and he did more to hinder Quitman in the end than he did to help.[55] Indeed, one must not forget the turbulent domestic situation that Pierce faced, including the fallout from the Kansas-Nebraska Act of 1854, the growing factionalism within the Democratic Party, and fears over the rising Republican Party.[56] Bruce Ambacher claims that it was Pierce's Cuban policy that emphasised the damage done to the Democrats by the Kansas-Nebraska

Act, and prevented the 'restoration of party harmony'.⁵⁷ Indeed, Pierce was ultimately rejected as the Democratic candidate in 1856, the first incumbent president to have faced this humiliation, as was Pierce's vice-president George Dallas, who associated himself closely with the expansionist 'Young America' movement during the campaign.⁵⁸ However, Pierce's Democratic successor James Buchanan also favoured Cuban annexation, calling on Congress three times in one term to make it happen, all to no avail. The issue of slavery stood at the forefront of Buchanan's presidency, and the annexation of Cuba would have to wait until after the Civil War had settled that question.

In 1868, only three years after the conclusion of the Civil War and the ratification of the Thirteenth Amendment abolishing slavery in the United States, Cuban lawyer Carlos Manuel de Céspedes declared the island's independence with his *Grito de Yara*. This was followed by the Ten Years' War between the Spanish and Cuban insurgents seeking independence, and a gradual end to slavery. During the height of the Cuban insurgents' success in April 1869, the month in which the revolutionary government of Céspedes adopted a new Cuban constitution, former President Andrew Johnson wrote:

> we [the United States] have long desired to gain Cuba. But now they have a rebellion there and Congress, seeking out the oppressed and downtrodden everywhere, is in favor of acknowledging the rebels of Cuba as a belligerent power. . . . We seem to have taken out a roving commission in search of the oppressed, and when we find them, our bowels yearn for them. . . . I want Cuba annexed, but I want it done in accordance with law. I suppose there are none here but want Cuba annexed and represented in Congress.⁵⁹

The outbreak of hostilities in 1868 saw an 'exodus' of Cubans to New York, Key West and New Orleans, serving as vital communities-in-exile for this as well as for later Cuban independence movements. In 1873, when the Spanish captured a ship funded by Cuban exiles in the United States, leading to systematic executions of those involved by the Spanish, tensions between the US and Spain 'neared breaking point'.⁶⁰ Though the Ten Years' War elicited sympathy and attention from the press in the United States, presidents Johnson and Grant both asserted the neutrality of the United States in the war, having neither the 'moral reserves nor the navy to intervene'.[61]

Overall, between the early musings of Jefferson and John Quincy Adams over the inevitability of Cuba gravitating towards the United States and the end of the Ten Years' War, the United States did not really progress in its mission to claim the island as its own. That said, the US had attempted to buy Cuba from the Spanish on more than one occasion, had intimated military action and also quietly supported covert operations in the form of filibustering missions. Nevertheless, a multitude of issues stayed the United States' hand in taking the final plunge to forcefully annex Cuba; even when there was a serious home-grown insurrection taking place on the island in 1868. Prior to 1861 inflaming the slavery question (or more accurately the *expansion* of slavery question) was a key issue. However, following the abolition of slavery in the United States, and the only partial emancipation of slaves by the Spanish at the end of the Ten Years' War, the *abolition* of slavery might well have become the rallying cry for annexationists instead. The primary supporters of Cuban annexation in the early nineteenth century had been southern whites, keen to add another slave state to the union, but in the years that led up to the annexation of Cuba in 1898, the debate took an altogether different turn (as explored in subsequent chapters).

It is clear from the examples explored here that US overseas imperialism had its roots far earlier in the nineteenth century than the Spanish-American War. The guano islands were the United States' first formal overseas acquisitions and the Guano Island Act of 1856 set interesting precedents for treating overseas territorial possessions differently from continental ones. Although the US never formally annexed Liberia, preferring instead to control it through a private company, it offers a unique example of an untaken path for American imperialism – as an overseas settler-colonial power. In North America, the settlement of US citizens had often prefigured annexation, yet future US annexations were of territories that were either uninhabited (like the guano islands), or – in the majority of cases – already populated, with no efforts being made to displace or replace their existing inhabitants. Finally, there is Cuba. Though the US did not successfully acquire the island in the period explored here, the US had looked to Cuba consistently as an almost inevitable future possession, in a similar manner to its attitude towards Canada. Combined, these three flirtations with overseas imperial expansion help provide a more rounded context for considering the debates that arose around 1898 regarding the annexations of Hawaii and the former Spanish colonies. American overseas imperialism did not suddenly arise as an issue in the 1890s; its pedigree was far older than that.

Notes

1. Oyebade and Falola, 'West Africa and the US', p. 20.
2. Yarema, *American Colonization Society*, p. 9.
3. Blyden, 'Back to Africa', p. 24.
4. Foster, 'Colonization of Free Negroes', p. 46.
5. Ibid. p. 52.
6. Massachusetts Colonization Society, *American Colonization Society*, p. 4.
7. Duignan and Gann, *US and Africa*, p. 65.
8. Paine, 'Colonization', p. 1.
9. Falkner, 'US and Liberia', p. 534.
10. Mower, 'Republic of Liberia', p. 268.
11. Ibid. pp. 268–9.
12. Falkner, 'US and Liberia', p. 539.
13. Magness and Page, *Colonization after Emancipation*.
14. 'Preliminary Emancipation Proclamation', *US National Archives*.
15. Foner, *The Fiery Trial*, pp. 258–60.
16. Boyd, 'Negro Colonization', pp. 361–5, p. 376, p. 382.
17. For example, Walter LaFeber's *American Age* only really gives passing reference to Midway Island (not even a 'guano' island), and Walter Nugent's excellent *Habits of Empire* gives only two pages (pp. 252–3) to the guano islands before linking them to Samoa.
18. This section includes discussion of Midway and Wake Islands, which are not technically 'guano islands' but share other similarities in terms of geographical location and constitutional status.
19. Skaggs, *Great Guano Rush*, p. 1.
20. Reprinted in: 'The Americans and the Guano Islands', *The Observer*, p. 3.
21. Burnett, 'Edges of Empire', p. 783.
22. Ibid. pp. 787–8.
23. Guano Island Act, *American Memory*.

24. O'Connell, 'Pacific Guano Islands', pp. 49–50.
25. Ibid. p. 55.
26. 'A Venture in Guano', *Washington Post*, p. 6.
27. Orent and Reinsch, 'Sovereignty over Islands in the Pacific', p. 443, p. 458.
28. 'US Insular Areas', pp. 60–3, *US Government Accountability Office*.
29. 'Lonely Midway Islands', *New York Times*, p. 4.
30. 'Midway is Ready', *New York Times*, p. 2.
31. 'US Insular Areas', p. 39, *US Government Accountability Office*.
32. The status of unincorporated territory is given attention in Chapter 5, where the outcomes of the Spanish-American War and the Insular Cases of the US Supreme Court are discussed in detail.
33. 'US Insular Areas', p. 10, *US Government Accountability Office*.
34. Kaplan, *Thomas Jefferson*, p. 173.
35. Leonard, *James K. Polk*, p. 184.
36. Hendrickson, *Spanish-American War*, p. 1.
37. Pérez, *Cuba in the American Imagination*, p. 30.
38. Silverstone, *Divided Union*, p. 224.
39. Leonard, *James K. Polk*, p. 183.
40. 'Loco Foco Motto', *Jeffersonian Republican*, p. 2.
41. Blight et al., *Cuba on the Brink*, p. 325.
42. Leonard, *James K. Polk*, 184; Nugent, *Habits of Empire*, p. 217.
43. See Chapter 5.
44. Chaffin, *Fatal Glory*, pp. 1–2.
45. Hendrickson, *Spanish-American War*, p. 2; May, *Manifest Destiny's Underworld*, pp. 226–7.
46. Chaffin, *Fatal Glory*, pp. 1–2.
47. Holt, *American Whig Party*, p. 250; Blight et al., *Cuba on the Brink*, p. 326.
48. Hendrickson, *Spanish-American War*, p. 3.
49. Nivison, 'Purposes Just and Pacific', p. 10.
50. Jones, *Crucible of Power*, p. 197.
51. Ostend Manifesto, *American History Leaflets*.
52. Walther, *Shattering of the Union*, p. 53.
53. Moore, 'Pierre Soulé', p. 203.
54. May, *Manifest Destiny's Underworld*, p. 120.
55. Ibid. p. 121. May argues that although Pierce toyed with the idea of supporting Quitman, he continually reneged on any action. There was also little support from other key administration figures such as the US Attorney General Caleb Cushing or Secretary of War Jefferson Davis.
56. Moore, 'Pierre Soulé', p. 214. The Kansas-Nebraska Act left the issue of whether the two named territories would become slave or free to

'popular sovereignty'. This in turn led to turmoil in Kansas, where large numbers of settlers moved into the region to back the competing factions and two rival governments were established.

57. Ambacher, 'George M. Dallas', p. 318.
58. Ibid. p. 324.
59. Johnson, 1869, cited in Bergeron, *Papers of Andrew Johnson*, p. 568.
60. Poyo, 'Key West', p. 298.
61. Blight et al., *Cuba on the Brink*, p. 326.

CHAPTER 4

A Two-Ocean Empire (1890–98)

In the years leading up to the Spanish-American War the mood in the United States shifted markedly, not only towards the sort of intervention in a Cuban rebellion that had been avoided in earlier decades, but towards annexation. Where the US had set a precedent for taking possession of overseas territories with the largely uninhabited guano islands, the period around 1898 saw the US take control of far more populous insular possessions. Hawaii proved to be the first in a rapid succession of annexations that led to substantial growth of the American empire overseas. In response, the period also saw the rise of a strong anti-imperialist movement that questioned how a nation founded on a rejection of empire could wear with pride such an overtly imperialist mantle. Hawaii might have been the vanguard of this major phase of overseas expansionism, yet its annexation also represented the end of a system that had been in place since the birth of the United States. It was the last territory to be fully incorporated into the United States and later become a state in its own right. The Spanish-American War not only set in place the perfect circumstances for expansion of the American empire, but it also proved to be the catalyst for a major recalibration of how American imperialism would look and operate as a new century dawned.

Hawaii

European knowledge of the remote island kingdom of Hawaii dates back to the discovery of the islands by British Captain James Cook in 1778, two years after the US Declaration of Independence. The attention of the United States turned to the archipelago not long thereafter. US interest in Hawaii grew and strengthened in tandem with the growth of its mainland empire and, during the post-Mexican War era of the mid-nineteenth century, the United

States made its first attempt to take formal control of the islands. Although it was the Spanish-American War that ultimately tipped the balance in favour of annexation, the decision should not be included simplistically as part of the same wave of Pacific annexations that occurred during and shortly after 1898. After all, interest in Hawaii from early missionaries, businessmen and expansionist politicians far pre-dated any interest in Guam or the Philippines.

By 1800 Honolulu had become the main stopover for American ships, where an early interest in furs was soon superseded by the whaling industry in the Pacific and the archipelago's lucrative cultivation of sandalwood.[1] As early as the 1820s, the British, whose foreign influence in the islands predominated, were well aware that Hawaii's utility as a trans-Pacific coaling station would prove attractive to the growing empires of the United States and Russia.[2] Aside from traders, the other significant group of early US migrants to the Kingdom of Hawaii were missionaries. They cultivated a religious and ideological presence that often preceded more formal interest in overseas territories for most imperial powers in the nineteenth century. Beginning with groups such as the American Board of Commissioners for Foreign Mission, established in Massachusetts in 1810, missionaries arrived who viewed the Hawaiian people as 'a nation of children "very small," and exceedingly dark hearted to instruct'.[3] Although at first the opinions of the missionaries concerning the approach to be taken towards the Hawaiian people differed from those of the more commercially minded, as time progressed the missionaries' designs soon began to meld with those of US businessmen.[4]

By the 1840s, the British saw the Sandwich Islands (as they referred to the Hawaiian Islands) as a place for them to maintain an influence, but not to the exclusion of other powers. Indeed, Britain ultimately sought to help support Hawaiian sovereignty.[5] In 1843, Britain and France made a joint declaration in recognition of Hawaiian independence, an agreement the United States declined to partake in, instead negotiating a separate Treaty of Friendship in 1849.[6] By this time, moves towards annexation were influenced both by ideas of Manifest Destiny and fears that the French might intervene in the islands first.[7] To this end, in 1851, it appeared that Britain might support US possession of the islands to prevent a clash with France, though key British figures had been troubled by US settler behaviour in the islands and one warned that 'the United States are very hard upon the natives of the countries they obtain'.[8] In the US itself, Californians were growing increasingly interested in Hawaii, citing the safety of their Pacific coast and possible trade advantages. These factors, when combined with a decline in the native Hawaiian population and their monarchy's fear of French manoeuvrings, meant that when Franklin Pierce became president in 1853 the time was ripe for Hawaiian annexation.

The Hawaiian and US governments drew up an annexation treaty in 1854 that would have seen Hawaii admitted as a full US state, with citizenship for Hawaiian subjects. A secret article in the treaty even provided for US protection if Hawaii were threatened prior to ratification.[9] However, the untimely death of the Hawaiian king, Kamehameha III, which resulted in the succession of a more pro-British monarch, put paid to the nascent annexation discussions that were underway.[10] Moreover, a number of additional factors, most pertinently the timing of the annexation talks during the difficult times of the Kansas-Nebraska Act, also helped foil any annexation deal in the mid-nineteenth century.[11]

Despite the failure of the annexation treaty in 1854, negotiations for a reciprocal trade agreement, and most importantly tariff-free trade in sugar, indicated a further strengthening of relations between Hawaii and the United States. Many in this period, including novelist and later anti-imperialist Mark Twain, envisaged Hawaii as an extension of the United States' western coast.[12] However, the road to an outward extension of the US Pacific coast was a rocky one, and in both 1855 and 1867 the two nations reached reciprocity agreements only for both to fail at the hands of the US Senate. On the first occasion this was largely down to opposition from Louisiana sugar planters, who saw pitfalls in the direct competition from Hawaiian sugar. In 1867, opposition came from businessmen who feared the loss of revenue from existing tariffs, and from expansionists concerned that the success of reciprocity might stymie future annexation attempts. Despite such concerns, many at the time, both in the US and in Hawaii, saw reciprocity as an encouraging step closer to annexation. Finally, following the 1874 election of the Hawaiian sugar lobby's preferred candidate for the Hawaiian throne, King David Kalakaua, the stage was set for the successful passage of a reciprocity treaty in 1876.[13] Importantly, this reciprocity treaty led to the growth in power and influence of the largely white sugar-planting elite in Hawaii, who served, in much the same manner as US economic migrants to Texas and California before them, as an internal catalyst for US annexation in the longer term.[14]

Kalakaua oversaw the beginning of the end of Hawaiian monarchical power, just as he sought to enhance his powers with the dividends of the reciprocity treaty. In 1884 the reciprocity treaty was renewed, giving another benefit to the United States: exclusive privileges over Pearl Harbor. However, in the wake of this new agreement, the powerful US-led sugar lobby in the islands also forced the king to enact a new constitution, the 1887 'Bayonet Constitution', under threat of armed rebellion. This new constitution led to a further increase in power for the white elite in the government of Hawaii.[15] Though the German foreign secretary Herbert Bismarck bemoaned the growth of US power in the islands, suggesting that the United States interpreted the Monroe Doctrine 'as though the Pacific ocean were to be treated as an American lake', the British prime minister, the Marquis of Salisbury, seemed less concerned, pointing out that by this point Hawaii was 'of no interest whatever to England'.[16]

Despite their gains in 1887, just two years later the sugar growers grew fearful of losing their special status and the Hawaiian minister to Washington, Henry Carter, met with the new secretary of state, James Blaine, to discuss further development of the reciprocity agreement. Blaine sought increased control over Pearl Harbor, and supported moves towards establishing a protectorate in Hawaii that would forbid the Hawaiians from entering external treaties without US approval and permit US troops to land in the islands to protect their sovereignty.[17] The Hawaiian monarch felt alarmed by the latter provision, and eventually renegotiated the Carter-Blaine Treaty of 1889 to include the former provisions, but exclude permission for the US to land troops in Hawaii for its 'own protection'.

The agreements of 1887 and 1889, however, proved remarkably short-lived in their effects. In 1890, the new McKinley Tariff Act saw sugar placed on the general US tariff-free list, with a subsidy for US growers further nullifying the favoured status that the 1887 reciprocity treaty had established for Hawaii. These measures ultimately led to an economic downturn in the islands.[18] In 1890 Kalakaua travelled to the United States, causing some apprehension among the Canadian government who felt that the US might use the visit to pressure the king into permitting US annexation of his kingdom. However, the king's death in San Francisco the following January put an end to this particular concern.[19]

King Kalakaua was succeeded by his sister, Queen Liliuokalani, who acceded to the throne in a time of increasing economic hardship. The McKinley Tariff had a devastating effect on the Hawaiian sugar-planter elite and renewed their enthusiasm for US annexation of the islands, leading to overtures to the US government from a secret Annexationist Club in the islands. The white planters in the islands distrusted the new, seemingly 'authoritarian and nationalistic' queen, who they suspected was in thrall to a Tahitian favourite and his allies, all of whom were decidedly anti-American.[20] Moreover, the attitude of the US government of the time became increasingly annexationist once again, with Secretary Blaine writing in August of 1891 that only three insular territories would be of value to the US: Cuba, Puerto Rico and Hawaii. Blaine saw Hawaii as the only territory likely to arise as a realistic proposition within his generation, noting: 'Hawaii may come up for decision at any unexpected hour and I hope we will be prepared to decide in the affirmative.'[21] Although Blaine was not in office to seize the moment when it arrived in January 1893, he had been replaced by an equally 'dedicated expansionist', John W. Foster. Guided by both a belief in a civilising mission in Hawaii, whose declining population he attributed to racial backwardness, and in the concept of Manifest Destiny, Foster was fully aware that his party's loss in the 1892 presidential election made annexation a highly unlikely prospect.[22]

Despite Foster's inklings, the issue of annexation did indeed arise during the lame duck period of Benjamin Harrison's presidency in early 1893. In response to a new constitution that aimed to be more favourable to native Hawaiians, the white planter elite rose up, with the support of US marines, to overthrow the queen and declare an American protectorate. However, despite most within the international community accepting US annexation of the islands as a *fait accompli*, the suspected complicity in the coup of John Stevens (the US minister to Honolulu) and the US State Department concerned many within the United States itself. To counter this, and to try and gain Senate consent before Democrat Grover Cleveland assumed the presidency on 4 March 1893, Foster did his best to remove any clauses and requests in the annexation treaty that might delay Senate ratification. However, defeat was ultimately snatched from the jaws of victory when Cleveland came to office and withdrew the treaty from Senate consideration. Cleveland then sent Congressman James Blount to Hawaii to investigate the situation, and when Blount later reported irregularities in the annexation agreement and that Hawaiians generally supported the queen, Cleveland announced that the United States would not annex Hawaii.[23] On 4 July 1894 the Republic of Hawaii was pronounced, and the question of annexation was again delayed for future reconsideration.

Why Hawaii was eventually annexed in 1898 is a question that still divides historians, many of whom have looked to the divided anti-imperialist lobby in the United States and the Spanish-American War of 1898 for answers.[24] Thomas Osborne contends that most historians consider the war as the primary motivation for eventual annexation, but he argues instead that trade was the 'primary' reason. Osborne suggests that the arguments behind military contingency as a primary factor, including that Hawaii was essential to supporting US troops in the Philippines and protecting the US Pacific Coast, are found wanting when the contemporary debate is studied more critically, and that the military connection was actually an indirect one. Instead he posits that, more importantly for policymakers, the annexation of Hawaii was the key to developing the China market and consolidating control of Pearl Harbor for the future.[25] However, William Morgan has challenged Osborne's viewpoint, and instead looks to a variety of factors, global, national and local, which contributed to the debate over Hawaiian annexation in the period 1893-8. Morgan highlights key, and often underplayed, themes such as an enhanced appreciation of Hawaii's naval-strategic value, the competition for power within Hawaii between native peoples, whites and Asians, and particularly the role of Japan and the 1897 US-Japan crisis.[26] Ultimately, it was these naval-strategic concerns – emphasised by the Spanish-American War – that pushed the US government into taking decisive action in Hawaii after decades of vacillation.[27]

President William McKinley finally took the decision to annex Hawaii in 1898, in spite of opposition from US-based sugar planters and those on the Pacific Coast who feared an influx of Asiatic labourers.[28] The onset of the Spanish-American War in April 1898 was integral to securing congressional support for Hawaiian annexation, though this still had to be done by a joint resolution of Congress, the same measure used to secure Texan annexation, since a treaty was unlikely to pass the US Senate where opposition came mainly from southern, western and Democratic members.[29] Oddly, even some later leaders of the anti-imperialist movement, such as Republican Senator George F. Hoar, favoured the annexation of Hawaii for reasons of defence. Hoar told the Senate that he believed, in the case of Hawaii, 'the fear of imperialism is needless alarm'; but as Foster Rhea Dulles argues, Hoar was absolutely wrong, and the annexation of Hawaii instead set a 'powerful precedent' for future annexations.[30] President McKinley finally signed the resolution on 7 July 1898, formally securing Hawaii for the United States in August of that year.[31] However, though Hawaii eventually gained statehood in 1959 along with Alaska, future annexations did not lead to future states. Instead, the annexations that followed the Spanish-American War gave birth to a new type of ambiguous and unequal relationship between the US and its overseas possessions.

The Spanish-American War

At the heart of many traditional narratives of United States imperialism is the idea that the US only really became an empire in 1898, in line with the 'aberration thesis' of historian Samuel Flagg Bemis.[32] Although this was the year in which the US annexed Hawaii, the main reason for the focus on 1898 is that it was the year the US took control of the remaining overseas colonies of Spain after victory in the short Spanish-American War. The causes of the war and, more importantly, the motivations that lay behind the US keeping the captured territories, contain a number of parallels that suggest continuity with the nature of US imperialism previously considered.

As Chapter 3 evidences, the Cuban Revolution of 1895–8 that preceded the Spanish-American War was not the first time Cubans had tried to throw off the yoke of Spanish imperialism. The Ten Years' War (1868–78) had proven a major stand against Spanish rule, although ultimately unsuccessful, and another 'Little War' followed between 1879 and 1880.[33] Yet it was a revolt in 1895 that belatedly proved to be the decisive instance in bringing about the long-expected US invasion of Cuba, the dream of many expansionists for more than a generation. Quite why this Cuban revolution succeeded in bringing on board the United States where others had not is, as ever, a multifaceted question.[34]

Although the 1895 revolution involved many of the same figures that had taken part in the Ten Years' War, some key changes had taken place in Cuba in the interim: the abolition of slavery, and a subsequent rationalisation and mechanisation of the sugar industry on the island, had seen a substantial increase in US investment in the island's economy. The political frustrations left unaddressed after 1878 and 1880, and exacerbated by economic fluctuations and disparities, led to the formation of José Martí's Cuban Revolutionary Party and eventual demands for freedom rather than autonomy, with their calls of 'Cuba Libre'.[35] However, the day after the full revolution began on 24 February 1895, US newspapers gave no indication that a moment 'that would be enshrined in history books as a starting point, a significant moment, a date', had passed, and for some time to come the US regarded this revolution as yet another bout of familiar Cuban upheaval.[36] However, the war that followed was markedly different, especially when it came to the role of the United States.

The US was initially keen for Spain to resolve the situation in Cuba, as it had done on previous occasions. When Spain was still confident of success, it appointed General Arsenio Martínez Campos, a Ten Years' War veteran, to crush the rebellion. Initially sent with views towards reconciliation, Campos failed to adapt to the guerrilla and economic warfare of the Cuban rebels and resigned in January 1896, a grave disappointment to his masters.[37] Campos was soon replaced with the altogether different General Valeriano Weyler y Nicolau, whose much more aggressive approach earned him the sobriquet of 'the Butcher', a title that he had more than merited for his previous brutal counterinsurgency work in the Ten Years' War as well as other postings prior to 1895.[38] Weyler was disdainful of Campos's benevolent style, and set about reorganising the Spanish army and intelligence services in Cuba as soon as he arrived in the islands.[39] Weyler famously used *reconcentrados* (concentration camps) to resettle rural Cubans and undermine support for rebels while desolating the remaining countryside: tactics that were forerunners of those used by the British during the latter stages of the Second Boer War. Such tactics caused shock and outrage in the United States, leading to calls for US intervention to stop the Spanish atrocities. Although the Spanish later recalled Weyler and introduced reforms towards increased self-government, these changes came too late in the day to pacify Cuban rebels. Furthermore, Cuban supporters in the US continued to propagandise the rebels' plight, while the insurgents themselves destroyed US property interests in Cuba in the hope of forcing an intervention from the United States.[40]

Historian David Healy argues that had the American public in 1898 seen 'no national advantage in imperialism, they would never have embarked upon it merely to do good; yet, had they seen no good in it, it is extremely doubtful that enough of them could have been persuaded to support it only for the sake of expediency'.[41] Similarly, the editors of one collected edition on the events of 1898 contend that the reasons for US intervention in what was a Spanish imperial matter continue to be the subject of some dispute among historians. From one angle the motivations were economic: the need for stability in a country with a sugar industry in which US businesses had substantial investments. From another, there is a need to contend with the view that the US saw itself as the 'harbinger of democracy and freedom', coupled awkwardly with ideas of racial superiority. Aside from these were additional concerns, such as strategic and military anxieties.[42]

Beyond these longer-term motivations for intervention, there was the more immediate impact of William McKinley's election victory in 1896, bringing the largely pro-imperialist party, the Republicans, back into office. McKinley's election brought about the somewhat begrudged rise of Theodore Roosevelt and led to heightened influence for proponents of a 'large policy' of US expansion.[43] Indeed, the role of the charismatic and media-savvy Roosevelt should not go understated, and his actions across this period consistently underlined his determination to advance American imperialism in the most single-minded manner. The Republican victory of 1896, and with it the rise of its substantial imperialist faction, was the most significant factor in finally bringing about US intervention in Cuba.

Although to suggest that there was any single overriding cause of the Spanish-American War is to oversimplify, there were some obvious catalysts. One of these was the so-called 'yellow' or sensationalist journalism propagated by the editors William Randolph Hearst and Joseph Pulitzer and their New York-based newspapers. In a bid to sell papers both publishers revelled in the shocking stories that emanated from the Cuban revolution, and actively sought the harrowing details Cuban sympathisers were so willing to supply. So keen was Hearst on the Cuban conflict that he is supposed to have instructed artist Frederic Remington in Cuba: 'You furnish the pictures and I'll furnish the war.'[44] These editors sent famous writers and artists to Cuba to cover the Cuban conflict, the first in US history to be covered with both still photography and moving images.[45] Coverage, especially from Hearst's papers, came to increasingly favour US military intervention; the publication of a report written by the Spanish minister to the United States, which was overtly critical of President McKinley, led to the minister's resignation soon afterwards.[46] Another catalyst for US intervention involved the sinking of a US warship, the *Maine*, in Havana Harbour. This incident was among the most evident causes of war in 1898. The *Maine* had been sent to Havana to protect US citizens and interests in the islands during late 1897, but on 15 February 1898 the ship exploded, causing the death of over 250 US sailors, probably due to an internal fire (and not a Spanish mine, as many in the US chose to believe).[47] Following this incident, and even fiercer urging from the press, the pressure mounted on President McKinley to act.

It is a mistake, however, to view the Spanish-American War as being all about Cuba. After all, the Spanish had possessions spread across the Pacific all the way to the very doorstep of China. A rebellion against Spain was also taking place in the distant Philippines, a place that, unlike Cuba, most Americans were largely unaware of prior to 1898. Just over a week after the *Maine*'s sinking, on 25 February, while Secretary of the Navy John D. Long was away having a 'mechanical massage', Assistant Secretary of the Navy Theodore Roosevelt sent a dangerously provocative cable to Admiral George Dewey. It included the following instruction: 'KEEP FULL OF COAL. IN THE EVENT OF DECLARATION WAR SPAIN, YOUR DUTY WILL BE TO SEE THAT THE SPANISH SQUADRON DOES NOT LEAVE THE ASIATIC COAST, AND THEN OFFENSIVE OPERATIONS IN PHILIPPINE ISLANDS.'[48] However, though the chain of events suggests that Roosevelt was the instigator of an attack on the

Philippines, he was 'merely amplifying' what had always been an element of the war plan.[49]

Despite such actions, and the fact that Roosevelt held those who vied for 'peace at any cost' in distain, McKinley's efforts to avoid war continued. These included yet another proposal to buy Cuba (for $300 million), though this did not gain Congressional support, and a proposed indemnity from Spain in compensation for the sinking of the *Maine*.[50] However, all of these proved to no avail and the Spanish, unwilling to guarantee Cuban independence, could only compromise so far as suggesting for Cuba something akin to the autonomy given at this time to Canada by the British. A weary McKinley, after further last-ditch attempts at avoiding armed conflict, accepted the inevitable, and on 11 April 1898 asked Congress for a declaration of war.[51] The so-called 'Splendid Little War' was all over by August of the same year, and the Spanish Empire was in American hands.

McKinley's views on the war have been the subject of some dispute among historians and, as Ephraim Smith suggests, much of this is down to the 'paucity of information on McKinley's personal opinions'. For Smith the burden of proof rests with those who 'have portrayed McKinley as a clever or confident imperialist'.[52] Walter LaFeber sees McKinley as determined to control foreign policy, basically opposed to war, but keen on the results that war would bring.[53] Ernest May's presentation of McKinley is that he gauged public opinion regarding intervention and anti-imperialism, and found the former to be the more popular. Overall, McKinley acted not through conviction but through pragmatism, reasoning that war would win him more votes in 1900 than peace would. Thus, whether it was his personal preference or not, the president followed the popular course, or as he more obliquely put it, 'in the end there was no alternative'.[54]

The Anti-Imperialists

The previous section of this chapter has briefly outlined the United States' entry to the Spanish-American War and some of the reasons for its intervention. But the war and its aftermath led to a rise in American anti-imperial feeling that ran very much counter to what actually occurred in 1898. Both imperialists and anti-imperialists justified their positions by appealing to ideas of

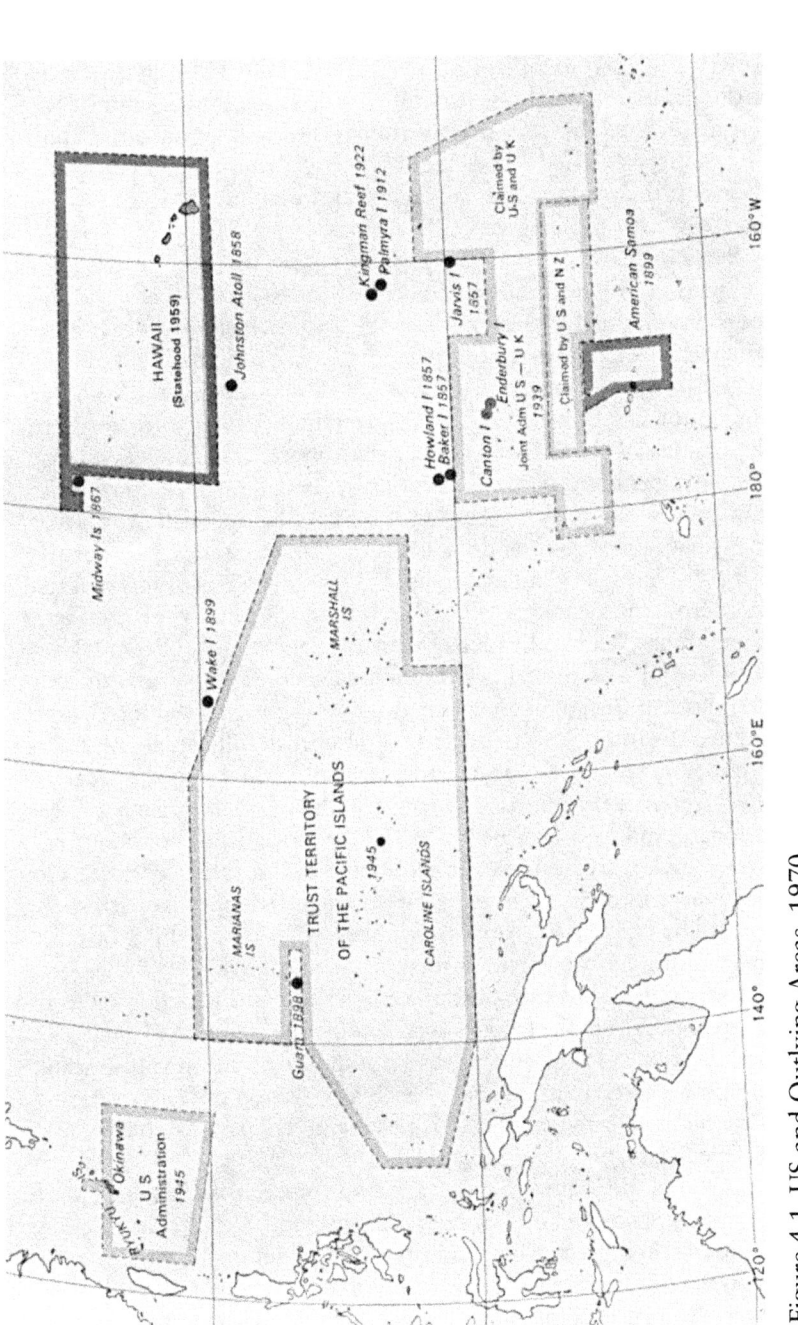

Figure 4.1 US and Outlying Areas, 1970

American exceptionalism, an idea that Fabian Hilfrich argues is so malleable as to allow for the paradoxical 'fundamental consensus' behind the very divisive debates over imperialism. While imperialists claimed an exceptional *right* to spread democracy overseas, their opponents saw an exceptional *duty* to refrain from aggressive interventionism.[55]

Robert Beisner describes the anti-imperialist movement as 'a campaign of opposition that flourished for two years before losing momentum after the election of 1900', a view challenged recently by Michael P. Cullinane, who argues that this overlooks its 'popularity, longevity, and enduring activism' in subsequent years. This latter contention certainly deserves to be given more prominence in future discussions of the movement. Both historians agree, however, that the movement had been germinating in the late nineteenth century, and only really took off during the Spanish-American War when Hawaiian annexation and rumours of plans to annex parts of the Spanish Empire began to circulate.[56] Many members of this crusade came from the Democratic Party, including 1896 and 1900 presidential nominee William Jennings Bryan and ex-President Grover Cleveland, but others, though less numerous, were Republicans, such as ex-President Benjamin Harrison and Massachusetts Senator George F. Hoar. In addition to politicians, a number of influential university presidents, labour leaders and former abolitionists joined the cause; they even had rich patrons to bankroll the movement, such as steel magnate Andrew Carnegie.[57] Though the movement's key public figures were largely men in their sixties and seventies (in contrast to to prominent imperialists like the far younger Teddy Roosevelt), some historians have stressed the overlooked roles played by a broader age and gender range within the movement.[58] While led by seniors, if not dominated by them, the anti-imperialist efforts of this era were of great import in the debates surrounding the direction of American imperialism. As Beisner puts it: 'It would be no mean feat to think of another issue that has united such a collection of Democrats and Republicans, progressives and conservatives, party stalwarts and independents, businessmen and labor-union chiefs.'[59]

Around the time of the war, Anti-Imperialist 'Leagues' were founded, predominantly in New England and New York, to allow various stripes of anti-imperialists to begin uniting around a common banner: to stop imperialism and the extension of sovereignty to overseas insular colonies, including Hawaii.[60] Their first major goal was to scupper the Treaty of Paris that would bring an end to the Spanish-American War, but also bring Spain's former colonies under US control (with the exception of Cuba; see Chapter 5). Article II of the treaty called for Spain to cede 'Porto Rico [sic] and other islands now under Spanish sovereignty in the West Indies, and the island of Guam in the Marianas or Ladrones', and Article III would see the purchase of the more distant Philippine archipelago for $20 million. Article IX dubiously noted that the 'civil rights and political status of the native inhabitants of the territories hereby ceded to the United States shall be determined by the Congress'.[61] The anti-imperialists felt that the passage of an unamended treaty by the Senate would deal their nascent fight an early knock-out blow.

With the existence of a substantial anti-imperialist lobby, the passage of the Treaty of Paris was far from straightforward and the Senate became the predictable focus of those seeking to alter or defeat the treaty, as final ratification required a two-thirds Senate vote in its support. Its passage became something of a partisan issue, but not entirely so, as Democrat William Jennings Bryan demonstrated. One of the most outspoken critics of US imperialism, Bryan made a late manoeuver to support ratification of the treaty that greatly displeased a number of anti-imperialists. Bryan's reasoning was that if the treaty was ratified and Spain removed from the issue entirely, the US could then swiftly resolve to grant independence to its temporary possessions when the Democrats returned to power. To this end, Bryan was decisive in convincing crucial senators to vote for ratification, though, as historian Paolo Coletta argues, the 'overpowering' public support for expansion and the role of key Republicans in forging crucial deals in the Senate should not go underestimated.[62] Several senators attempted to add resolutions to the treaty clarifying what exactly the US planned to do with the Spanish islands, the most notable of these being Senator Augustus Bacon of Georgia's:

> [that] the United States hereby disclaim any disposition to exercise sovereignty, jurisdiction, or control over said islands, and assert their determination, when a stable and independent government shall have been duly erected therein entitled to recognition as such, [to] transfer to said government, upon terms that shall be reasonable and just, all rights secured under the cession by Spain, and to thereupon leave the government and control of the islands to their people.[63]

However, this resolution just missed out on being attached to the treaty, when Vice-President Hobart, somewhat predictably, voted it down following a tied vote in the Senate. The Treaty of Paris, without the Bacon resolution, was signed on 10 December 1898, and the first phase of the anti-imperialist movement had been defeated.

The victory of the imperialists over the treaty left the anti-imperialists divided over how best to proceed, with some seeking to veer the movement towards campaigning for improvements to the colonial regimes of the islands now under US control.[64] Indeed, with annexation now a reality, the anti-imperialists altered their aims to both critiquing US policy in the islands, particularly in the Philippines, and campaigning for their independence (see Chapter 5). During this recalibration in 1899, the remaining anti-imperialist groups amalgamated into the American Anti-Imperialist League (AIL) and began pamphleteering, conferencing and lecturing to anyone who would listen.[65] However, like the movements before it, the AIL was 'too heterogeneous in membership ever to speak with a single voice', meaning that 'valid generalizations about it are correspondingly difficult to formulate'.[66] For example, there were those within the campaign, such as Cleveland and Carnegie, who supported 'imperial expansion by non-colonial means' (or economic imperialism), but the key, New England-based leaders of the movement did not agree with this viewpoint at all.[67]

The variety of reasons offered in opposition to American imperialism paralleled the diversity of pro-imperial arguments. The most important of the latter in winning both public and political support were the strategic benefits and prestige to be gained from empire, and the commercial benefits for all parties concerned, especially access to the China market. Less telling, but often used by politicians to justify the benevolence of the endeavour, were factors such as: the former Spanish colonies needing to be annexed to be save them from the Spanish, anarchy, or other 'less benevolent' empires; that annexation would spread American values, religion, democracy and 'civilisation' to the inferior inhabitants of these territories; and even that unity might be enhanced at home by expansion overseas.[68] For most of these reasons, there was a reasonable counter-argument to be had, and there was almost always an anti-imperialist at hand to provide it.

The most compelling and unsurprising case for anti-imperialism was simply that it was un-American. The AIL, from 1899 onwards, tended to focus on the 'constitutional contradiction of imperialism and democracy'.⁶⁹ Many anti-imperialists, like most imperialists, accepted that Filipinos and Puerto Ricans could not be integrated as full legal citizens, largely for racial reasons. However, the anti-imperialists reasoned that, as such, it would be unfair to bring them into the United States as 'subjects' under different laws and regulations. The United States was born of a rejection of imperialism and rule from afar, so how could it, in good faith, institute its own form of distant imperial rule against the consent of the governed, however changed in form it might be from that of the British in 1776? As author Mark Twain, who had proved more sympathetic to the admission of Hawaii under equal terms, put it in October 1900: 'I have read carefully the treaty of Paris, and I have seen that we do not intend to free, but to subjugate the people of the Philippines. We have gone there to conquer, not to redeem'.⁷⁰

Another aspect of imperialism that saw the United States go against its traditions in the eyes of anti-imperialists was the abandonment of a largely hemispheric isolation. Entangling alliances, after all, had been warned against by Washington and Jefferson, and a new Pacific border would bring the US toe-to-toe with the very empires the Monroe Doctrine sought to see slowly slip away.⁷¹ An empire, in short, would bring expensive foreign wars. The Germans had already been quick to stake a potential claim to any unwanted Philippine islands in 1898, a fact that helped McKinley decide to take them all.⁷² The Japanese, with victories over China and Russia during the turn-of-the-century period, were a competitor power in Asia and the annexation of Hawaii, Guam and the Philippines brought them far closer than was comfortable for many. Added to such issues of self-interest were fears of the potential detrimental effects overseas annexations would have on the US domestically.⁷³ Some anti-imperialists argued that the United States should not distract itself with imperialism when domestic affairs required more immediate attention. For historian Christopher Nichols, this vision of domestic civic and economic reform, coupled with the ideas that the US should never practice colonialism or form entangling alliances, guided the majority of those who spoke and wrote about anti-imperialism.⁷⁴

Whereas pro-imperialists might have argued for the potential for racial uplift under US stewardship, anti-imperialists were less certain that the 'inferior' races could cope with complex US ideals and systems. Of equal concern to some anti-imperialists was whether these wards of empire, rather than becoming Americans, would 'bastardise' the 'American race' and flock to the mainland. Historian David Turpie looks to a southern Democrat, Edward Ward Carmark of Tennessee, as an example of how the 'southern worldview' of the turn of the century made the South a hotbed of anti-imperialism of a somewhat different nature to that in New England. Although many themes in his speeches echoed the 'democratic deficit' themes discussed above, Carmack also pointed critically to the benefits imperialism brought to primarily *northern* businessmen and drew parallels between US military occupation of the Philippines and post-Civil War Reconstruction in the US South.[75] Perhaps more predictably, southern anti-imperialists also focused heavily upon the dangers of importing another 'race problem' by annexing the former Spanish colonies; this in a period when lynch law and Jim Crowism was reaching its height.[76] For such reasons, African Americans, who in many ways sympathised with the plight of the subjugated, viewed imperialism through the lens of their own 'deteriorating status at home' and found it hard to find a place in either the imperialist or anti-imperialist camps, each with their particular racist undertones.[77] Indeed, the anti-imperialists were in many respects 'no more liberal' than the expansionists, and both were guided by 'pseudo-Darwinian' views of racial hierarchy.[78]

Many anti-imperialists felt that the re-election of the 'imperialist' incumbent President William McKinley in November 1900 would sound the death knell to any hopes of a speedy withdrawal from overseas imperialism. Therefore, as early as May 1899, the anti-imperialists weighed up their strategic options for the forthcoming election and even considered a problematic third-party challenge. The problem for many was that, although the likely Democratic candidate, Bryan, was an anti-imperialist, he was also the turncoat of the Treaty of Paris; for many anti-imperialists, the only positive thing about Bryan was his anti-imperialist rhetoric. The most famous speech of Bryan's career, however, was not about imperialism, but about 'free silver', when he electrified the Democratic Convention in 1896 by telling them that the US would not be crucified on a 'cross of gold'. Sadly, for Bryan at least, many anti-imperialists were far from convinced about his views on economics. Tompkins describes the choice for many anti-imperialists in 1900 as one between Scylla and Charybdis, where even the most hardened anti-imperialists, such as the Republican George F. Hoar, could not bring themselves to vote for Bryan, even if he was the undisputed 'anti-imperialist candidate'.[79]

In the Philippines, where rebels continued fighting as hard against their new imperial masters as they had against the Spanish before 1898, Filipinos remained buoyed by tales of the anti-imperialist movement and the independence that a Bryan victory would surely bring.[80] The Democratic Party Platform of 1900 stated their position on imperialism clearly and at length: 'We assert that no nation can long endure half republic and half empire, and we warn the American people that imperialism abroad will lead quickly and inevitably to despotism at home', and roundly condemned Republican policy towards the former Spanish colonies. The Republican Platform read quite differently, leading with how the party had improved the US economy, and addressing foreign policy directly only towards the end. It approved of Hawaiian annexation, called the Spanish annexations the only option for a nation that accepted its duty and 'responsibility before the world', and vaguely mentioned that the 'largest measure of self-government consistent with their welfare and our duties' should be given to the Philippines and Puerto Rico.[81] In the end, despite the partisans in the imperialism debate deeming it so, the 1900 election was not one about imperialism alone, as the Republican Platform indicates. However, even if it was not as decisive as it might seem, the 1900 result was the final nail in the coffin of the anti-imperialist movement for many who, after this point, accepted that the US was inevitably on an imperialist course.[82]

Just as the Republicans' victory in 1896 had set in motion the shift in US politics necessary to allow for the annexation of Hawaii and US entry into the Spanish-Cuban and Philippine conflicts, so their re-election in 1900 gave them a mandate to re-enforce this change in direction. The Spanish-American War had allowed the proponents of US expansionism to realise their vision under the auspices of humanitarian intervention and, in response, the anti-imperialist movement proved unable to mobilise sufficient support to halt their progress. However, as the next chapter illustrates, debates over the fate of the former Spanish colonies did not end in 1898. The multiple justifications for and against the annexations were echoed for years to come in discussions over how exactly the US would rule its new overseas empire.

Notes

1. Whitehead, 'Hawaii', p. 159.
2. Tate, 'Sovereignty of Hawaii', p. 327.
3. Kashay, 'Agents of Imperialism', pp. 280–1.
4. Ibid. p. 281.
5. Tate, 'Sovereignty of Hawaii', pp. 329–30; though the British had briefly exerted more formal control in 1843.
6. Chock, 'One Hundred Years of Illegitimacy', pp. 463–4.
7. Whitehead, 'Hawaii', p. 164.
8. Tate, 'Sovereignty of Hawaii', pp. 329–30.
9. La Croix and Grandy, 'Political Instability', p. 167.
10. Whitehead, 'Hawaii', p. 164.
11. The Kansas-Nebraska Act raised the issue of 'popular sovereignty' regarding the expansion of slavery into US territories and whether the territories would ultimately become free states or slave states. This led to a major crisis in Kansas, referred to most frequently as 'bleeding Kansas'.
12. Whitehead, 'Hawaii', pp. 165–6. However, James Caron, 'Blessings of Civilization', pp. 51–2, argues that historians, such as Jim Zwick, who have painted this picture of Twain have relied on evidence that is far from compelling, and which he critiques in detail in his article.
13. La Croix and Grandy, 'Political Instability', pp. 166–8.
14. An observation made by Whitehead, 'Hawaii', p. 169.
15. Ibid. p. 170.
16. Cited in: Tate, 'Sovereignty of Hawaii', p. 335.
17. Crapol, *James G. Blaine*, p. 123.
18. Tindall and Shi, *America*, p. 655.
19. Tate, 'Sovereignty of Hawaii', p. 337.
20. Devine, 'John W. Foster', pp. 31–2.
21. Crapol, *James G. Blaine*, pp. 124–5; Devine, 'John W. Foster', p. 29.
22. Devine, 'John W. Foster', p. 30, p. 33. In this period the incumbent 'lame duck' post-election government remained in office until 4 March of the following year.
23. For a detailed outline of the efforts of Foster during this period see: Ibid.
24. See the latter part of this chapter for detailed discussion of both.
25. See: Osborne, 'Trade or War?', pp. 285–6; and Osborne, 'Main Reason for Hawaiian Annexation', pp. 161–78. For a critique of Osborne see Beisner, 'Book Review', pp. 1475–6, where Beisner discusses Osborne's monograph of the same year that has the same central thesis as the 1970 and 1981 articles cited here.

26. Morgan, *Pacific Gibraltar*, pp. 3–5. Morgan suggests a range of interconnected factors: 'a strong anti-imperialist tradition, the rise of new, technology-driven navalism, a peculiar intellectual climate, and a desire to increase exports to absorb domestic overproduction'. The 1897 'crisis' related to moves towards the annexation of Hawaii and is explored by Morgan in Chapter 14.
27. Naval-strategic concerns and trepidation about the rise of Japan were also drivers behind Theodore Roosevelt's expansionist policies at the turn of the century, as explored in later chapters.
28. Whitehead, 'Hawaii', p. 171.
29. Meiser, *Power and Restraint*, p. 34. A traditional treaty would require support from two thirds of the US Senate.
30. Dulles, *America's Rise to World Power*, p. 44.
31. Whitehead, 'Hawaii', p. 172. Technically Hawaii retained its republican government until 1900, when territorial status was officially given to the islands.
32. See: Bemis, *Diplomatic History of the United States*.
33. For details of the 'Little War' see: Ferrer, *Insurgent Cuba*, Chapter 3.
34. For a useful overview of the historiography of the war see: Pérez, *The War of 1898*, p. ix.
35. Offner, *An Unwanted War*, pp. 2–3.
36. Hoganson, *Fighting for American Manhood*, pp. 1–2.
37. Leonard, *Encyclopedia of Cuban-US Relations*, p. 231.
38. Tone, *War and Genocide in Cuba*, p. 155. Tone gives a very useful character profile of Weyler.
39. Foner, *The Spanish-Cuban-American War*, pp. 76–8.
40. LaFeber, *The American Age*, p. 197.
41. Healy, *US Expansionism*, p. 5.
42. Smith and Dávila-Cox, *Crisis of 1898*, pp. 10–11. An excellent but somewhat dated historiography of this period can also be found in: De Santis, 'The Imperialist Impulse', pp. 64–90.
43. Gould, *Spanish-American War*, p. 5. The phrase 'large policy' was used by imperialists such as Senator Henry Cabot Lodge and Theodore Roosevelt, to refer to their favoured policy of territorial expansion to further US interests overseas. They saw the War of 1898 as a chance to put this policy into operation (see especially: Pratt, 'Large Policy of 1898', pp. 219–42).
44. Fellow, *American Media History*, p. 169.
45. Harrington, 'Photography', p. 419.
46. Ross, 'New York Journal', p. 418.
47. LaFeber, *The American Age*, p. 199.
48. Roosevelt cited in: Morris, *Rise of Theodore Roosevelt*, p. 629.

49. Smith, 'Assistant Secretary of the Navy', pp. 47–8.
50. Morris, *Rise of Theodore Roosevelt*, p. 631. See Chapter 3 for previous efforts to buy Cuba.
51. For detailed coverage of events leading up to the declaration of war see: Trask, *War with Spain*, Chapter 2.
52. Smith, 'William McKinley's Enduring Legacy', p. 205. See also: Fry, 'William McKinley', pp. 77–98; Gould, *Spanish-American War*; Hamilton, *McKinley, War and Empire*.
53. LaFeber, *The American Age*, pp. 196–202. LaFeber reasons that McKinley needed to protect business interests in Cuba and to be seen to be acting by the US public, while noting that it would also give the president a 'free hand' to deal with a potential Japanese and German threat to the fabled China market.
54. May, *Imperial Democracy*, p. 259.
55. Hilfrich, *Debating American Exceptionalism*, p. 2.
56. Beisner, *Twelve against Empire*, pp. iv–viii; Cullinane, *Liberty and American Anti-Imperialism*, pp. 1–2.
57. Of particular note among labour leaders is Samuel Gompers, the leader of the American Federation of Labor; see especially: Whittaker, 'Samuel Gompers', pp. 429–45.
58. Zimmerman, 'Who Were the Anti-Imperialists?', pp. 589–601, debunks the age theory in his exploration of anti-imperialists in Chicago, while Murphy, 'Women's Anti-Imperialism', pp. 244–70, evaluates the complex place of women in the movement.
59. Beisner, *Twelve against Empire*, pp. iv–vi. Beisner's work explores the role of key figures in the anti-imperialist movement, but excludes those he sees as politically partisan, such as Bryan.
60. Hunt, *Ideology and US Foreign Policy*, p. 39; Welch, *Response to Imperialism*, p. 44; Healy, *US Expansionism*, p. 219.
61. Treaty of Paris, 1898, *Avalon Project*.
62. Coletta, 'Bryan, McKinley, and the Treaty of Paris', pp. 131–2.
63. Cited in: Ibid. p. 135.
64. Cooke, 'An Unpardonable Bit of Folly and Impertinence', p. 314.
65. Healy, *US Expansionism*, p. 219.
66. Ibid. p. 219; Welch, *Response to Imperialism*, p. 44.
67. Schirmer, 'On the Anti-Imperialist Movement', p. 85.
68. Offner, *An Unwanted War*, p. 22, discusses Protestant missionaries as supporters of US imperialism (with the exception of the Quakers). For unity at home see: Hunt, *Ideology and US Foreign Policy*, p. 42.
69. Murphy, 'Women's Anti-Imperialism', p. 245.
70. Twain, excerpt from the *New York Herald*.
71. Dulles, *America's Rise to World Power*, p. 44.
72. Marks, *Velvet on Iron*, p. 6.

73. Dulles, *America's Rise to World Power*, p. 44.
74. Nichols, *Promise and Peril*, p. 73.
75. Turpie, 'Howling Upon the Scent of Another Victim', pp. 412–14.
76. Burns, 'Without Due Process', p. 234.
77. Gatewood, 'Black Americans', p. 545.
78. Lasch, 'Anti-Imperialists', p. 321. Many on both sides believed in a scientifically justifiable hierarchy of race that was growing in influence in the late nineteenth century, seeing 'Anglo-Saxon' whites as those who had fought, survived and adapted in order to reach the top of this social order.
79. Tompkins, 'Scylla and Charybdis', pp. 143–7. The titular phrase is a classical allusion meaning (roughly) a choice between two equally bad fates.
80. See especially: Gates, 'Philippine Guerrillas', pp. 51–64.
81. 'Republican Party Platform of 1900', *American Presidency Project*.
82. Murphy, 'Women's Anti-Imperialism', p. 245.

CHAPTER 5

Spanish Plunder (1898–1917)

The previous chapter outlined the motivations for US intervention in the Spanish-American War of 1898, and the opposition that arose in response to the annexations that resulted from the conflict. Yet the United States viewed each of Spain's imperial possessions quite differently after the euphoria of victory had abated. America had, from the very early nineteenth century, continued to turn its imperial gaze away towards Cuba. However, after the war it was Cuba that was most assured of its 'independence' and it was instead the other Spanish possessions, in which the United States had hitherto shown little interest, that the US eventually annexed as part of the its overseas empire. The Philippines, after a bloody insurgency now commonly referred to as the Philippine-American War of 1899–1902, was the only other piece of America's Spanish plunder to gain its independence, but not until after the Second World War. As for Puerto Rico and the distant island of Guam in the Pacific (as discussed in Chapter 8), both became and remain curious entities, neither state nor free, and still a part of the United States to this day.[1]

Cuba

If any country was at the centre of the Spanish-American War it was Cuba. Cuba's rising against Spain, and its brutal repression, led the yellow press in the US to cry for intervention. It was in Cuba's capital that the USS *Maine* 'exploded', piling further pressure on President McKinley to declare war on Spain (see Chapter 4). Despite an attitude of covetousness by some in the United States towards Cuba, in 1898 the war was not for Cuban annexation but for Cuban freedom, stability and regional harmony. Indeed, it seemed as if this independence might well have been assured at the same time the United States decided to join the conflict. On 19 April 1898, Democratic Senator Henry Moore Teller sponsored a resolution attached to the authorisation for the US entry into the Spanish-Cuban conflict. The Teller Amendment began by expressing moral outrage over Spanish actions in Cuba that could 'no longer be endured' by the United States. Then followed a four-part resolution: first, that the Cuban people had the right to be 'free and independent'; second, that the US demanded Spanish withdrawal; and third, that the US President was otherwise authorised to intervene to assure the first and second parts were accomplished. However, it is the fourth part of the Teller Amendment which was to prove most interesting:

> That the United States hereby disclaims any disposition or intention to exercise sovereignty, jurisdiction, or control over said Island except for the pacification thereof, and asserts its determination, when that is accomplished, to leave the government and control of the Island to its people.[2]

This promise persuaded many Cubans and Americans that the intervention of the United States in Cuba, despite preconceptions of many to the contrary, came with 'no strings attached', a promise that in practice was 'never quite so clear-cut or so morally unambiguous'.[3] Indeed, for many in Cuba and the United States, the island never truly gained full independence until the later revolution of 1959.

The 1898 war with Spain was a short and one-sided affair with few doubts as to who would eventually emerge victorious. The only question remaining revolved around what the United States would do with Cuba once the war was over. Early signs suggested the matter might not be all that straightforward for Cuban nationalists. The US was keen to stop the Cuban General, Calixto Garcia, from accepting the Spanish capitulation, instead preferring that the Spanish surrender to the United States directly.[4] Once the Spanish had relinquished Cuba by mid-July, the US army effectively occupied the island, and this was formalised in a ceremony when the outgoing Spanish captain-general handed the keys of Havana to US General John Brooke in December. Cuba appeared to have passed swiftly from one type of imperial rule to another. However, Article I of the

Treaty of Paris, signed that same month, seemed again to reiterate the promise of the Teller Amendment:

> Spain relinquishes all claim of sovereignty over and title to Cuba. And as the island is, upon its evacuation by Spain, to be occupied by the United States, the United States will, so long as such occupation shall last, assume and discharge the obligations that may under international law result from the fact of its occupation, for the protection of life and property.[5]

Teller's pre-war amendment spoke of 'pacification' and now the post-war peace treaty talked about 'occupation', and though both insinuated these interventions would be finite, the precise length of the American stay had yet to be decided. Perhaps politicians would now decide that events had moved on so significantly since Teller's amendment was drafted that even the prospect of Cuban annexation was back on the table. For historian Louis Pérez Jr., the initial US intervention marked a noticeable shift in 'terms' regarding the war's purpose (even the *name* Spanish-American War), from a Cuban 'struggle for independence' to a US war of 'conquest' with Spain, with a new main aim being that Cuba did not fall into the hands of a third party.[6] From the start, the United States had been careful not to give recognition to the Cuban revolutionary government, a policy that was continued by the military during the war.[7] Importantly, this policy allowed the United States full flexibility in dictating the terms of peace.[8] Pérez rightly notes that while the US exclusion of Cuban insurgent commanders led to the estrangement of the pro-independence *insurrectos*, at the same time the Americans were becoming ever closer to the anti-independence Cuban elites who feared that anarchic conditions might result from self-government. At home, many Americans who had temporarily seen the Cubans as freedom-loving independence fighters now began to claim that Cubans were a racially heterogeneous group unlikely to be able to govern themselves.[9] As the year 1899 dawned the fate of Cuba was far from certain, despite the well-sounding words of the Teller Amendment.

The Cuba that the United States inherited had been devastated by the long Cuban revolution and the far shorter US-led war effort which ended it. The US administration tasked with helping Cuba back onto its feet was at first led by General Brooke, who undertook preliminary measures such as a census of the Cuban population and the disbanding of the Cuban army.[10] Brooke and his successor as military governor from December 1899, General Leonard Wood, enacted a number of important domestic reforms, ranging from penal and legal changes to the improvement of health and education provision on the island.[11] However, alongside his more benevolent alterations, Wood was also keen to centralise power and take as much personal control of Cuba as possible. He was reporting directly to the Secretary of War by June 1900.[12] Those involved in running post-war Cuba began to think and act as if the Teller Amendment was best forgotten, with General Brooke coming to believe that Cuba would ultimately accept annexation – a position that Wood held even more strongly.[13] Even more moderate US figures such as General James H. Wilson, a departmental commander in Cuba, favoured the formation of a protectorate and a customs union as preliminary steps towards ever-closer amalgamation. However, among Cubans, such sentiments came almost exclusively from the conservative elites that courted the United States in order to re-establish their own power in Cuba, under US rule if need be.[14]

During the period of military government in Cuba, the economic presence of the United States boomed: by the end of the occupation, US investment in Cuba was more than double what it had been before the war, primarily in tobacco and sugar. Indeed, Wood actively promoted tariff reciprocity to help bolster US-Cuban trade, seeing US trade and investment as the key to stabilising the island.[15] However, some in the United States opposed gratuitous profiteering in the wake of the war. Foremost among the opposition was Republican Senator Joseph Foraker, an anti-annexationist, who in 1899 proposed an amendment to the Army Appropriations Bill. This amendment forbade the US government from granting concessions or franchises in Cuba during the US occupation, as well as reiterating the Teller pledge to leave after 'pacification' was complete. However, despite its altruistic intentions, big business was able to circumvent the Foraker Amendment – through devices such as the 'revocable permit' or the exemption of mining from the Foraker provisions – with the help of Wood and Secretary of War Elihu Root.[16] This sort of military support for US economic intervention and dominance on the island became the primary route for maintaining control over the island, as well as the rest of the Caribbean, for years to come.

Wood and Root felt that rather than unleashing power on the uneducated and (as they saw it) racially inferior masses, the best chance for success in Cuba was to entrust power to the conservative Cuban elite and the remaining Spanish population.[17] In order to achieve this, literacy and limited property-owning provisions were included in the all-male franchise for the 1900 elections, limiting the electorate to around 5 per cent of the population. However, despite the best efforts of Wood and Root, the municipal elections in June 1900 and the constituent assembly election that December both saw substantial victories for parties advocating immediate independence. This result caused Wood to lament that those who had ultimately taken leadership were 'the absolutely irresponsible and unreliable element'.[18] With the Cubans not making the decisions the Americans had hoped they would, and with the continued success of the independence movement showing no signs of ebbing as 1901 progressed, the time had arrived for a re-conceptualisation of US-Cuban policy in the United States.

Although not a cornerstone in US history, the Platt Amendment, named after Republican Senator Orville Platt, is certainly a cornerstone in Cuban history; as historian Richard Gott puts it, *La Enmienda Platt* has been familiar to Cuban schoolchildren for over a century as evoking 'the humiliation of the settlement imposed on Cuba at the close of the US occupation'.[19] Although Platt drafted it, the real ideas behind the amendment belonged to Root, who saw in it a way to maintain US interests while securing the 'independence' required by the Teller Amendment.[20] In 1901, Congress passed the Platt Amendment as a rider attached to the Army Appropriations Bill (the same legislative tactic used to pass the earlier anti-exploitation Foraker Amendment).[21] The amendment defined 'future relations' between the US and a free Cuba and contained stipulations restricting Cuba's future treaty-making powers, ability to annul US-made laws, and future debt accrual. Perhaps the clearest evidence of the real intent of the Platt Amendment, however, can be found in Article III:

> That the government of Cuba consents that the United States may exercise the right to intervene for the preservation of Cuban

independence, the maintenance of a government adequate for the protection of life, property, and individual liberty, and for discharging the obligations with respect to Cuba imposed by the treaty of Paris on the United States, now to be assumed and undertaken by the government of Cuba.[22]

The Platt Amendment required Cuba to give the United States *carte blanche* to intervene in the future, if and when the US deemed it necessary, and the Cuban government were required to insert the amendment into their constitution when independence was granted. Such demands caused outrage among Cuban independence advocates, but, as one patriot put it, they faced a stark decision: either a protected Republic, or no Republic at all.[23] For Root, US interests and the very safety of Cuba itself required 'constitutional limitations which would never be put into the [Cuban] Constitution except on our insistence or suggestion'.[24] Cuba's constituent assembly accepted the US-inflicted amendment by a single vote, and on 20 May 1902, Tomás Estrada Palma became an independent Cuba's first president. The Platt Amendment again formed part of a 1903 treaty between the newly independent Cuba and the United States. However, for some veterans of the struggle for independence, such as General Juan Gualberto Gómez, the amendment had 'reduced the independence and sovereignty of the Cuban Republic to a myth'.[25]

Granted, Cuba had gained independence in 1902 when the rest of the Spanish Empire had been annexed by the United States, but this independence came at a cost. The Platt Amendment allowed for US intervention in Cuban affairs in 1906, 1912, 1917 and 1920, before finally being expunged as part of Franklin Roosevelt's Good Neighbor Policy in 1934. The extent to which Cuba was still regarded as a pseudo-colony of the United States was captured nicely in the title of the 1928 volume *Our Cuban Colony: A Study in Sugar*. The author of this volume, historian Leland H. Jenks, noted 'a widespread popular belief [in the US] that Cuba is part of an incipient American Empire'.[26] Although formal independence and self-government had been granted, the United States remained the economic master of Cuba and patron of its disreputable dictators for decades to come, in a manner not unlike its treatment of the rest of the Caribbean (see Chapter 7).

Puerto Rico

The extensive literature on the Spanish-American War period tends to focus upon the larger Spanish possessions of Cuba and the Philippines. In contrast, the less populous annexed territories of Puerto Rico and Guam (discussed in Chapter 8) garner far less attention. Cuba was, after all, the main focal point of US attention before and during the Spanish-American War, while the Philippines became the main focus afterwards, as the largest annexed territory and one in which the US fought a protracted war to suppress the islands' independence fighters. In contrast, Puerto Rico seemed less important – more a by-product of the war, which the US annexed with little trouble at the time. However, overlooking Puerto Rico underestimates both its important role in defining what US overseas imperialism would come to look like in the early twentieth century, and the fact that in the twenty-first century it remains the United States' more populous unincorporated imperial territory.

For the Spanish, Puerto Rico was first and foremost a garrison island whose value lay in the protection it gave to its empire's shipping. The island became a formal colony of Spain in 1815 and, thereafter, Spanish influence and interest continued to grow. By 1870, following the brutal suppression of the 1868 pro-independence 'Lares Revolt', the islands were a full province of Spain with legal recognition of Puerto Rican political parties.[27] Despite increased Spanish interest and investment, Puerto Rico never became the powerhouse of economic output that Cuba was and, as economic historian James Dietz persuasively argues, the primary reason it did not develop an independence struggle at the same time as the rest of Latin America was because the island lacked a large elite economic class whose interests were no longer served by the colonial government. However, after 1870 the growing economic elite began a political, rather than armed, struggle to increase their autonomy. Although such efforts intermittently met with Spanish hostility – such as 'The Terrible Year of 1887' – just over a week before the Spanish-American War began, the Spanish granted Puerto Rico full representation in the Spanish Cortes along with a bicameral legislature for the island itself.[28]

For the Americans, Puerto Rico was somewhat significant, even if its fate did not weigh as heavily on the minds of the nation as that of Cuba. During the nineteenth century Puerto Rico was regarded much like Cuba (see 'Early Cuban Intrigue' in Chapter 3), as a potential strategic asset. It also, unlike the Philippines, lay snugly inside the bounds of the Monroe Doctrine and the broadly accepted US sphere of influence. In 1867 Secretary of State Seward attempted to purchase two Puerto Rican islands (Culebra and Culebrita) along with some of the Danish Virgin Islands, and during the presidency of Benjamin Harrison, Puerto Rico ranked alongside Cuba and Hawaii as one of the three potential overseas acquisitions the US might advisedly pursue.[29] Puerto Rico was not a bad substitute for Cuba as a base in the Caribbean.[30] From the moment negotiations between Spain and the United States began in 1898, despite the former's hope of keeping the island, the US made it clear that Puerto Rico was to be annexed. The Puerto Ricans seemed to largely welcome US troops and, moreover, the Spanish had no way of stopping the United States from keeping the island if it chose to do so.[31]

Imperialist Senator Henry Cabot Lodge suggested leaving Puerto Rico in the same position as Hawaii, organised as a territory with the theoretical potential for statehood but unlikely to attain it. Indeed, political and public opinion was nowhere near as hostile to this annexation as that of the Philippines, and even the anti-imperialist William Jennings Bryan favoured annexation of Puerto Rico if the island's population consented.[32] However, another way in which Puerto Rico differed from Cuba and the Philippines was that its people were divided about the desirability of independence from the United States. For Puerto Ricans, three main routes became the focus of debate: independence, full union or something in between. Regardless of Puerto Rican opinion, from the time of the Treaty of Paris through until April 1900, a US military government under the War Department ran Puerto Rico. For historian Jacqueline Font-Guzmán, despite early promises from the US military to respect Puerto Ricans, what followed was in her view 'a brutal process of cultural assimilation and repression', including anti-sedition measures, the imposition of the English language and a more general 'Americanisation' of the education system.[33] This is a view bolstered by Ramón Bosque-Pérez, who notes the US deployment of a new police force under military control that set about spying on those harbouring anti-American sentiments.[34]

In 1900, after a short period of military rule, the passage of the Foraker Organic Act gave Puerto Rico a civil government. Given the divided nature of the US Congress on the matter of annexation, it was no surprise that this act was a compromise. The Foraker Act enabled the United States to 'selectively govern Puerto Rico as a foreign country for an indeterminate amount of time', and, importantly, tariffs – though reduced – remained in place to begin with.[35] The US government wanted to keep the island but not to allow it full 'member's rights'; the tariff was the first early sign of Puerto Rico's semi-outsider status, even though Congress removed it the following year. The Foraker Act also gave Puerto Rico a governor and an executive council, effectively an upper chamber, appointed by the US President with an in-built majority of US citizens. In addition, it gained its own elected House of Representatives and a judiciary, as well as being allowed to send a non-voting resident commissioner to Washington. Despite the trappings of self-government, the US Congress reserved the right to scrap any legislation that emanated from the island if it saw fit. This government system allowed the United States to keep close control of Puerto Rican affairs, and a similar system was set up a few years later in the Philippines. Puerto Ricans became citizens of Puerto Rico under the Foraker Act, but not US citizens.

Puerto Rico's unusual status, like that of the other US island possessions gained during the Spanish-American War, was ultimately established through an array of Supreme Court decisions referred to as the Insular Cases. These cases, spanning the years 1901–22, essentially upheld and extended the formulation of Puerto Rico as something other than a future state of the union. In perhaps the most important of these cases, *Downes v. Bidwell* (1901), the Supreme Court declared that: 'So long as Congress has not incorporated the territory into the United States, neither military occupation nor cession by treaty makes the conquered territory domestic territory in the sense of the revenue laws. But those laws concerning "foreign countries" remain applicable to the conquered territory until changed by Congress.' In this important case, the court settled the issue of whether the Constitution followed the flag to the new insular possessions: if they were not 'incorporated' then the answer was 'negative'. Puerto Rico, along with the other former Spanish territories of Guam and the Philippines, became 'unincorporated territories', neither within nor outwith the United States.[36]

The issue of citizenship is important to consider at this stage, as it was with the creation of 'unincorporated territories' that the admission of new territories ceased to come with a guarantee of future US citizenship. Those living in territories annexed following the Mexican-American War, or more contemporaneously Hawaii, were automatically granted US citizenship once they had established territorial governments. However, this did not follow for Puerto Rico and the other Spanish-American War annexations. In *Downes v. Bidwell*, Justice Henry Billings Brown stated that the new US annexations raised 'grave questions' about the 'differences of race, habits, laws and customs' of their inhabitants, and he instead made a clear distinction about rights which were peculiar to 'Anglo-Saxon jurisprudence'.[37] For E. Robert Statham Jr., the key reason for differentiating between incorporated territories and unincorporated territories was deeply rooted in contemporary notions of racial hierarchy: the 'distinction between Anglo-Saxon Americans and other human beings'.[38] Although US citizenship was eventually granted to all US overseas territories (except American Samoa), this citizenship still only becomes 'full and complete' if territorial inhabitants move to one of the fifty states.[39] Only in 1917 did the US belatedly grant Puerto Ricans citizenship, with the passage of the Jones-Shafroth Act, and for other territories this came far later. Puerto Ricans were left only with the option of rejecting this citizenship, an unsavoury prospect that would leave such a person without most of their civil rights.[40]

To this day, Puerto Rico's status remains that of an 'unincorporated territory' and the island's inhabitants remain divided on whether to campaign for change. According to Rubén Martínez, the majority of the Puerto Rican people still favoured independence until the 1940s, when the independence movement was *de facto* criminalised.[41] In the 1950s Puerto Rico drew up a new constitution and became, in 1952, a 'Commonwealth' of the United States. This name is entirely unhelpful, as it remained in much the same relationship with the United States as it always had, though with a further reformed and more autonomous system of government.[42] It would be a mistake, however, to see Puerto Rico's gradual acceptance of US imperialism as largely peaceful. Indeed, events in the 1950s illustrated that the issue of Puerto Rico's future was far from settled. During this decade, nationalist Puerto Ricans led by Pedro Albizu Campos orchestrated a series of uprisings, leading the island's government to call in the national guard. This refusal to accept US domination reached its height in March 1954 when four nationalists entered the US House of Representatives, unfurled a

Puerto Rican flag and began firing pistols at those present, wounding five Congressmen.[43] Certainly, much interest remains as to what the future holds for the relationship between the United States and the island. Four separate referendums (1967, 1993, 1998 and 2012) have been held since 1952 in order to determine some way forward for the island's curious status, but none has chosen decisively to move away from the status quo. Both the US Democratic and Republican parties addressed the issue of Puerto Rican status in their 2012 election platforms, but for now the future remains as uncertain as it seemed back in 1898.

The Philippines

Unlike Cuba and Puerto Rico, the Philippines lie substantially further from US shores and, prior to 1898, most Americans knew little of this distant archipelago lying outside even the most generous interpretation of the Monroe Doctrine's boundaries. President McKinley himself described the Philippines as 'somewhere away around on the other side of the world'.[44] However, unlike the similarly distant and obscure guano islands, Midway or Guam, the Philippines were also home to a large, diverse population of around eight million people.[45] In terms of the acquisitions from the Spanish-American War, the Philippines proved to be the trickiest of all. The US populace remained divided on their value as a colony and the Filipinos far more reluctant to accept the yoke of a new empire. Nonetheless, despite great reservations and some increasingly pressing strategic issues regarding their defence, the US annexed the Philippines after the war and the islands did not gain their independence until 1946.

Spain ruled the Philippines for hundreds of years, but by the late nineteenth century, as in Cuba, the islands were beset with rebellion and the Spanish began to respond in an uncompromising fashion. Unlike in Cuba, the Spanish failed to develop the islands economically. Instead, the Philippines became an 'enormous mission' dominated by Catholic friars, towards whom most of the revolutionary sentiment was directed.[46] By 1896, the insurgency against the status quo had reached a critical momentum; however, it was only between 1896 and 1899 that pro-independence sentiment became widespread in the islands.[47] The ascendant Filipino nationalists, led by Emilio Aguinaldo, sought to take advantage of Spanish weaknesses in this period to liberate the islands and form a new republic in the Pacific.

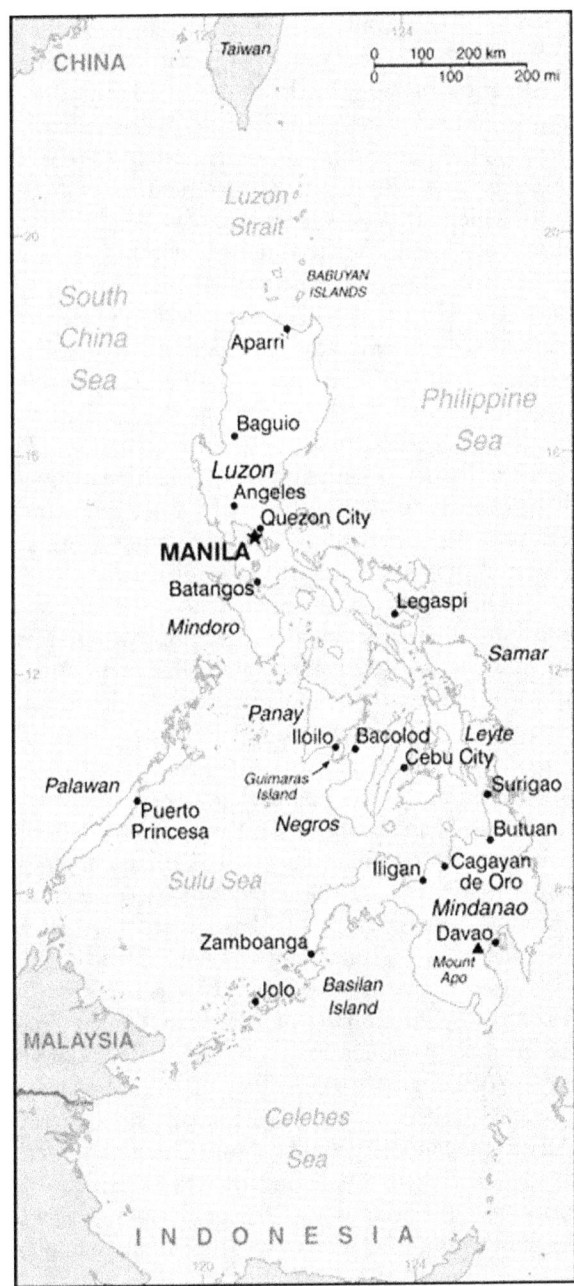

Figure 5.1 Philippines

Though Cuba appeared to be the epicentre of the Spanish-American War, its first major tremor was felt in the Philippines. In the first real action of the war, the Battle of Manila Bay, Admiral George Dewey led his Asiatic Squadron to overwhelm the Spanish on 1 May 1898. In light of this success, Aguinaldo's rebels declared the formation of a new Philippine government on 12 June. Despite the speed at which success was arriving, further US forces were required to press home the seemingly inevitable victory. Troops duly departed from the west coast of the United States, and by the beginning of August sufficient US forces were in place for the final push. The Spanish were already prostrate in Manila, surrounded by Aguinaldo's nationalist troops. Aguinaldo later claimed to have come to an understanding with the Americans that, when the Spanish had been defeated, the ultimate goal was Philippine independence and not the supplanting of one type of imperial rule for another.[48] The Spanish, for their part, were reluctant to reach terms with Aguinaldo, preferring instead to come to an agreement with the United States, echoing the narrative of events in Cuba that summer. On 13 August, the Spanish and the increasingly suspicious Filipino rebels oversaw a curious 'mock' battle, where the Americans launched a tokenistic bombardment of Manila before moving in to seize the capital city unopposed. The following day, the Spanish officially surrendered to the Americans rather than Aguinaldo.

The acquisition of the Philippine Islands was not at the forefront of debates over the Spanish-American War. Even the arch-imperialists said little, if anything, about annexation of the Philippines prior to the fall of Manila.[49] Though the Philippine capital of Manila had certainly been of interest as a naval base, there were doubts about whether Manila or Luzon (the island on which it lies) could be taken without the rest of the archipelago.[50] Nevertheless, with Manila under US control by the summer of 1898, familiar imperialist arguments arose from 'large policy' stalwarts such as Theodore Roosevelt and Henry Cabot Lodge, who cited the importance of, for example, strategic benefits, access to the much-touted China market, and a sense of duty to the Filipino people.[51] Paolo Coletta argues that, aside from such advocacy, the ultimate driver behind President McKinley's decision to annex the islands was US public opinion, which supported the annexation of the Spanish acquisitions while still borne high on post-war euphoria.[52] However, as historian Fabian Hilfrich has subsequently shown, McKinley used a series of speaking tours of the West and the South to influence public opinion in favour of the annexations rather than simply yielding to it.[53] Indeed, McKinley was not simply a follower of public opinion but, like his successor Theodore Roosevelt, proactively latched on to the prevailing popular sentiment and then drove it forward.

Article III of the Treaty of Paris, which ended McKinley's 'splendid little war', ceded the Philippines in their entirety to the United States in return for a $20 million payment within three months of the treaty's ratification.[54] In a businesslike fashion, the entirety of this Spanish imperial archipelago thus passed uninterrupted into the burgeoning American empire. Although for some in the anti-imperialist movement the annexation of the Philippines was anathema to US ideals, for the pro-imperialists like Senator Lodge it was nothing of the sort. In a speech to Congress given in March 1900, Lodge stated that 'the record of American expansions which closes with Alaska has been a long one, and to-day we do but continue the same movement. The same policy runs through them all'.[55] Walter Williams also draws compelling parallels between the treatment of the Filipino resistance forces and Native Americans in the US during the nineteenth century, claiming that the treatment of Native Americans provided a precedent for taking over territories without incorporating 'natives', granting them US citizenship or guaranteeing them constitutional protections.[56] Ultimately the Philippines, like Puerto Rico, became an unincorporated territory, with the details of this new legal position defined by the succession of US Supreme Court Insular Cases in the following decade or so.[57]

On 4 February 1899, shortly before ratification of the Treaty of Paris, open conflict had broken out between the US troops and Aguinaldo's nationalists, and this unrest continued for many months to come. Historian David Silbey describes the ongoing insurrection in the islands as 'a war of frontier, and of empire', bringing together the experience of US westward expansion and the relatively novel form of overseas imperialism of the 1890s.[58] The 'Philippine War', as Brian McAllister Linn refers to it, can be roughly dated from the outbreak of hostilities between Aguinaldo's troops and those of the US in February 1899, until the final surrender of the rebels and full establishment of US civil government on 4 July 1902.[59] During this time the nationalist rebellion took on an increasingly guerrilla form and became confined primarily to non-metropolitan areas. The United States' actions in subduing the rebellion, including the use of 're-concentration' tactics similar to those used by Weyler in Cuba, caused an outcry when they broke in the US press.[60] Hostility towards Filipino insurgents in the US military reached its apogee in the use of the 'water cure', or 'waterboarding', as it is now better known.[61] US military rule was established in Manila under the command of General Arthur MacArthur before being handed over to General Ewell Otis in 1900, with no certain end date to military control in mind. The United States had acquired a new type of territory, enforced against the will of at least part of its indigenous population, and the question over how best to proceed over the coming years remained remarkably fluid.

In 1899 President McKinley sent an investigative commission to the islands, headed by Cornell University president Jacob Gould Schurman, with the original aim of stopping another war. However, by the time Schurman's commission arrived, their primary aim had already been thwarted and the commission aimed instead to work out how to win over the Filipinos to US rule.[62] Schurman, who had initially opposed the islands' annexation, became convinced the US could not now leave the islands in good faith, but should move away from military rule and bring in a measure of self-government.[63] In 1900 a second commission, led by Ohio judge William Howard Taft, prepared the way for US civil government in the archipelago.[64] Taft, like Schurman before him, felt that despite the misfortune of having acquired the Philippines, McKinley had been doing his duty to the islands by bringing them under US rule. With their annexation complete, Taft believed that the best way forward was the rapid implementation of a 'policy of attraction' to win over the Filipinos, building upon the ideas of Schurman.[65] Ongoing 'unrest' delayed the establishment of US civil rule in the islands for some months, but on 4 July 1901 President McKinley installed Taft as the islands' first US Civil Governor. Taft took control of the subdued parts of the archipelago, while Major General Adna Chaffee maintained control of those parts still in open insurrection. A year later, President Roosevelt declared the conflict at an end, though even after this time fighting continued intermittently on the more remote islands.

Taft's governorship was relatively successful, and during his time he implemented a 'policy of attraction' that involved working with the existing, pragmatic elites in the islands to bring about a range of reforms to the economy, the education system, healthcare and the legal system.[66] In addition to such 'attractive' measures, a degree of political representation was also to be introduced for the Filipino people. The 1902 Cooper Organic Act set out that a popularly elected assembly, susceptible to a veto by a US-dominated upper house (as in Puerto Rico), would be established when suitable conditions were in place. The assembly proved to be the most volatile part of Taft's policy of gradually incorporating Filipinos into positions of power, dubbed 'Filipinization'. While sympathetic Filipino elites tended to be appointed to tokenistic positions, the assembly was more susceptible to popular opinion. Despite the best efforts of the US civil government to thwart pro-independence parties, these parties won a sweeping majority in the first popular elections to the assembly in 1907. After this point, despite Taft and his successors' continued efforts, the issue of independence dominated the Filipino political arena. Nationalist Filipino assemblymen finally saw potential for movement on the issue of independence when the Democrats swept to power in the four-horse race that was the 1912 US election.[67]

By 1912, US overseas imperialism had diminished as a central campaigning issue. Former Republican president and arch-imperialist Theodore Roosevelt, now running on a Progressive ticket, had, like most of the American public, changed his mind about the Philippines.[68] At least as early as 1907, Roosevelt had decided that with the continued growth of Japanese power in the Far East and increasing tension arising over the mistreatment of Japanese nationals on the US West Coast, the Philippines constituted a weak link in the armour of the United States. As a result of this, and the fact that Roosevelt was keenly attuned to US public opinion, he now argued that the Philippines should be set on the road to independence.[69] The indefensible nature of the Philippines was later confirmed by the Naval War College in their 1910 Orange Plan, which concluded that if Japan attacked the Philippines the islands would be easily taken.[70] Against the tide of public and military opinion, moves towards independence were delayed under the presidency of Taft (1909–13), who maintained his belief that the

US needed to commit to long-term imperial rule in order to fulfil its duty to the islands. However, the election of President Woodrow Wilson in 1912, coupled with a Democratic majority in Congress, meant that by March 1913 the party most closely associated with anti-imperialism was back in power for the first time since Grover Cleveland left office in 1897. Furthermore, Wilson selected as his new secretary of state William Jennings Bryan, perhaps the most prominent of all anti-imperialists.

Democrat William Jones led a renewed pro-independence effort in the US House of Representatives and sought to pass legislation that would guarantee future independence for the islands. In 1916, despite the best efforts of a small 'retentionist' lobby, the Jones Act (Philippine Organic Act) made it official US policy to grant the islands independence in the future. This was to follow a furtherance of the 'Filipinization' policy initiated by the US civil government and allow for an elected Senate to replace the existing US-dominated upper house.[71] When the Republicans re-occupied the White House in the 1920s, progress towards independence slowed somewhat. Republican administrators like Philippine Governor-General Leonard Wood, the former military governor of Cuba, proved reluctant to devolve further powers to the Filipino people, but Filipino Senate leader Manuel Quezon was determined to keep pushing. However, despite the efforts of some administrators in the 1930s, including High Commissioner Paul McNutt, to revisit 'retentionist' ideas, the resurgence of the US Democratic Party in 1932 led instead to a revitalising of the move towards independence.[72]

The Tydings-McDuffie Act of 1934 set up the islands as a 'commonwealth', not unlike the 'dominion' status used by the British in places like Australia, granting the Filipinos an elected president and, crucially, independence by 1946.[73] The act left the Filipinos in a quite irregular relationship with the United States: not independent but decidedly 'alien' while under continued US control.[74] The first president of the Commonwealth, Manuel Quezon, was a pragmatist who balanced his overtly nationalist rhetoric alongside a close understanding with the Americans, and he hoped the reality of independence remained relatively far off. The main reason for his uncertainty over independence, other than economic concerns, was the threat Theodore Roosevelt had identified back in 1907: Japan. The Japanese expanded into northern China in the

1930s, and, by 1937, they became embroiled in a full-scale conflict there. This Sino-Japanese situation concerned those engaged in the debate over the future of the Philippines and their forebodings materialised in dramatic form in December 1941 when Japanese attacks on Pearl Harbor left the Philippines assuredly indefensible. By March 1942, the US general in charge of the islands' defence, Douglas MacArthur, son of the islands' first military governor, left the islands along with President Quezon. The Philippines returned briefly to US hands following the long struggle to wrest them back from the Japanese between 1944 and 1945, but independence had already been agreed upon.

Despite the ever-changing situation in the islands, on 4 July 1946 the Philippines formally gained their independence from the United States. However, the US maintained such economic dominance in the islands that its 'requests' for continued military bases in the Philippines after independence, including the important naval base at Subig Bay, were practically non-negotiable.[75] Added to this continued military presence, in 1951 the two nations signed a mutual defence treaty, further cementing a continuing bond between the republic and its former colonisers. Not until 1992 did the Philippines finally achieve the withdrawal of US troops from their remaining military bases, just under a century after Dewey had struck the first blow for US imperialism back in 1898.

The Spanish-American War annexations provide the leading examples of American imperialism, a fact which even the aberration theorists – who regarded this period as a temporary lapse in US history – concede.[76] However, the effects of these annexations were far from temporary. Cuba might have gained its imperfect independence in 1902, yet even there the issue of Guantanamo Bay provides a lasting reminder of US imperialism (see Chapter 8). The Philippines fought a long and bitter guerrilla war against the US and their politicians campaigned for decades before finally achieving independence in 1946. In Puerto Rico, of course, the mantle of US empire lives on, despite dividing public opinion there to this day. Yet the Spanish-American War annexations were not the end of such overseas territorial aggrandisement, and the same Caribbean and Pacific theatres continued to see further US imperialist interventions throughout the first decades of the twentieth century and beyond.

Notes

1. For the sake of a closely shared history, Guam will be discussed in Chapter 8 along with the Mariana Islands, even though it formed part of the plunder of 1898.
2. Teller Amendment, *History of Cuba*.
3. Gott, *Cuba*, p. 102.
4. Lipman, *Guantánamo*, p. 21.
5. See: Treaty of Paris, 1898, *Avalon Project*. Although the treaty was signed on 10 December 1898, ratifications were not exchanged until 11 April 1899, only a year after McKinley's war message to Congress. See Fitzgibbon, *Cuba and the US*, p. 28.
6. Pérez, *Cuba and the US*, p. 97.
7. Aguilar, 'Cuba c. 1860–c.1930', p. 36.
8. Offner, *An Unwanted War*, p. 182.
9. Aguilar, 'Cuba c. 1860–c.1930', p. 37.
10. Fitzgibbon, *Cuba and the US*, p. 29.
11. For details of Wood's time in Cuba see McCallum, *Leonard Wood*, Chapter 7.
12. McCallum, *Leonard Wood*, pp. 175–6.
13. Gott, *Cuba*, p. 106.
14. Benjamin, *The US and Cuba*, p. 8.
15. Ibid. p. 9.
16. Leonard, *Encyclopedia of Cuban-US Relations*, pp. 76–7, p. 226.
17. McCallum, *Leonard Wood*, p. 165, describes Wood as 'an unabashed Anglo-Saxon Social Darwinist'; Benjamin, *US and Cuba*, p. 7; Gott, *Cuba*, p. 108.
18. Pérez, *Cuba and the US*, p. 103.
19. Gott, *Cuba*, p. 110.
20. Fitzgibbon, *Cuba and the US*, p. 81.
21. Hitchman, 'Platt Amendment Revisited', p. 343.
22. Platt Amendment, *Our Documents*.
23. Aguilar, 'Cuba c. 1860–c.1930', p. 39.
24. Pérez, *Cuba and the US*, p. 108.
25. Gott, *Cuba*, p. 111.
26. Jenks, *Our Cuban Colony*, p. 5.
27. Waugh, *Family of Islands*, p. 265; Dietz, *Economic History of Puerto Rico*, p. 74.
28. Dietz, *Economic History of Puerto Rico*, pp. 73–6.
29. Monge, *Puerto Rico*, pp. 22–3.
30. Healy, *US Expansionism*, p. 113, notes that Puerto Rico had in fact featured as a replacement for Cuba as the basis of an invasion in a – somewhat far-fetched – German war plan of 1899.

31. Offner, *An Unwanted War*, pp. 211–21.
32. Healy, *US Expansionism*, pp. 54–5.
33. Font-Guzmán, *Experiencing Puerto Rican Citizenship*, p. 25.
34. Bosque-Pérez, 'Political Persecution', p. 16.
35. Venator-Santiago, *Puerto Rico*, p. 54.
36. For an excellent up-to-date review of Puerto Rico and the Insular Cases, see: Burnett and Marshall, 'Between the Foreign and the Domestic', pp. 1–38. For a more detailed overview of the Insular Cases, see also Sparrow, *Insular Cases*; Neuman and Brown-Nagin, *Reconsidering the Insular Cases*.
37. Statham, *Colonial Constitutionalism*, p. 15.
38. Ibid. pp. 15–16.
39. Ibid. pp. 16–17. As Statham notes, US citizens in overseas territories have no formal representation in the US Congress, pay no federal taxes, have no electoral votes for the selection of the president, and have no control over judicial representation. For American Samoans' anomalous status see Chapter 6.
40. Pérez y González, *Puerto Ricans in US*, p. 29. The Jones Act did little else to change the lot of Puerto Rico. It increased the elected elements of the legislature, but retained for the United States government the ability to nullify Puerto Rican legislation.
41. Martínez, 'Puerto Rico's Decolonization', p. 102.
42. For a list of powers the United States still holds over Puerto Rico see: Miranda, 'Powers Held by the US', pp. 152–3.
43. Immerwahr, 'Greater United States', pp. 373–4.
44. Karnow, *In Our Image*, p. 100.
45. Wolff, *Little Brown Brother*, p. 19.
46. Ibid. p. 17.
47. Salamanca, *Filipino Reaction to American Rule*, p. 163.
48. Burns, 'An Imperial Vision', p. 71; Karnow, *In Our Image*, pp. 110–11.
49. Karnow, *In Our Image*, pp. 108–9.
50. Coletta, 'Acquisition of the Philippines', p. 345.
51. See: Karnow, *In Our Image*, pp. 108–9.
52. Coletta, 'Acquisition of the Philippines', pp. 346–7.
53. Hilfrich, *Debating American Exceptionalism*, p. 123.
54. Treaty of Paris, 1898, *Avalon Project*.
55. Lodge 1900, cited in W. L. Williams, 'US Indian Policy', p. 817. Williams's article presents a number of the arguments made in the *fin de siècle* period that supported the idea of Philippine annexation as in line with other annexation processes in US history.
56. Williams, 'US Indian Policy', p. 819. See also Chapter 1.
57. For a brief overview, see the section on Puerto Rico.
58. Silbey, *War of Frontier and Empire*, p. xiii.

59. Linn, *Philippine War*. See also: Schirmer, *Republic or Empire*; Welch, *Response to Imperialism*.
60. Brands, *Bound to Empire*, pp. 56–7.
61. Kramer, *Blood of Government*, p. 140. Interestingly, a similar debate over waterboarding appeared again in the twenty-first century surrounding the US treatment of prisoners in Guantanamo Bay.
62. Go, *American Empire*, pp. 34–5.
63. See especially: Hendrickson, 'Reluctant Expansionist', pp. 405–21. For a detailed account of military rule in the islands see: Gates, *Schoolbooks and Krags*.
64. Burns, 'Adapting to Empire', p. 420.
65. Burns, 'Winning "Hearts and Minds"'.
66. Ibid. For detailed coverage of US policy in the islands between 1899 and 1903 see: Miller, *'Benevolent Assimilation'*. For the subsequent period, other than works cited here, see also: Stanley, *Nation in the Making*; Gleeck, *American Half-Century*; Golay, *Face of Empire*.
67. The four main contenders were Woodrow Wilson (Democrat), William H. Taft (Republican), Theodore Roosevelt (Progressive) and Eugene Debs (Socialist, who gained 6 per cent of the popular vote). Though between them the incumbent Republican president Taft (23.2 per cent) and former Republican president Roosevelt (27.4 per cent) gained over half of the popular vote, the division caused by them running against one another meant that Wilson's 41.8 per cent share of the popular vote gained him a resounding 82 per cent of the Electoral College vote.
68. Roosevelt failed in his attempt to win the Republican nomination in 1912 (won by Taft) and immediately bolted the party to run as the candidate for the new Progressive Party.
69. Burns, 'Adapting to Empire', pp. 427–8.
70. Brands, *Bound to Empire*, p. 177.
71. See especially: Burns, 'Retentionist in Chief', pp. 163–92.
72. Kotlowski, 'Independence or Not?', p. 504.
73. Ibid.
74. Kramer, *Blood of Government*, p. 427.
75. Brands, *Bound to Empire*, pp. 220–1.
76. A theory propounded by historian Samuel Flagg Bemis and promulgated in subsequent years by scholars such as Julius Pratt and Ernest May. For discussion see: Morgan, *Into New Territory*, p. 8.

CHAPTER 6

An Empire among Equals (1899–1917)

Following its sudden accumulation of territories in 1898, the United States established itself as an imperial power with island possessions in the Caribbean and the Pacific. The annexations of American Samoa and the US Virgin Islands bring to light an important theme in US expansion that the Spanish-American War somewhat overshadows: 'preclusive imperialism', defined here as taking control of an area to stop another power from doing so instead. As the archimperialist Senator Henry Cabot Lodge put it in 1895: '[The great nations] are rapidly absorbing for their future expansion and their present defence all the waste places of the earth ... As one of the great nations of the world, the United States must not fall out of the line of the march.'[1] The annexations of parts of the Samoan and the Virgin Islands reflect Lodge's thinking. There were no pressing economic or strategic benefits to annexing these islands and, if anything, they became more superfluous after the annexations of Hawaii, the Philippines and Puerto Rico. Instead, to some extent like the acquisition of the Panama Canal and its surrounding 'zone', the overriding impetus for annexation of parts of the Samoan and Virgin Islands was strategic, preclusive imperialism. In this regard – in Panama, Samoa and the Virgin Islands – the most pressing rival power in the wake of the Spanish-American War was Germany.

Germany came late to the imperial race, so by the late 1880s the empire built by the Iron Chancellor, Otto von Bismarck, consisted of scattered possessions in the western Pacific and central and southern Africa, many of which had been left untargeted by the early movers such as France and Britain.[2] However, following the death of Kaiser Wilhelm I in 1888, the new Kaiser, Wilhelm II, oversaw the chancellor's fall from grace. The young Kaiser sought a place for Germany among the other great imperial powers as part of a far more aggressive foreign policy: *Weltpolitik*. Wilhelm's motives display some similarity to those of Senator Lodge. Where Bismarck's *Realpolitik* had relied largely on diplomacy to acquire overseas territories, Wilhelm's *Weltpolitik* meant the very real possibility of force. As a result, German ambitions in the Pacific and Caribbean led the United States to become more forthright in annexing overseas territories in this period than it might otherwise have been.

American Samoa

The Samoan Islands are a group of Polynesian islands that lie 2,300 miles south-east of Hawaii, and fall into two main sections: the larger western islands and the smaller eastern islands. American interest in Samoa, like many islands in the Pacific, dated back to the mid-nineteenth century when trading agents arrived in 1839, and the US certainly saw the potential of the archipelago as the base of a future Pacific coaling station. The US was not alone in its interest and US agents, later termed 'consuls', were joined by representatives from Britain and Germany in the islands' principal city of Apia (on the large western island of Upolu).[3] The Germans, in particular, sought to increase their political influence over the islands by utilising their increased naval power, and they took the lead in the 'tug-of-war' over Samoa that subsequently developed.[4] As well as dealing with European competition, the US also had to navigate the tumultuous internal politics of Samoa, which rarely settled for long in this period.[5]

In this competitive and fractious environment, one American business, the Central Polynesia Land and Commercial Company (CPLCC), managed to purchase territory amounting to about a third of the archipelago's total land.[6] The resulting increase in US commercial investment in Samoa led to growing pressure on the US government to establish some form of protectorate in the islands. However, this particular lobbying group collapsed when the CPLCC itself went bankrupt in the early 1870s.[7] Interest in Samoa was far from over, though, and shipping magnate William H. Webb moved to establish a presence in the islands for his steamers.[8] In 1872 US Navy Captain Richard W. Meade came to an agreement with a Samoan chief to establish US shipping rights to the harbour at Pago Pago, a town on the largest of the eastern Samoan islands, Tutuila.[9]

President Ulysses S. Grant sent Albert B. Steinberger as a US agent to follow up on Meade's agreement, an agent whom historian Peter Stuart singles out as, debatably, one of twelve men that 'expanded the United States overseas'. Indeed, Steinberger proved a less-than-reliable representative of the Grant administration's relatively modest exploratory intentions. He sided with Samoan islanders against the US land speculators and gave the Samoans the impression that the United States intended to form a protectorate in the islands.[10] On leaving the islands after three months in 1873, Steinberger proceeded to negotiate with German commercial interests, with a view to forming a more workable government in Samoa. When he returned in 1874 to much popular acclaim from native Samoans, Steinberger's manoeuvrings to create a more coherent government proved relatively successful. He helped forge a new arrangement for appointing a king, alongside a bicameral parliamentary system with himself as premier from 1875.[11] However, Steinberger's radical departure from his country's official stance and equally outlandish self-aggrandisement made him a multitude of enemies in the islands, especially among non-native communities. These enemies, primarily US and British business interests, conspired to bring Steinberger down by denouncing him as a 'charlatan' interested in enriching himself, and they badgered the Samoan king into agreeing to his speedy deportation.[12] Ultimately, both Steinberger's actions and the king's reaction furthered divisions between Samoan factions and stoked up anxieties between the US and its European rivals in the region.

Tensions between the three powers seeking control of the islands escalated further after the time of Steinberger. From 1884 onwards, Bismarck embarked on a period of imperial activism that promoted the idea of a protectorate over Samoa, leading to an attempted coup against King Malietoa Laupepa. The United States' position was consistent: it did not seek a US protectorate over the islands, but also felt that no other nation should establish one. In 1886 another US representative, Consul Bertold Greenebaum, overstepped his remit, provocatively hoisting the Stars and Stripes in response to the positioning of a German man-of-war in Apia's harbour, though his actions were swiftly undone when word arrived from Washington. Finally, in the summer of 1887, the US convened a conference in Washington to settle the Samoan question, proposing a tripartite protectorate and the return of Malietoa Laupepa. However, the British and German delegations rejected this proposal, resulting in a thoroughly inconclusive end to proceedings.[13]

By 1889, rivalry between the powers had increased to such an extent that the United States sent the USS *Trenton* to Apia. Britain and Germany responded in kind. These manoeuvres heightened the tensions in the archipelago without any real desire for war, creating a very tense 'stalemate'.[14] As it turned out, the weather intervened to play a critical role in the Samoan standoff, with a typhoon sinking or grounding the powers' ships. With the pacifying intervention of strong winds, a second international conference on the Samoan situation was organised between the powers. When taking into account the presence of rivals in the archipelago, particularly the strong German position in western Samoa, the United States chose to focus attention on its existing interests at the deep-water bay of Pago Pago. In subsequent negotiations, the division between existing spheres of influence proved decisive: the eastern Samoan islands would be the focus of US claims while the Germans pressed theirs in the larger western islands.[15] The British role in the Samoan negotiations by now existed simply to provide leverage for annexations elsewhere in the Pacific.

Despite the strong US position in eastern Samoa, on 20 February 1889 the *New York Times* reproduced a State Department publication outlining the United States' lack of interest in forming a protectorate there:

> The interest lately manifested in the Samoan Islands renders pertinent a reference to several incidents which disclose the position heretofore maintained by the United States concerning that group. The advocates of the assumption of a virtual protectorate over those islands by the United States appear to have lost sight of the fact that this Government, in pursuance of its traditional and established policy regarding remote foreign possessions, has at least five times refused to assume such a relation.[16]

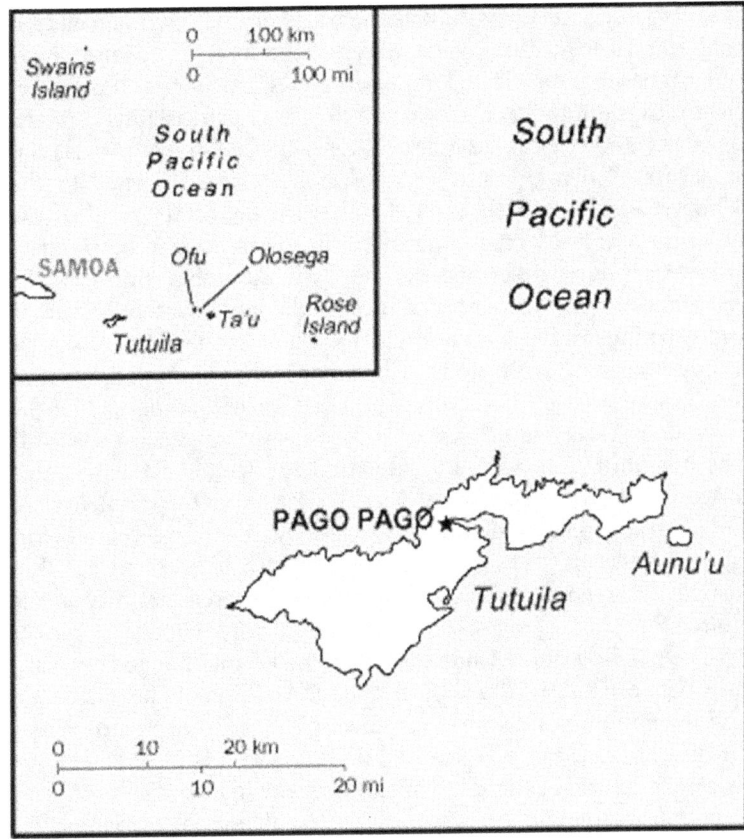

Figure 6.1 American Samoa

Clearly, the Cleveland administration desired a treaty that would maintain Samoan independence; however, Cleveland had lost in his bid for re-election in 1888, and he was now a lame duck with less than a month left in office.[17] When the Republican Benjamin Harrison moved into the White House in March 1889, the Republicans swiftly drew up a new treaty. The *Washington Post* described the draft 'agreement' as guaranteeing 'an autonomous administration of the islands under the joint control of Germany and America, England acting as arbitrator in the event of difference arising'.[18] The

Post also outlined a new-look Samoan government with an elected king and viceroy, along with a senate composed of island chiefs and a chamber of elected representatives. Although this agreement moved more firmly towards a division of the islands between Germany and the United States, it remained relatively provisional in nature. When the anti-imperialist Cleveland returned to the White House in March 1893, he clarified his disapproval of the situation that had arisen during the four years he had been out of office. Cleveland described the Harrison administration's Pacific machinations as: 'in plain defiance of the conservative teachings and warnings of the wise and patriotic men who laid the foundations of our free institutions'. Cleveland's administration believed the US had already gone too far, and that the Samoans, like the Hawaiians, were quite capable of governing themselves.[19] It was not until over a decade later that the United States decided it would depart from what Cleveland's State Department had called 'traditional and established policy regarding remote foreign possessions'. The US did not establish a protectorate, but instead annexed the islands as an unincorporated territory of the United States.

The position of the United States in the Pacific changed dramatically between 1889 and 1899, with the annexation of Hawaii, Guam and the Philippines. Samoa was now no longer to be regarded as a far-distant land, but a logical link in a growing US Pacific empire: by now a sensible sphere in which to engage in a spot of preclusive imperialism. In January 1899, the internal politics of Samoa led once again to a rise in imperial tensions when a rival claimant challenged the new Samoan king, Malietoa Tanumafili I. The US, fearful that a pro-German king would replace him, sent the cruiser *Philadelphia* to Samoa in order to 'represent the United States interests there', as the *Los Angeles Times* put it.[20] The nations actually came to blows in March and April, and American and British ships went so far as to shell the town of Apia. Although fighting ended in May, it was clear that the relatively malleable 1889 agreement between the United States, Germany and Great Britain produced a situation that satisfied no one in the long term.

In December 1899 the three imperial powers in Samoa finally drew up a new agreement, this time with more lasting results, at least for the islands left under US jurisdiction. The main islands of western Samoa were ceded to the German Empire, along with the principal town of Apia. The United States took control of the six eastern islands, with full control of the island that was home to its existing base in Pago Pago. As for Britain, its interest in the islands ended for a time, in return for control of some Tongan islands.[21] In 1900 and 1904 the United States agreed upon Articles of Cession with many of the high-ranking chiefs in eastern Samoa, taking effective control of what became termed 'American' Samoa.[22] The lack of attention thereafter shown to its newest imperial acquisition was underscored by the fact that the US Congress only formally approved these cessions more than two decades later, in 1929.[23]

The US had given Puerto Rico and the Philippines gradual measures of self-government in the first decades of the twentieth century, but it was not until the 1950s that American Samoa ceased being run by US naval governors. In 1931, anthropologist Margaret Mead wrote an article entitled 'Civil Government for Samoa', giving a relatively positive presentation of US naval rule there. However, Mead also supported an unsuccessful bill sponsored by Senator Hiram Bingham that aimed to provide self-government in the islands under a US-appointed governor along with dual citizenship for US-administered Samoans.[24] Bingham's bill was perhaps the closest to US citizenship American Samoans ever got. In 1951, President Harry Truman issued Executive Order 10264, shifting control from the Navy to the Secretary of the Interior, but unlike Guam, which gained an Organic Act in 1950, American Samoa still remains without one to this day.[25] Although since 1967 American Samoa has been governed under its own constitution, without an Organic Act it remains the only *populous* US overseas territory that has a population designated as US 'nationals' rather than 'citizens'.[26] In June 2015 a group of American Samoans unsuccessfully challenged this in a US federal court, where the judges noted in their decision that the government of American Samoa itself opposed such a move, due largely to fears it would affect traditional land-ownership laws.[27] The relatively low levels of US intervention in American Samoa since its acquisition in 1900 indicate that preclusive imperialism was by some distance the most compelling reason for the US's decision to embark upon this particular chapter in its imperial history.

Panama

Even before rising to the presidency following the assassination of William McKinley, Theodore Roosevelt subscribed to a 'large policy' that aimed to bring the United States on to a par with European nations in terms of a military and strategic presence across the globe.[28] Having penned his own work on *The Naval War of 1812* (1882), lauded Alfred Thayer Mahan's influential tome, *The Influence of Sea Power upon History* (1890), and then served as McKinley's Assistant Secretary of the Navy, Roosevelt became convinced that for the United States to project power effectively it required a large navy.[29] In one recent study, historian James Holmes argues that Roosevelt sought to project US power into a region of interest and exclude its great-power rivals.[30] Because the United States was a transcontinental nation with imperial possessions in both the Pacific and the Caribbean, a naval force capable of patrolling two oceans was required to realise this vision. To save having to circumnavigate South America to sail from California to Florida, the US had long envisaged a short cut. On becoming president, Roosevelt seized upon pre-existing plans to build a canal to improve existing rail links across the Central American isthmus, either in Nicaragua or through the Colombian province of Panama. Roosevelt biographer Kathleen Dalton argues that the president's urgency in trying to secure an inter-oceanic canal also 'came from his reading of German intentions' in Latin America.[31] Like US expansion into American Samoa, however, the acquisition of the Panama Canal would involve working with people who lived in the region, whilst also negotiating with the same two imperial powers: Great Britain and Germany.

For Roosevelt and his supporters, simply owning shares in a canal would not suffice. The US required a canal that would always be open for US military and commercial shipping, and this could only be guaranteed with a US flag flying over the entrances to such a waterway. After all, the British had been 'obliged' to occupy Egypt in 1882 as a result of political instability there and then form a quasi-protectorate over the entire country to secure control of the extremely valuable Anglo-French Suez Canal, which provided its main shipping route to India. Roosevelt and his administration believed a Central American canal for the US, just like the Suez

Canal for Britain and France, could prove a vital strategic passage for inter-oceanic naval movements and also a long-term investment in streamlined international trading.

Before the US could realise its own inter-oceanic canal in Central America, it had to gain freedom of action from Great Britain. The existing Clayton-Bulwer Treaty of 1850 mandated that Britain would be party to any potential canal project. In the years following this treaty, US interest in the region continued to grow and it began to feel the existing arrangement needed renegotiation. US investors built a railroad across Panama and, by 1880, President Rutherford B. Hayes stated that it was US policy to obtain 'a canal under American control' for commercial reasons.[32] By the time of McKinley's presidency, Anglo-British relations had advanced substantially and, just as the British had stayed rather quiet over the Spanish-American War, the American government reciprocated by staying out of Britain's torrid conflict in South Africa with the Boer Republics. Nevertheless, despite growing and convenient bonhomie between the two empires, the US Senate was, as Walter LaFeber notes, 'never reluctant to kick the British Lion as long as it was already badly wounded'.[33] Indeed, Secretary of State John Hay saw the Second Boer War (1899–1902) as an ideal opportunity to renegotiate the issue of an isthmian canal in the first Hay-Pauncefote Treaty (1900). This was superseded, after further Senate grumbling about the issue of fortification of said canal, by the November 1901 treaty of the same name. With this second treaty the United States became free to build its own canal, subject to securing an appropriate site.

Though Panama was an obvious location for an inter-oceanic canal, the Republic of Nicaragua also garnered a great deal of attention as an alternative location. However, the mastermind behind the Panama Canal scheme, French businessman Philippe Bunau-Varilla, utilised all of his lobbying skills to help convince a sceptical US Congress that the volcanic state of Nicaragua was less attractive than Panama. Bunau-Varilla even sent a message to the US Senators debating the issue with a Nicaraguan stamp affixed. This stamp pictured an active volcano, leading some to infer that a Nicaraguan canal might be subject to volcanic disruption. Bunau-Varilla's concerns about Nicaragua were, however, largely prompted by his position as a stockholder in the French company that owned the rights to build a canal in Panama. As a result of his efforts Bunau-Varilla managed to convince the US Congress to opt for the Panamanian route at a price of $40 million, compared to the more than $100 million that had been the asking price of the company's previous owners.

The issue of permission from Colombia, on whose territory the canal was to be constructed, proved to be the final hurdle to overcome before Roosevelt's great work could commence. In early 1903 this looked to be all but secure with the signing of the Hay-Herrán Treaty, agreeing to a six-mile-wide zone for the price of $10 million and an annual sum of $250,000.[34] However, the Colombian Senate was not as convinced as its US counterpart and rejected the treaty allegedly because its members were unimpressed with the amount offered. Historian Frederick Marks notes that some suspected Colombia rejected the treaty because of Germany's increased influence over Colombia, as its chief creditor, and this helped to increase Roosevelt's concerns over German designs on the region.[35] With the rejection of the treaty, Roosevelt and Hay were forced to rethink their strategy and the ultimate solution was that if Colombia refused to acquiesce, then maybe an independent Panama would.

On 2 November 1903 a Panamanian revolution occurred, vitally aided by the United States, which blocked sea access to the Colombian reinforcements. On 7 November, Roosevelt took the remarkably rapid step of recognising the new republic, making clear to many that the revolution took place in full expectation, or foreknowledge, of such US reactions. Moreover, President Roosevelt spent a good deal of his Annual Message to Congress that December explaining his support for a Panamanian revolution. Roosevelt harked back to a treaty signed in 1846 with New Granada, the precursor state to Colombia, which he felt gave the US 'a substantial property right carved out of the rights of sovereignty and property which New Granada then had'.[36] The treaty's main purpose, he noted, was to confirm neutrality in the Panamanian isthmus for the purposes of transit. Roosevelt then listed a seemingly unending number of riots and rebellions, many of which led to US incursions into the area between 1850 and 1902 to support the Colombian government. However, when the Colombian government failed to ratify a treaty giving the United States permission to take a strip of their country and build a canal across it, Roosevelt's government deemed the time ripe to change the approach of the previous half-century and support the long-repressed Panamanians. Even when trying to justify his approach, Roosevelt made it hard for neutral outsiders to see his support for the Panamanian revolution of 1903 as anything more than cynical and self-serving.

Given the United States' unequivocal support for the Panamanian revolution in 1903, it is unsurprising that the new Panamanian ambassador to the United States happened to be Philippe Bunau-Varilla, mentioned previously as an employee of the company that owned the rights to the canal in Panama. The Hay-Bunau-Varilla Treaty that followed saw the newly independent Panama give the United States exactly what the Colombian Senate had refused. For the price of $10 million and $250,000 per annum, the United States purchased a ten-mile-wide zone in which to build a canal, along with, crucially, what the *Los Angeles Times* referred to as 'abundant sovereignty over the canal strip. . . . Within this zone the power of the United States is absolute, as if the zone were part and parcel of this country.'[37] The US had finally achieved its best-case scenario, control over a US-owned canal zone that would allow them to protect and possibly build upon their empire from a position of strength.

Reaction to both the purchase of the Panama Canal Zone and the methods by which it was obtained caused mixed reactions in the United States. For a minority, the canal purchase represented a 'nefarious . . . a quite unexampled instance of foul play in American politics'.[38] For most, like Roosevelt himself, the ends justified the means and there were few challenges to the patriotic, Rooseveltian story of the Panama Canal. Few Americans paid much attention to Panamanian claims that America had 'stolen' the canal in 1903 or had infringed upon Panama's sovereignty over its national territory. For many years the United States continued to control the site of its great national triumph, and to exercise its self-appointed role as 'policeman' of the West.[39]

Robert A. Friedlander notes that many early-twentieth-century historians accused Roosevelt of some of the 'most perfidious conduct known to international law and individual morality'.[40] He suggests, however, that Roosevelt was not so duplicitous and cunning as some implied, but was rather clear in his approach to the matter throughout, and this evaluation is supported by the speedy recognition of an independent Panama by a number of other states. Similarly, historian Serge Ricard notes that 'Roosevelt would always claim, not

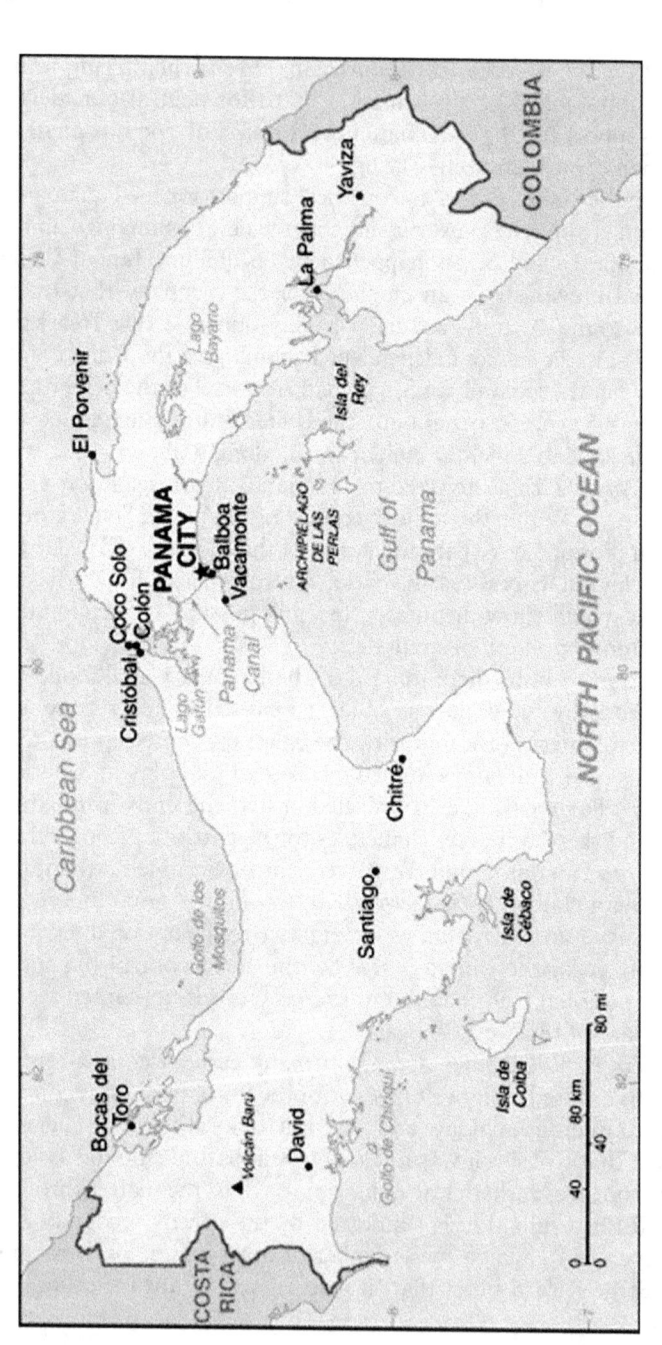

Figure 6.2 Panama

altogether unconvincingly, that given the Panamanians' unanimity in favor of the canal and the generosity of the American offer, the Colombian government, far from being despoiled, had only its mendacity, greed, and stupidity to blame for American intervention on behalf of Panama's independence from Colombia.'[41] Roosevelt might have been clear about what he wanted, but any claims of altruism should not be accepted. Even if his actions aided Panamanian independence, this was simply a by-product of his desire to build a canal, rather than the result of any genuine selflessness. The US had certainly acted in an underhand manner to get what it wanted, and Panama's resentment regarding US control of their territory in the decades that followed amply demonstrates this.

The Hay-Bunau-Varilla Treaty came into effect on 26 February, 1904. A few days later President Roosevelt appointed the first Isthmian Canal Commission under the supervision of the Secretary of War, and appointed the Zone's first governor, George W. Davis. The canal itself was not officially opened until a decade later, when the Republican government that had overseen its acquisition had been removed from office. From the outset, Roosevelt had made it clear that the US had both the right and desire to modify the legal system within the Panama Canal Zone (PCZ) and, despite the Democratic Party controlling the federal government from 1913, there was no sign of a change in direction when President Wilson issued an executive order approving the nature of the 'permanent administration' of the zone in 1914.[42] It cannot go unremarked that the US had spent more money on the canal project by 1914 than any public works programme to that point in its history – an estimated $6.3 billion in 2006 money, according to a recent review by economic historians.[43] In short, the Panama Canal needed to be made to earn back its investment. The United States maintained control of the PCZ until the end of the century, but queries over its rights to the zone began when the ink on the 1903 treaty had barely dried. In a few short months the Panamanian government challenged the right of the United States to establish ports, customs houses and other pieces of infrastructure in the PCZ. For Panama, anything not specifically ceded in the treaty remained within its control. For the US, Panamanian 'titular' sovereignty over the PCZ remained strictly limited by the treaty terms. Similar arguments over sovereignty recurred across the decades, which saw a series of new treaties, executive agreements and readjustments to the relationship.[44]

After the Second World War the situation began to change in relation to the canal, which became increasingly difficult to justify in the face of increasing Panamanian nationalism and global anti-colonial sentiment, as well as in regard to a simultaneous decrease in the canal's military-strategic significance. As Robert Strong explains, after World War Two, transferring military ships across the isthmus became increasingly unnecessary as the US maintained substantial forces in both the Atlantic and Pacific.[45] In 1964, nationalist riots broke out in the PCZ over the raising of the US and Panamanian flags in Balboa High School, an educational facility for US students in the PCZ. This led to four days of fighting, which saw four US and twenty-one Panamanian soldiers killed along with numerous civilians, as well as substantial damage to property. Following this unrest, Lyndon Johnson became the first US president to pledge that the United States would not hold onto the PCZ in perpetuity, a substantial shift in the official position maintained since 1903.[46]

From the time of Johnson's pledge onwards, the trajectory of the debate over the canal turned from one of US adherence to the 1903/4 interpretation of US sovereignty, to the issue of when and how Panama might regain sovereignty over the PCZ. Talks continued during the Republican presidencies of Richard Nixon and Gerald Ford. Yet dissenting voices remained, such as Republican presidential hopeful Ronald Reagan, who, in 1974, raised the PCZ as a campaign issue to try and wrest his party's nomination from Ford with the argument: 'We built it ... we paid for it, it's ours, and we should tell [General] Torrijos and company that we are going to keep it.'[47] However, with Ford's eventual loss to Democrat Jimmy Carter in the 1976 election, the new administration built upon the groundwork of its predecessors, leading to the treaties eventually signed by Carter with the Panamanian dictator General Omar Torrijos in 1977.

In 1978 the US Senate ratified the Carter-Torrijos treaties that set on course what political scientist Steve C. Ropp calls a 'symbolic' handover of sovereignty in the PCZ. Though sovereignty of the zone area returned to Panama, the US maintained rights to operate and defend the canal itself, as well as continuing to exercise control over schools in the zone. The treaties came into effect in 1979 and General Torrijos described the outcome as 'a little pebble which we shall be able to carry in our shoe, and that is better than the stake we have had to carry in our hearts'.⁴⁸ Most importantly, the treaties set a time limit on the continued US presence in Panama: Panama would regain full sovereignty of the canal when the treaty expired on 31 December 1999, much earlier than previous presidents had postulated.⁴⁹ Thus, at the very end of the twentieth century, one of the United States' most significant and controversial territorial possessions finally reverted to the control of the nation that the United States had been instrumental in establishing back in 1903.

The US Virgin Islands

President Woodrow Wilson, who approved the continuation of US sovereignty over the Panama Canal Zone in 1914, came to be known in later years as a champion of self-determination, a concept understood by many to signify his general opposition to imperialism. However, as historian Erez Manela illustrates, Wilson's rhetoric of self-determination after the Great War disappointed many of those living in European imperial possessions that had initially been so hopeful of widespread decolonisation.⁵⁰ Wilson's actions were inconsistent when it came to European empires: he called for self-determination for the colonies of US enemies, but not for those of its allies. A similar inconsistency could be found in Wilson's handling of US colonies. The US promised the Philippines their future independence in 1916, but the following year, the United States annexed a new overseas possession. Following ratification of a treaty with Denmark in January of 1917, the United States agreed, as stated in Article 5 of the convention, to pay the sum of 'twenty-five million dollars of gold coin of the United States' for the Danish West Indies.⁵¹ With this treaty, the supposed champion of self-determination had completed the first fully diplomatic purchase of new US territory since Seward bought Alaska back in 1867.

Today the three larger islands of St Croix, St John and St Thomas, along with various smaller islands, together comprise the 133 square miles of the US Virgin Islands. Originally named the Virgin Islands by Christopher Columbus, they had been settled and resettled by various European colonial powers since their discovery in 1493. Denmark ultimately took control of the archipelago, and ruled the islands for the best part of 200 years. Like many other islands in the Caribbean, the Danish West Indies imported African slaves to work on sugar plantations, and it was only when the price of sugar began to fall and unrest grew (partially due to emancipation in the British West Indies in 1833), that the Danes abolished slavery there in 1848. Over the following decades, the islands generally ceased to be of real economic benefit to Denmark and the country raised the issue of their sale on numerous occasions. Between 1848 and 1917 there were several occasions on which it looked as though the United States would be the buyer. However, it was the last of these occasions that saw perhaps the most unlikely imperialist, Woodrow Wilson, finally seal the deal.[52]

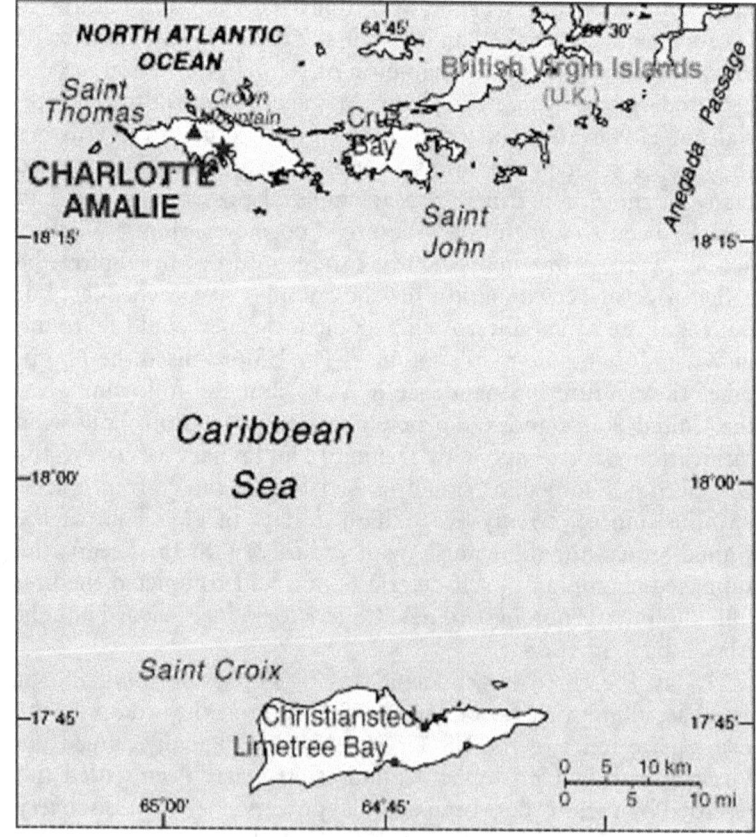

Figure 6.3 US Virgin Islands

The history of US attempts to acquire the small archipelago in the Caribbean dates back as far as the Lincoln administration. Secretary of State William Seward, the mastermind behind the Alaska purchase of 1867, suggested the idea at a dinner party in early 1865. However, the disruption caused by the assassination of the president, and the near-assassination of Seward himself by former confederate soldier Lewis Powell, caused the plan to be sidetracked for several months.[53] Although the Danish government was not particularly interested in letting go of its imperial possessions at the time, it offered the US a deal in 1867 whereby the US could have two of the islands, St John and St Thomas, for $7,500,000. In 1867 King Christian IX of Denmark proclaimed to the citizens of St John and St Thomas Denmark's resolution to 'cede our Islands . . . to the United States of America', but with the crucial caveat that he would first seek the agreement of the people there.[54]

Despite Seward's reservations, the votes went ahead on the two islands in early 1868, and the inhabitants of both voted overwhelmingly in favour of cession. The 1867 treaty, unlike later treaties considered in 1902 and 1917, would have given the Virgin Islanders the chance to become citizens of the United States, something that was edited in future treaties to become more vague.[55] Following the plebiscites in St John and St Thomas, the treaty was submitted to the Danish *Rigsdag* (lower house) and US Senate for ratification. The former ratified it, but the Senate Foreign Relations Committee, under the stewardship of Senator Charles Sumner, reported back on the treaty adversely and the Senate subsequently refused its ratification.[56] This early effort to acquire these territories showed the islands had something to offer that appealed to the United States. In this early period the islands' harbours appeared to be the basis of US interest, and as the century reached its close the strategic importance of Caribbean ports appeared to be ever more central to the concerns of the US government.

In March 1898, the same committee that had condemned the 1867 treaty to frustration thirty years before revived the dormant proposals for acquisition of the strategic Caribbean outposts. With the committee now under the command of Theodore Roosevelt's close friend Senator Henry Cabot Lodge, the islands were now heralded as a valuable strategic possession for use as a naval and coaling station. In 1900, in a letter to the *New York Times*, one Francis Wayland Glen discussed the rumours that Denmark was willing to part with its possessions for $3,000,000. Glen suggested that the purchase would be 'another step in the direction of complete emancipation of this hemisphere'. He then went onto conclude that, with positive potential for trade, such a purchase would be 'a wise and beneficent investment'.[57] By January 1902 a new convention had been agreed with Demark, this time ceding all three islands to the United States for the comparatively cheap price of $5,000,000. On this second occasion the US Senate promptly ratified the new treaty, leading the *Washington Post* to laud what appeared to be the US acquisition of 'one of the most important naval strategic points in the Western Hemisphere'.[58] However, once again the legislative process struck down the deal, this time on the other side of the Atlantic in the Danish *Landsting* (upper house), where the vote was tied at 32:32. A combination of factors led to this, including memories of 1867, the king's personal reluctance to sell and the lobbying of various business interests.[59] With this disappointing result, ratification of the islands' purchase was once again defeated and the issue was placed on the back burner for another decade.

The near-miss of the 1902 purchase led to some debate within the United States as to why exactly it might want this tiny archipelago. Peter J. Nevins wrote to the *New York Times* to enquire as to the point of obtaining the Danish islands when the country had only recently acquired a better possession in the form of nearby Puerto Rico. Nevins felt acquiring a population of 'very ignorant negroes' who, according to merchants from Britain and Germany, were 'truculent and undesirable people' would be a burden that was unlikely to be offset by the boon of 'one good harbor' on the island of St Thomas. Nevins also raised the issue of suspected US designs upon Haiti and its 'barbaric horde' of inhabitants, concluding that it was better to leave the Danish islands and Haiti 'to work out their own salvation. There is such a thing as knowing when we have enough.'[60] Similar objections to the supposedly 'inferior' populations of new possessions had also been raised regularly in debates about Philippine annexation, debates that in 1902 were still very fresh in American minds.

When the Virgin Islands debate first resurfaced in the news during 1916, following the reopening of negotiations with Denmark the previous year, newspapers reported that the 'disposition of the Wilson Administration toward the question of acquiring [them] ... never has been disclosed'. The *New York Times* speculated that there was some evidence that the administration had been moving in this direction, such as the 'supervisory' treaty with Nicaragua, and pending legislation for similar powers over the affairs of Haiti (see Chapter 7). In fact, Haiti offers a particularly useful parallel as there was concern within the US over the role of the German population in that nation that had contributed to the invasion of US marines in 1915. If Wilson's administration was set on a course to intervene in other Caribbean island nations, why not the Virgin Islands that the Danes appeared to be keen to offload by 1916? In the eyes of many Americans, intrigue from the direction of Germany to purchase the islands would be tantamount to conquest, and therefore a violation of the Monroe Doctrine.[61]

Edgar Robinson and Victor West, writing in 1917, suggested that neither the Monroe Doctrine nor existing trade interests compelled the US to purchase the islands. Instead they argued that the purchase was first and foremost part of the Wilson administration's preparedness program: protecting the Panama Canal and taking useful harbours from potential European combatants.[62] Almost a century later, historian Cathal Nolan characterised Wilson's policy towards the Caribbean and Latin America somewhat differently, as: '[intervening] repeatedly, violently, and excessively without ever facing a comparable threat of European military intervention'. Nolan even suggests that such actions took place in spite of the fact that the Virgin Islands were 'a relatively minor backwater where no major power other than the United States saw its vital interests at stake or was any longer prepared to use force'.[63] In reality, neither interpretation is wholly satisfactory in explaining the acquisition of the US Virgin Islands.

Following the ratification of a third and final treaty with Denmark in 1917, Secretary Lansing justified the annexation of the US Virgin Islands by outlining his two key explanations of their importance: firstly, as a naval base for military and merchant vessels and, secondly, to stop other interested powers jumping in instead: preclusive imperialism.[64] The first element had formed the mainstay of arguments for annexation in the Civil War era and during Theodore Roosevelt's administration. However, the second element is more specific to this period in time. After all, the successful purchase was completed only three months before the United States entered the First World War against Germany. Nevertheless, both of the explanations for US acquisition are interlinked. If the islands had not boasted important harbours, Germany would have had little interest in them and, although the extent of the German interest in the Virgin Islands was dubious, the US believed such an interest existed. Thus, the annexation was a result of a mistaken – yet genuine – fear of German ambitions in the Caribbean. Tellingly, on 3 February 1917 (not long after the confirmation of the treaty in January), Wilson broke off diplomatic relations with imperial Germany; and in March, the famous Zimmermann Telegram implicated Germany in a plot to form an alliance with Mexico in a potential future conflict with the United States. On 6 April the US Congress declared war on Germany, perhaps safer in the knowledge that the Germans had no foothold in the Americas.

In buying the territory, rather than allowing the islanders their independence under US supervision, the US stepped beyond its more tentative imperialism in Haiti and Nicaragua. For the people of the Virgin Islands at the time, the United States' purchase of their territory was looked upon hopefully, especially given that for the last few decades their economy had been in steady decline. In contrast, from the US perspective, this new territory became defined by the idea that it would serve as a military base, rather than any particular interest in its economic resources.[65] The Virgin Islands were annexed as an 'unincorporated' territory in line with the other post-Hawaiian annexations: ruled by the United States, but not placed on the same road to statehood as territories admitted prior to the Spanish-American War. Similar to other unincorporated territories, the privileges of those who resided in the US Virgin Islands rested with the US Congress, which did not grant US citizenship rights to most Virgin Islanders until 1927.[66] The US Department of the Navy controlled the islands until 1931, when they were finally transferred to the Interior Department. However, unlike American Samoa, the US granted the Virgin Islands an Organic Act in 1936, which gave the islands a largely autonomous government.[67] In 1970, after more than half a century under US rule, the US Congress granted the islands their own governor, and in 1976 it passed legislation allowing the Virgin Islands' legislature to draft their own constitution. The Virgin Islands remain, to date, the most recent formal US territorial acquisition in the Caribbean. However, as Chapter 7 shows, the US Virgin Islands proved the exception rather than the rule for twentieth-century US imperialism in the Caribbean, which continued in a different form well beyond 1917.

Notes

1. Lodge, 1895, cited in Schlesinger, *Cycles of American History*, pp. 143–4.
2. The German overseas empire at its height, prior to World War One, comprised substantial sections of a number of modern-day states including: (in Africa) Cameroon, Togo, Namibia, Rwanda, Burundi, Tanzania; (in the Pacific) Papua New Guinea, Samoa, the Marshall Islands, Micronesia, Palau and Nauru.
3. Kennedy, *American Consul*, pp. 186–7.
4. Steinmetz, *The Devil's Handwriting*, p. 297.
5. Schellinger and Salkin, *International Dictionary of Historic Places*, p. 725. The islands had fallen into a deep-rooted factional struggle following the death of King Malietoa Vainuupo in 1841.
6. Stuart, *Planting the American Flag*, p. 42.
7. Meleisea and Meleisea, *Lagaga*, pp. 82–3.
8. Stuart, *Planting the American Flag*, p. 40.
9. Meleisea and Meleisea, *Lagaga*, p. 83.
10. Stuart, *Planting the American Flag*, p. 43 and Chapter 3 generally. Among the other figures Stuart discusses are Richard Meade (also involved in Samoa), William A. Jones, the architect of the Jones-Shafroth Act which gave Puerto Ricans citizenship (as well as the Philippine Organic Act, which did not do the same for Filipinos) and Theodore Roosevelt Jr., the first governor of Puerto Rico and later governor of the Philippines.
11. Meleisea and Meleisea, *Lagaga*, pp. 83–4; Stuart, *Planting the American Flag*, p. 44.
12. Stuart, *Planting the American Flag*, pp. 45–7.
13. Pletcher, *The Diplomacy of Involvement*, p. 86.
14. Kennedy, *American Consul*, p. 139.
15. Laughlin, 'US Government Policy', p. 30.
16. 'Our Samoan Relations', *New York Times*, p. 3.
17. Cleaver, *Cleveland's New Foreign Policy*, p. 37.
18. 'The Control of Samoa', *Washington Post*, p. 1, makes the case that the 1889 tripartite agreement was more correctly an 'agreement' than a treaty, as rather than regulating the relations between two nations, it regulated the behaviour of three towards a fourth.
19. Cleaver, *Cleveland's New Foreign Policy*, pp. 37–8.
20. 'Great Danger', *Los Angeles Times*, p. 1.
21. In 1920 the islands became a League of Nations mandate under the control of New Zealand. Since 1907 New Zealand had been a self-governing 'dominion' within the British Empire and, at the time, left foreign policy largely in the hands of the British.

22. Laughlin, 'US Government Policy', p. 30. Laughlin's article discusses the formation of social structures and government systems in the islands during this early period in depth. However, official control of American Samoa would take until 1928 to establish.
23. Kiste, 'United States', p. 245.
24. Gilliam and Foerstel, 'Margaret Mead's Contradictory Legacy', pp. 118–19.
25. This makes American Samoa not only 'unincorporated', like Puerto Rico, but 'unorganised' as well.
26. Those born in the Northern Mariana Islands have the right to opt to be 'nationals' rather than 'citizens' if they wish (under certain conditions).
27. Associated Press, 'People from American Samoa'.
28. Pratt, 'The "Large Policy" of 1898', pp. 219–42.
29. Roosevelt, *Naval War of 1812*; Mahan, *Influence of Sea Power*. Both books have been reproduced many times since their original publication.
30. Holmes, *Theodore Roosevelt and World Order*, p. 143.
31. Dalton, *Theodore Roosevelt*, p. 255.
32. Maurer and Yu, *The Big Ditch*, p. 687.
33. LaFeber, *The American Age*, p. 241.
34. Herrán was a Colombian diplomat in Washington.
35. Marks, *Velvet on Iron*, p. 7.
36. Roosevelt, 'Third Annual Message'.
37. 'Hay and Varilla Sign Canal Treaty', *Los Angeles Times*, p. 1.
38. Davis, *The Circus Age*, p. 210.
39. Hogan, *Panama Canal in American Politics*, p. 57.
40. Friedlander, 'Reassessment of Roosevelt's Role', p. 535.
41. Ricard, 'The Roosevelt Corollary', p. 20.
42. Ealy, 'Law in the Panama Canal Zone', p. 284, p. 292.
43. Maurer and Yu, *The Big Ditch*, p. 688.
44. Shay, 'The Panama Canal Zone', pp. 17–20. Shay outlines this in an article written in the 1970s, when the debate reached its zenith.
45. Strong, 'Jimmy Carter', p. 270.
46. McPherson, 'Courts of World Opinion', pp. 83–4.
47. Strong, 'Jimmy Carter', p. 271.
48. Ropp, 'Ratification of the Panama Canal Treaties', pp. 283–4.
49. Strong, 'Jimmy Carter', p. 274.
50. Manela, *The Wilsonian Moment*.
51. 'Convention between the US and Denmark', *US Department of the Interior*.
52. 'A Brief History', *Danish National Archives*.
53. Dookhan, *History of the Virgin Islands*, p. 251.
54. 'Danish West Indies', *New York Times*, p. 1.

55. Statham, *Colonial Constitutionalism*, p. 52. US citizenship was ultimately obtained in 1927.
56. Dookhan, *History of the Virgin Islands*, p. 254.
57. Goldwin Smith cited in: Glen, 'The Danish West Indies', p. 8.
58. 'Treaty Signed for Danish West Indies', *Washington Post*, p. 2.
59. Dookhan, *History of the Virgin Islands*, pp. 257–8.
60. Nevins, 'Danish West Indies Question', p. 38. For more on Haiti, see Chapter 7.
61. 'Sale Planned Twice Before', *New York Times*, p. [0]1.
62. Robinson and West, *Foreign Policy of Woodrow Wilson*, pp. 117–18.
63. Nolan, 'Learning to Lead', pp. 149–50.
64. Bank of Commerce, *The Virgin Islands*.
65. Dookhan, *History of the Virgin Islands*, pp. 265–6.
66. Miller, 'Virgin Islands', p. 297.
67. Dookhan, *History of the Virgin Islands*, pp. 275–98.

CHAPTER 7

Occupation over Annexation (1912–73)

This chapter explores the nature of US imperial intervention in the Caribbean and how it developed in the early twentieth century. Although in 1917 Woodrow Wilson took the step of formally annexing the US Virgin Islands, his administration also oversaw the apogee of US long-term occupation of other islands in the Caribbean. This form of imperialism came to characterise US interventionism overseas in the later twentieth century. To illustrate this, the latter half of the chapter looks at the second phase of medium-to-long-term occupations that occurred in the wake of the Second World War, particularly those of the US sector of West Germany and the nation of Japan.

Caribbean Occupations

The impact of Germany's aggressive expansionism was not limited to the preclusive imperialist annexations by the United States detailed previously. During the early twentieth century, the United States began a series of long-term Caribbean occupations that were also, at least in part, motivated by a preclusive attitude towards European intervention, particularly that of Germany. However, such *occupations* were easier to justify than *annexations*, due largely to the Roosevelt Corollary to the Monroe Doctrine. The corollary added an underlying threat of armed intervention to the traditional idea that the US had the right and duty to safeguard the 'independence' of the central and southern American republics from European intervention. It also clearly expanded the remit of the US to maintaining the stability of these smaller nations. As Theodore Roosevelt put it to Congress in 1904:

Chronic wrongdoing, or an impotence which results in a general loosening of the ties of civilized society, may in America, as elsewhere, ultimately require intervention by some civilized nation, and in the Western Hemisphere the adherence of the United States to the Monroe Doctrine may force the United States, however reluctantly, in flagrant cases of such wrongdoing or impotence, to the exercise of an international police power.[1]

Roosevelt's words stirred up suspicion in Central America, with some seeing his corollary as a blanket permit for US intervention. Indeed, so unsettling was Roosevelt's proclamation that he eventually played down the 'police power' role outlined in his speech during his second term as president. However, despite Roosevelt's rhetorical backtracking, the period after his speech saw his eponymous corollary put into effect on numerous occasions.[2]

The US often referred pejoratively to the small Central American and Caribbean states where they intervened as 'Banana Republics', due to the huge sway over their affairs held by colossal US businesses such as the United Fruit Company. Some historians hence refer to this period of US interventions and occupations as the 'Banana Wars'.[3] There were certainly very marked economic motivations for US intervention, either to stabilise these countries and protect US investments, or to stave off European debt collectors with their own gunships. Moreover, the increased level of competition between Mexico and the United States in the region at this time increased fears during the First World War that the Mexicans might reach some form of agreement with the Germans. Although the US often cited moral and humanitarian concerns as a factor in the interventions, both economic and strategic interests stood at the forefront when it came to sending US troops in to occupy and prop up puppet dictators in the region. Only after the First World War, in the 1920s, was there a general move within the US government to reduce the level of US interference in the Caribbean, and this can be attributed to the high levels of internal criticism within the United States as well as frustration from many Latin American nations.[4] Nevertheless, the US was not willing to leave a country until a regime was in place that would provide the stability and amenability the US desired, and in many cases the road to withdrawal was anything but smooth.

Cuba had been granted a conditional form of independence in 1902 with the Platt Amendment, the terms of which were incorporated into a 1903 treaty between the two nations. The Platt Amendment effectively granted the United States the right to intervene in Cuban affairs when it saw fit, providing a more legally binding justification than the Roosevelt Corollary to the Monroe Doctrine, and the amendment proved to be a clause that the United States was more than willing to put into effect. The first incursion came in 1906 while Theodore Roosevelt was still in the White House. Secretary of War William Howard Taft led this second occupation, becoming the provisional governor of Cuba, and his leadership, as Louis Perez notes, 'resulted in the wholesale displacement of Cubans from the upper reaches of political office'.[5] The US anticipated a short-term intervention in order, as the Platt Amendment intended, to secure peace and stability in Cuba following a revolt against the fraudulent re-election of President Tomás Estrada Palma.[6] Following Taft's return to Washington, Charles E. Magoon, a Nebraska lawyer, maintained what Roosevelt wanted to be seen as a temporary civil, not military, US administration on the island until the end of the occupation in 1909.[7]

Following a short military intervention in 1912 to quell a rebellion led primarily by black Cubans who felt the Cuban government discriminated against them, the second major post-Platt intervention in Cuba came between 1917 and 1922 and is known as the 'Sugar Intervention'.[8] As in 1906, widespread discontent following a corrupt election sparked events, on this occasion causing the Cuban Liberal Party to rebel. Although exercising more restraint than during the 1906 intervention, President Woodrow Wilson still felt the need to intervene in 1917 to guard the US sugar plantations on the islands.[9] This desire to protect the plantations was both economic and strategic, as the First World War reached ever closer to the North American continent following the German announcement of unrestricted submarine warfare in February 1917. This final US occupation of Cuba lasted through until 1922, but the intervention was just the first of many US occupations following Theodore Roosevelt's announcement of his corollary to the Monroe Doctrine. Similar US incursions followed in Nicaragua, Haiti and the Dominican Republic. Like Cuba, all three of these republics had a history of US interest, but it was only in the early twentieth century that the

United States actually occupied them.¹⁰ These lengthy occupations augured a new form of US imperialism that came to dominate the twentieth century and beyond.

Nicaragua

US interests in Nicaragua can be traced back as far as Thomas Jefferson, who earmarked the territory in 1788 as the ideal place for a trans-isthmian canal. However, it was the nation's instability following its independence from Spain in 1821 that led to the first 'real' US occupation in the 1850s. This incursion was the result of a filibustering mission headed by an expansionist former newspaper editor from the United States, William Walker. Walker intervened in an internal Nicaraguan political dispute, and then usurped control of the nation for several months. Ultimately, US businessman Cornelius Vanderbilt undermined Walker's grip on power in order to frustrate leading business rivals who had supported the filibusterer. This episode constituted Nicaragua's first 'dramatic encounter' with US imperialism.¹¹ However, 1912 proved to be the truly pivotal year for US-Nicaraguan relations when a short civil war in the Central American state led to the first full-scale US invasion, one that lasted longer than any other US intervention in Central America during the twentieth century.

Prior to the renewal of US interventions from 1910 onwards, Mexico had acted as the main external power broker in Nicaragua. The Mexican dictator of the era, Porfirio Díaz, provided both political and diplomatic support to Nicaraguan leaders who preferred stronger ties with Mexico to interference from the United States.¹² Anti-US sentiment was also evident in the efforts of the Nicaraguan Liberal leader, José Zelaya, to attract European investors into building a new canal to rival the US efforts in Panama.¹³ By 1906, Zelaya had further frustrated the United States by cancelling a US lumber business contract in the region, but the real problems arose with a change at the US State Department, when the less interventionist Elihu Root was replaced with the more hawkish Philander C. Knox following the election of President William Howard Taft.¹⁴

In 1909, in response to death sentences being served on two US citizens who had led filibusters to the region, the US severed diplomatic relations with Nicaragua and threatened intervention, leading to Zelaya's resignation. Months of high tension in the country followed. The United States ultimately intervened by sending troops to help revolutionaries seeking to overthrow Zelaya's elected successor, José Madriz, under the premise of protecting American lives. By 1910, the US intervention had placed Juan Estrada in control as a seemingly more amenable puppet leader. However, the unpopular Estrada soon stepped down from the presidency after proving unable to provide his internally divided country with adequate leadership.[15] This continued civil disruption led President Taft to give the go-ahead for marines to head in and support the pro-US regime of yet another leader, Adolfo Díaz, in 1912.[16] Taft likened the situation to the Boxer Rebellion in China a decade or so earlier, and would have sent in infantry units if the marines had not secured key assets so quickly.[17] This occupation, unlike the short-term 1909–10 intervention, lasted effectively until the early 1930s.

In 1911 Secretary of State Knox negotiated the Knox-Castillo Treaty, which would have linked secured loans from US banks with a customs receivership agreement; but the US Senate refused to ratify the treaty, as senators believed this would create a quasi-financial protectorate over Nicaragua.[18] However, banks implemented the loan regardless, and by 1912 the US banking houses were in near-control of Nicaraguan finances. In February 1913 the Taft administration made its final attempt to increase control over Nicaragua with the Chamorro-Wietzel Treaty, through which the US would buy the option to construct an inter-oceanic canal and naval bases in Nicaragua. For similar reasons to the defeat of the earlier Knox-Castillo agreement, however, this treaty failed in the US Senate. When Woodrow Wilson arrived in the White House in March 1913, he signalled to many that Roosevelt and Taft's interference in the region would come to an abrupt end. Wilson appeared to offer clear opposition to both Roosevelt's 'Big Stick' diplomacy and Taft's 'Dollar Diplomacy' in Latin America.[19] Instead Wilson proposed a Pan-Americanist 'good neighbour' policy that suggested a new sort of relationship with Latin America with a decidedly less imperialist tone.[20]

Both Wilson and his secretary of state, William Jennings Bryan, disliked the economic hold the US had on Latin America, but they ultimately struggled to find an alternative way forward in Nicaragua. When the failed Chamorro-Wietzel Treaty was resuscitated as the

Bryan-Chamorro Treaty, anti-imperialist Republican senator William Borah described the situation thus: 'We took some battleships and went down to Nicaragua and put a certain faction in power and now we are making a treaty with that faction, in other words we are making a treaty with ourselves.'[21] Bryan similarly saw the banking houses that dominated Nicaraguan finances as 'thieves', but Wilson rejected his suggestion that the US government provide loans directly to Nicaragua, and Bryan's other idea of a Platt Amendment for Nicaragua faced unyielding opposition in the Senate Foreign Relations Committee.[22] Nevertheless, with increasing fears over the Great War in Europe and German interests in a trans-isthmian canal, the US finally signed the Bryan-Chamorro Treaty, without a Platt-style amendment, in 1914 and ratified it in 1916.[23] The final version of the treaty set out the right of the US to build a canal, to construct a naval base on the Gulf of Fonseca and to take out a long-term lease over the Nicaraguan Corn Islands.[24] The passage of the treaty was greeted with disgust by many Latin American nations and led to the dissolution of the Central American Court of Justice, as the US had simply ignored its decisions over Nicaragua. The ratification of Bryan's treaty 'cemented U.S. control over Nicaragua' and Wilson's policy, far from renouncing that of Roosevelt and Taft, actually entrenched it, with US Marines remaining in Nicaragua throughout the 1920s.[25]

In 1927, President Calvin Coolidge, under attack from members of his own party in the US Senate, sent former secretary of war Henry Stimson to Nicaragua to seek an agreeable withdrawal strategy. However, one dissatisfied military lieutenant, Augusto Sandino, would not compromise with US demands to retain President Díaz, and his attack on remaining US marines undid Stimson's good work.[26] Over half a decade later, a new Stimson-designed policy did eventually lead to the final removal of the marines in 1933, under the presidency of Franklin Roosevelt. Indeed, such moves in the 1930s characterised Franklin Roosevelt's actions in aid of a Good Neighbor Policy echoing that which Wilson had failed to follow two decades before. However, despite relatively fair elections that brought a democratic leader, Juan Sacasa, to the presidency following the removal of the US marines, real power actually lay with the head of the Guardia Nacional, Anastasio Samoza. By 1937 Samoza had seized dictatorial power for himself, and his dynasty would dominate Nicaraguan politics until the Sandinistas toppled it in 1979.[27]

Haiti

The history of US-Haitian relations has been troubled since the earliest days of both nation states. Following the successful revolt of enslaved people that led to independence from French rule in 1804, the influential slave-owners of the southern United States found it difficult to deal with a free black-run nation on its doorstep, and the US ended up enforcing a 65-year embargo on Haiti in 1806.[28] Not until 1862 were diplomatic relations established between the US and Haiti by President Abraham Lincoln, during the US Civil War.[29] Shortly after the war, Haiti offered up the enticing naval base of Môle-Saint-Nicolas in return for an effective protectorate. The usually expansionist secretary of state, William Seward, unusually turned down this proposal in 1868 on the grounds that it would prove unconstitutional.[30] Later that year, President Andrew Johnson suggested in his annual message to Congress that the US might annex both Haiti and its neighbour the Dominican Republic. However, for the rest of the nineteenth century talk of annexation never went much further than the naval base at Môle, with Secretary of State James Blaine scheming unsuccessfully for a lease of the base between 1889 and 1891. For most in the US, annexation of the republic of Haiti appeared to be more trouble than it was worth, due largely to the island nation's chaotic internal politics.[31]

After more than a dozen naval 'visits' to 'protect American lives and property' in the years after the Civil War, in July 1915 the United States sent marines to the republic, just as it had with Nicaragua a few years earlier.[32] Woodrow Wilson, the supposed champion of self-determination, initiated this particular intervention rather than the more likely candidates of Theodore Roosevelt or the father of 'Dollar Diplomacy', William H. Taft. Historian Brenda Gayle Plummer convincingly traces the Wilson administration's road to invasion back to 1913, when Secretary of State Bryan replaced the long-term black US representative in Haiti with a white man 'until affairs there could be straightened out'.[33] The US cited similar reasons for intervening in Haiti as it had in Nicaragua: widespread violence, and the consequent danger to US residents and business interests in the country.[34] However, US fears of Haiti falling into enemy hands were also significant, and preclusive imperialism provided part of the rationale for every Central American intervention following the Roosevelt Corollary to the Monroe Doctrine. From the start, Haitian nationalists remained hostile to the US takeover, and intermittent guerrilla warfare punctuated the early occupation, leading to the razing of settlements and shooting of rebels.[35]

Between 1915 and 1916, the US formulated a Haitian treaty that effectively committed them, morally and legally, to continued military occupation of the island until 1936.[36] However, the treaty 'negotiations' made Wilson's second secretary of state, Robert Lansing, remark that it was 'more or less an exercise of force and an invasion of Haitian independence'.[37] The US took control of Haitian finances, created a *Gendarmerie* (constabulary) that was controlled by the US marines, and installed a US-friendly president who, in short order, dissolved the elected Haitian legislature. Historian Mary Renda contends that the occupation of Haiti was 'one of several important arenas in which the United States was remade through overseas imperial ventures in the first third of the twentieth century', and this was certainly the case across the Caribbean.[38] During the occupation, US marines put down various insurgent guerrilla groups, introduced Jim Crow-style segregation laws, and even instituted forced labour. African Americans in the United States became some of the foremost critics of the Wilsonian occupation, including members of the National Association for the Advancement of Colored People (NAACP). African American intellectual W. E. B. Du Bois even wrote directly to the president urging him not to act without the 'cordial support of the Haytian [sic] people'.[39] On a political level, the US propped up an unpopular regime that suspended the constitution and free speech, introduced curfews, and censored the press.[40] The US also used its control over Haitian finances to intervene in areas that were far outside of its remit, such as education and schooling.[41] The American occupation of Haiti came in the period after a number of hostile US encounters overseas and therefore, by 1915, it certainly had a good deal of experience to call upon regarding imperial interventionism.[42]

In January 1918 President Wilson released his Fourteen Points for the post-Great War world, peddling the idea of self-determination for the oppressed. In the same year, the United States also oversaw the enforcement of a new Haitian constitution, which bore little resemblance to Wilson's more enlightened proclamations in January. The most important provisions of the constitution were the legalisation of foreign land ownership, indefinite suspension of the elected Haitian legislature, temporary suspension of the irremovability of judges, and the legalisation of all acts of the US military occupation.[43] The success of this regime was largely because of the efficacy of the US-led Haitian *Gendarmerie*, which was more effective than its counterparts in Nicaragua and the Dominican Republic in consolidating power and crushing rebels. Ultimately the US attempted to 'Haitianise' the *Gendarmerie* in the occupied nation in order to facilitate a more rapid handover of military power and to expedite the removal of the US marines.[44] In 1930 President Hoover sent a commission to ascertain when best to withdraw from Haiti, and by 1931 the two states were able to agree to a fairly rapid 'Haitianisation' of the nation that saw the US officially withdraw the marines in 1934, whilst retaining strong economic ties and influence over Haiti for years to come.[45]

The Dominican Republic

The final major occupation of this period was that of Haiti's island neighbour, the Dominican Republic (Santo Domingo).[46] Unlike the long occupation of Haiti, US marines occupied the Dominican Republic for a relatively short period, and they exited in the 1920s prior to the initiation of Franklin Roosevelt's version of a 'Good Neighbor Policy' towards Latin America. Unlike the United States' fractious history with Haiti following their slave-led revolution, the Dominican Republic had often been the object of US desire rather than disdain.

In the antebellum period, the United States involved itself in a number of tentative steps to secure rights over Samana Bay in the Dominican Republic, but anti-imperialists in the US Senate and media rejected an approach made by President Franklin Pierce's administration in 1854. Following a brief period between 1861 and 1865, when the republic was re-annexed by Spain, Dominican presidents routinely attempted to convince the United States to annex their nation in a form of proactive preclusive imperialism of their own. After the Civil War the expansionist secretary of state William Seward touted the idea of leasing a naval base in the Dominican Republic or establishing a formal protectorate and, as noted above, in 1868 President Johnson proposed the annexation of both Haiti and the Dominican Republic. However, the decisive move came in 1869 when President Ulysses S. Grant attempted to purchase the Dominican Republic and incorporate it into the United States. On this occasion the US Senate rejected Grant's plan, with opposition to it being led by Senate Foreign Relations Committee Chair Charles Sumner, who believed that annexation would lead to a domino effect in the Caribbean and future entanglements with European powers.[47] Despite this setback, Grant supported the efforts of the Samana Bay Company to establish a harbour in the republic in order to bolster the case for annexation under the pro-US regime of President Buenaventure Báez, although these efforts also came to nought when Báez was overthrown in 1874.[48]

The decision to dispatch US marines to affect 'political stability' in the Dominican Republic arose in much the same way as in Cuba, Nicaragua and Haiti. Both Taft and Wilson had sent commissions to the republic to bring about political change and establish financial supervision, but ultimately the US intervened with a marine-led occupation in 1916 when General Desiderio Arias threatened to topple the US-backed President Juan Jiménez. When the Dominican leadership would not accept Wilson's assumption of control over key government functions, the US formed a military government under Captain Harry Knapp, who proceeded to suspend democratic institutions and free speech.[49] But once in control, the United States lacked clear goals.[50] For the first couple of years following the initial intervention, the marines' counterinsurgency operations mirrored those in Haiti with the idea that eventually a US-trained *Gendarmerie* would take their place, but the Dominican rebels continued to occupy the marines well into the 1920s.[51]

By the end of World War One the fear of Europeans interfering in the Caribbean had all but evaporated, and the strategic benefits of the occupation had disappeared. Additionally, the political mood in the United States moved against Wilson's Democrats. In the 1920 election campaign, following a speech in which Democratic vice-presidential candidate Franklin Roosevelt seemed to suggest the US could control the votes of twelve Latin American nations in the proposed League of Nations, the Republican presidential nominee Warren G. Harding vowed to end the mistreatment of the Latin American republics.[52] By the time Harding took office, public opinion had also turned decisively against the occupation following press reports of US atrocities and the launch of a Senate investigation into conditions on the island. Harding hereafter grew committed to improving relations in the region and negotiated the US exit from the Dominican Republic with the support of Sumner Welles, who successfully oversaw the eventual transition to self-government by 1924.[53]

These cases of Caribbean intervention offer the most telling examples of a new strain of US imperialism that arose in the early decades of the twentieth century: medium- to long-term military occupation and temporary US governance, with the ultimate goal of independence under a pro-US government. In Haiti, though, the military government stage was forgone to move straight to a puppet dictatorship propped up by a US marine-led constabulary force. The end of the Second World War, and the bipolar world order that followed, saw the US take the precedents of this non-annexationist military government policy to far larger and more remote nations than the 'Banana Republics' where it had begun such experimentations.

Germany

Like the 'Banana Republic' occupations, the post-World War Two occupations were both preclusive and self-serving. As the Cold War began, the United States increasingly sought the 'containment' of communism and granted support for pro-US regimes around the globe. The US occupations of the post-war era were initiated with a clear sense that if the Americans did not intervene, the Soviets would almost certainly do so instead. With the defeat of the Axis powers in 1945, the United States undertook occupations of key Axis territories, including parts of Germany and the whole of Japan. Moreover, the allies also occupied parts of the former German, Japanese and Italian empires: Austria, Korea, Taiwan and the city-state of Trieste. The focus here is on Germany and Japan, as they amounted to the longest and most high-profile occupations of the period.

The United States had already had a little practice in occupying Germany in the aftermath of the First World War, when US soldiers formed part of the joint occupation force in the Rhineland, with a special American zone around the city of Coblenz.[54] However, plans for the post-World War Two era were envisaged on a far larger scale. In October 1943, at a meeting of Allied foreign ministers in Moscow, the British, Americans and Soviets agreed to the principle of a joint occupation of the whole of Germany, an idea that made steady progress at the Teheran Conference some weeks later.[55] Following Teheran, the European Advisory Committee met in London, where US Ambassador John G. Winant and others considered how joint occupation would actually work. Roosevelt showed a preference for occupying the north-western region of Germany, but eventually the US conceded this sector to the British. The United States provisionally took control of the south-west and the USSR the east. During these meetings, Roosevelt and Churchill also mooted other ideas, including the formal division of Germany into two, or as many as five, different states.[56] However, the most radical and punitive alternative vision for post-war Germany came from US Treasury Secretary Henry Morgenthau. Introduced at the Second Quebec Conference in September 1944 without the Soviets present, the Morgenthau Plan called for the partitioning of Germany into two states (northern and southern), the cession of core industrial areas to bordering nations, the internationalisation of the Ruhr, and the complete deindustrialisation of the nation.[57] This plan would certainly stop Germany rising to dominate and devastate Europe for a third time in the twentieth century, but destroying German industry so comprehensively also raised the spectre of a prolonged Europe-wide economic crisis. The US and Britain feared this might, in turn, ignite the flame of communism in western Europe.

The eventual plan for Germany that was unveiled by the Allies at the Yalta Conference in February 1945 was quite different from Morgenthau's, and was instead more reminiscent of the ideas set out at Moscow in 1943. The new aspects of the Yalta agreement saw a French zone added to the western part of Germany, leaving the Soviet Zone largely intact, and an understanding that all four powers would form an Allied Control Council (ACC) to coordinate Allied policy in Germany. Berlin, the German capital, was also to be divided between the four powers, though geographically the city lay entirely within the eastern Soviet Zone of Germany. However, despite Yalta's seeming show of unity between the powers regarding an Allied policy towards Germany, the United States actually drafted its own directive on US policy for occupied Germany (JCS 1067) several months earlier. This directive, issued in September

1944, outlined the occupation and partial deindustrialisation of Germany as a 'defeated' rather than a 'liberated' nation and, for historian Michael Beschloss, 'had much the sound of the Morgenthau Plan'.[58] JCS 1067 also gave the proposed US military government in post-war Germany 'supreme legislative, executive, and judicial authority' in order to achieve its aims.[59] As a result of the existence of JCS 1067, the essence of the Morgenthau Plan, if not its totality, was not truly rejected until July 1947, when the directive ceased to be in effect.[60] However, as shown below, when the military government took control, it soon found that any entirely punitive plan for Germany was impractical on a number of levels.

After Germany's surrender on 8 May 1945, the Potsdam Conference formally established the four zones of occupation and set out Allied aims to disarm, partially deindustrialise and democratise Germany. The ACC, made up of the four occupying powers, would run Germany for an unspecified amount of time until a suitable German-run government could be re-established.[61] The key changes effected at Potsdam were for US administrators in Germany to be given more latitude in two key areas: the economy and the political sphere. Where JCS 1067, like the Morgenthau Plan, largely proscribed German economic recovery and political organisation, the Potsdam agreement seemed to offer more room for gradual revival in these controversial areas.[62] Rebecca Boehling puts a somewhat different emphasis on this change, arguing that the prioritisation of economic reconstruction soon trumped policies such as denazification and democratisation.[63] The conflicting projections of US policy in JCS 1067 and at Potsdam reflect the dual desires among Americans for some sort of punishment for Germany, and to stop the spread of communism into western Europe. However, it was the economic arguments that ultimately prevailed in determining US policy.

The US Zone of occupation in Germany consisted of the neighbouring regions of Bavaria, Württemberg-Baden and Hesse, with an effective zone 'capital' in Frankfurt am Main. The US also controlled the non-contiguous ports of Bremen and Bremerhaven, which were otherwise surrounded by the British Zone, as well as a sector in western Berlin, which sat within the Soviet Zone.[64] General Lucius D. Clay became the first Military Governor of the US Zone and its US government. Clay could not rule like a despot, in part because of

US public pressure but also because Germany was in such financial difficulties that it would hardly survive a truly punitive regime. The US public called for three key restrictions that would affect Clay: demobilisation of troops (leading to manpower shortages), pressure to uphold a moral code, and the need to consider the long-term economic commitment the US was willing to make to the occupation.[65] Clay was also eager, from the outset, to loosen the restrictive shackles of JCS 1067 as he, like a number of others on the ground in Germany, believed that German industry had to be allowed to recover to a reasonable extent, if only to prevent the starvation of the German people.[66]

With the US Zone firmly established, the American occupation regime set about imposing a policy of political democratisation, complemented by a secondary policy of re-education led by social scientists, which would promote 'democratic values' in the post-Nazi era.[67] Between 1945 and 1946 German political parties began to reform, but there emerged marked differences between those that organised in the western zones and those permitted to act freely in the Soviet Zone, leading early on to a divergence of the political destinies of the four zones.[68] The United States moved faster than other allies to set out a speedy transferral of political power to the Germans. When Secretary of State James Byrnes announced such plans publicly during a speech in Stuttgart in September 1946, it led to staunch criticism from Poland.[69] Byrnes also outlined the need for a higher level of German economic recovery, if only to meet its own needs and its reparation obligations, and stressed the ultimate goal of US policy as being the economic union of the Allied zones and a common financial policy.[70] Byrnes' speech essentially loosened the shackles of JCS 1067 even further and set the US on course for the complete rejection of a policy of revenge.

Following Byrnes' speech, the United States stepped up both the economic and political rebuilding of western Germany. In January 1947 the United States and Britain united their zones economically, creating an economic 'Bizone', a move that effectively created a 'shadow state' by 1948.[71] Indeed, from mid-1947 onwards the US zone became increasingly integrated with the British, and later, the French zones. The United States had by this point adopted a clear strategy towards the whole of western Europe, including western Germany, in the form of the Truman Doctrine and the Marshall

Plan. The former set out US intentions to support any democratic nation under duress, while the latter offered a substantial aid package to expedite economic recovery; both measures designed to stymie the spread of communism. For the Soviets, both of these broader policies were imperialist in design and when it came to Germany, the USSR saw what it considered even more compelling evidence of creeping US imperial ambition in the years that followed.

In 1948 the French joined 'Bizonia', creating 'Trizonia', and the US extended Marshall Aid to the western zones, while the Soviets refused to accept invitations either to unite or receive aid from the US. In June 1948 the United States, Britain and France announced a reformed single currency for Trizonia, a step that prompted the Soviets to cut off the western-controlled zones of Berlin entirely bounded by the Soviet Zone. However, after around a year of the Soviets' 'Berlin Blockade', in the summer of 1949 Stalin called off the exercise, and by September 1949 Trizonia became the Federal Republic of Germany (FRG) with its capital not in divided Berlin but in the more reserved enclave of Bonn. Formal US military occupation of the FRG ended in 1952, but it was only on 5 May 1955 that the US and other western powers recognised German sovereignty, almost a decade after the initial occupation had begun.[72] The United States had undertaken the imperialistic occupation of West Germany first and foremost to preclude the Soviet Union, and the Soviets had done likewise in the east. Indeed, both the US and USSR successfully created long-lasting spheres of influence once their preferred systems were firmly in place, and both maintained a substantial military presence for decades to come.

Japan

Although Allied planning for a post-war Japan dated back to at least May 1943, the main focus of the Allies, at least initially, had been on Germany and Europe.[73] Therefore, by the end of the war, many questions remained unanswered, particularly when it came to the foreign relations of post-war Japan and the role of the Japanese Emperor.[74] Following Japan's unconditional surrender after the US bombing of Nagasaki, General Douglas MacArthur, leader of the victorious Allied forces, flew to the defeated nation on 15 August to organise the demilitarisation and occupation of the Empire of the

Rising Sun. Far from threatening a punitive regime in Japan, like Morgenthau's plan for Germany outlined above, MacArthur hoped to bring US democratic ideals and civilising zeal to what he saw as a 'racially inferior' nation, in much the same way Americans had suggested for the Philippines in the wake of the Spanish-American War.[75] MacArthur also remained open to working with the Japanese Emperor, Hirohito, and establishing a form of 'indirect rule' through the emperor and the Japanese government.[76]

In common with US policy in Germany, 'democratisation' supposedly meant tasking the US military government to purge all vestiges of the previous authoritarian regime. Unlike in Germany, however, the US was both more able and more determined to act unilaterally in Japan: there were no four allied control zones.[77] Nevertheless, even working alone, the US was unable to come to a fully unified approach to a post-war Japanese policy. MacArthur's desire to work with Hirohito and maintain the 'emperor system' clashed with the US government's public aims to democratise Japan as quickly as possible. Eventually MacArthur triumphed, and the Japanese Constitution of 1946 enshrined MacArthur's three primary goals: continuation of the emperor as head of state, official renunciation of aggressive wars, and the abolition of the Japanese feudal system.[78] MacArthur then followed up this constitution with a determined effort to emphasise his transition from 'warrior to peacemaker', presenting a determined effort to eliminate militarists and ultranationalists during the occupation era.[79] As historian Justin Williams notes, the traditional view of MacArthur's constitution focused on its creation of the Diet, or parliament, as the 'chief organ of state power' as well as its guarantee of civil rights. However, as Williams goes on to argue, many revisionist historians have, in his view unfairly, been reluctant to accept such a positive interpretation of US reforms and focused instead upon the limitations and contradictions of the US democratisation process.[80] Despite such criticisms, the Japan that emerged from this period of US imperial rule was far more democratic that the one the US had entered in 1945.

Regardless of MacArthur's supposedly benevolent intentions, this era constituted the first time Japan's national sovereignty had ever been compromised, and its people were still subjected to 'humiliation' under the military government of a foreign power. The US occupation of Japan was felt in a whole range of areas, especially in the early years. For example, the United States controlled Japanese foreign policy and the movement of its people as well as monitoring and censoring their communications.[81] It might have appeared a benevolent, even light-touch, occupation to the world, but to many in Japan the occupation felt far more heavy-handed. In parallel with the experience of the US occupation in Germany, economic affairs became an unwanted but essential diversion from the headline democratisation project. Although MacArthur was keen to leave the economy to the new Japanese government to handle, an economic crisis and the widespread strikes that followed it saw the new regime threaten to undermine MacArthur's vision of a peaceful and stable democratic Japan. MacArthur was therefore forced to intervene against the Japanese labour movement on a number of occasions.[82] As well as strike-breaking, the occupation period saw the enactment of other radical but less autocratic interventions that altered the Japanese economy, most notably agrarian reforms and the dissolution of the *zaibatsu* – powerful business conglomerates of imperial Japan.[83]

One notable side-effect of the US occupation of Japan was that it provided opportunities for second-generation Japanese Americans (*Nisei*) in the US, many of whom had been 'interned' as a potential menace to the United States during the war following President Roosevelt's infamous Executive Order 9066 of 1942. As historian Eiichiro Azuma notes, for many *Nisei* the occupation was a 'godsend', providing a range of interpreting and translating jobs. The *Nisei* acted as useful intermediaries between the Americans and the Japanese and utilised their position to re-emphasise their allegiance to the United States.[84] Another positive side-effect of the US occupation of Japan relates to the liberation of Japanese women. The inclusion of the Equal Rights Amendment in the new Japanese Constitution is one example of this, a measure that went beyond what the US was ultimately willing to accept for its own citizens.[85]

The occupation of Japan lasted until 1952 and wrought a massive transformation of the political nation from what had existed prior to the Second World War. As historian John Dower notes, the remarkable success of this transformation cannot solely be ascribed to the Japanese familiarity with 'top down' revolution dating back to 1868, but must also be attributed to the all-encompassing reforms, not just legally and institutionally, but to the education system, everyday culture and the very Japanese way of thinking. Nevertheless, Dower also remarks upon the glaring contradiction of an overarching scheme of democratisation being imposed autocratically by an all-powerful regime led by an almost-absolute ruler, or 'viceroy', in the guise of MacArthur.[86] In the context of the Cold War, this instance of US imperial occupation, like that in West Germany, accomplished its aims of securing an anti-communist ally. However, the ongoing presence of US troops long after the end of formal occupation also echoed the situation in Germany, and continues to cause tension to the present.

The Bonin and Ryukyu Islands

Although the US occupation of the major Japanese islands ended in 1952, it continued to occupy the Bonin and Ryukyu Islands into the 1960s and 1970s. The Bonin Islands – home to the highly symbolic Iwo Jima, which featured in the famous photograph of troops raising the Stars and Stripes during World War Two – are a group of tiny dispersed Pacific islands which the US occupied until 1968. As the Vietnam War intensified, the Japanese pushed President Lyndon Johnson for the return of these less strategically important islands as a precursor to the later return of the Ryukyu Islands. Johnson's advisers suggested that the president should heed these calls, but in return demand greater Japanese trade with the US and ask that the Japanese increase their defence spending.[87] In June of 1968 the US returned the Bonin Islands to Japan by executive order and turned its attention to the more valuable Ryukyu Islands.

The Ryukyu Islands, which stretch from southern Japan to Taiwan, were central to the very earliest relations between the US and Japan. When US Commodore Matthew C. Perry 'opened' Japan to US trade in the 1850s, he also, in a lesser-noted episode, advocated the occupation of the Ryukyu Islands. The status of the islands remained vague following Allied declarations after the wartime conferences of Cairo, Yalta and Potsdam, and even after the Treaty of San Francisco in 1951, which outlined the fate of most of Japan's remaining 'imperial' possessions. The San Francisco Treaty suggested that making the Ryukyu Islands a UN Trust Territory under US control was a possibility, just as many other Pacific Islands had been since 1947 (see Chapter 8), but the US showed no interest in pursuing this route and Secretary of State John Foster Dulles instead stressed the temporary nature of the continued occupation.[88]

Far more so than the Bonin Islands, the Ryukyu Islands constituted an incredibly useful strategic base for the United States in the post-war era. In order to check Soviet designs in the Pacific, monitor Chinese tensions with Taiwan, and engage fully in the Korean and Vietnam Wars, the United States set great store by its control of the gem of the Ryukyu Islands: Okinawa. Even after relenting to Japanese demands for the islands' return in 1972, the United States continued to maintain a vast military presence on the island of Okinawa in the form of over thirty bases and around 28,000 military personnel (see also Chapter 8).[89] Its presence there continues to offer the US an important strategic presence in the western Pacific, but has in recent years caused friction with Japan and, even more recently, with China, which has claimed that Okinawa and the rest of the Ryukyu Islands should lie under their sovereignty.[90]

The policy of 'occupation' rather than 'annexation' became the favoured policy of the United States after the experiments in Germany and Japan. A comparison can be drawn, for example, between the post-Second World War occupations and the US-led occupation of Iraq between 2003 and 2004, though the differences are quite marked in terms of both US pre-planning and in the level of internal armed opposition the US occupations faced.[91] In some respects, increasingly indirect and diluted versions of the post-Second World War occupations came to characterise US interventions overseas throughout the twentieth century. However, rather than look at the ever-decreasing circles of 'formal' US imperialism, the final chapter shows how the story of US imperialism has continued on in other forms. Indeed, the US annexed the last vestiges of its formal empire in the 1970s and it has continued to expand its presence overseas, through military bases, and even below the ocean, well into the twenty-first century.

Notes

1. Roosevelt, 'Fourth Annual Message'.
2. Holmes, *Theodore Roosevelt and World Order*, p. 104.
3. See: Langley, *Banana Wars*.
4. Munro, 'American Withdrawal from Haiti', p. 1.
5. Pérez, *Cuba Under the Platt Amendment*, p. 103.
6. Schoultz, *That Infernal Little Cuban Republic*, pp. 25–7.

7. Hernández, *Cuba and the US*, pp. 144–6.
8. The best treatment of Wilson's policy in Cuba can be found in: Pérez, *Intervention, Revolution, and Politics*.
9. Meiser, *Power and Restraint*, p. 181.
10. One recent article exploring the role of justice systems in all three of these occupations is: McPherson, 'The Irony of Legal Pluralism', pp. 1149–72.
11. Gobat, *Confronting the American Dream*, pp. 1–3, p. 40, p. 100. For a recent narrative account of Walker's attempts to establish control over the region see: Dando-Collins, *Tycoon's War*.
12. Buchenau, 'Counter-intervention against Uncle Sam', pp. 208–9.
13. Harrison, 'Wilson and Nicaragua', pp. 25–6.
14. Buchenau, 'Counter-intervention against Uncle Sam', p. 219. This view of Knox is echoed in Dinwoodie, 'Dollar Diplomacy', p. 237.
15. Harrison, '1909 Nicaragua Revolution', pp. 56–7; Buchenau, 'Counter-intervention against Uncle Sam', p. 230.
16. For a full investigation of Taft's foreign policy as president see: Scholes and Scholes, *Foreign Policies of the Taft Administration*. For a brief overview of Taft's place in US imperial endeavours see: Burns, 'William Howard Taft', pp. 850–1. Díaz was previously Estrada's deputy until the latter resigned in 1911.
17. Munro, 'Dollar Diplomacy in Nicaragua', p. 228.
18. Sanchez, 'Philander C. Knox', p. 311.
19. The term 'Big Stick' refers to Roosevelt's use of the phrase 'speak softly and carry a big stick', suggesting that US diplomacy needed to be supported by the potential for military intervention. Taft defined 'Dollar Diplomacy' as making a mark overseas via investment and trade rather than by military means.
20. Harrison, '1909 Nicaragua Revolution', p. 59; Munro, 'Dollar Diplomacy in Nicaragua', p. 230; Baker, 'Wilson Administration and Nicaragua', pp. 339–42. The term 'good neighbour' is more frequently linked to President Franklin Roosevelt's Latin American Policy, but was used in the nineteenth century also to refer to a US-Latin American relationship that did not rely on US interventionism but was based on a more equal footing.
21. Baker, 'Wilson Administration and Nicaragua', p. 344.
22. Harrison, 'Wilson and Nicaragua', pp. 25–6.
23. Smith, 'Bryan-Chamorro Treaty', pp. 63–6.
24. The lease of the Corn Islands was never really acted upon in a significant way, and the islands were returned to Nicaragua in 1970.
25. Schoultz, *Beneath the United States*, p. 227.
26. Ibid. pp. 263–5. The 'Sandinistas' that overthrew the Nicaraguan dictatorship in 1979 took their name from Sandino.
27. Pike, *FDR's Good Neighbor Policy*, p. 169.

28. Reding, 'Exorcising Haiti's Ghosts', p. 16.
29. See: Byrd, 'Black Republicans, Black Republic', pp. 545–67. The most obvious reason for recognition coming in the Civil War is the US Republican Party's turn towards more overt abolitionism during the conflict. However, as Foner notes in *Fiery Trial*, p. 222, there were some who saw Haiti as a potential site for the colonisation of African Americans after the war.
30. Plummer, *Haiti and the United States*, pp. 52–3.
31. Johnson, 'Fourth Annual Message'; Schmidt, *US Occupation of Haiti*, pp. 30–1.
32. Schmidt, *US Occupation of Haiti*, p. 31.
33. Bryan cited in: Plummer, 'Afro-American Response', p. 128.
34. Ibid. p. 125.
35. Plummer, *Haiti and the United States*, p. 103.
36. Schmidt, *US Occupation of Haiti*, p. 11. The treaty is usually referred to as the Haitian-American Convention (or Treaty).
37. Lansing, cited in Langley, *Banana Wars*, p. 128.
38. Renda, *Taking Haiti*, p. 12.
39. Ibid. p. 188.
40. Plummer, 'Afro-American Response', pp. 129–31.
41. See: Pamphile, 'America's Policy-Making in Haitian Education'.
42. Schmidt, *US Occupation of Haiti*, p. 8.
43. Ibid. p. 11.
44. Daugherty, *Counterinsurgency*, pp. 70–5. 'Haitianise' meaning to turn control gradually over to Haitians.
45. Munro, 'American Withdrawal from Haiti', p. 6. McPherson, 'Herbert Hoover', pp. 623–39, argues that Hoover deserves far more credit for initiating the 'Good Neighbor Policy' (GNP) of non-intervention and treating Latin America with mutual respect in the late 1920s and early 1930s, rather than simply accepting the traditional presentation of the GNP as solely the brainchild of FDR.
46. The republic is often referred to in texts from the earlier period as Santo Domingo, which was its earlier name under Spanish rule.
47. Atkins and Wilson, *Dominican Republic and the US*, pp. 17–27.
48. Guyatt, 'America's Conservatory', p. 974. Guyatt's article traces the debate over Dominican annexation in this period, outlining key debates over Reconstruction, race and citizenship in the United States.
49. Roorda, *The Dictator Next Door*, p. 16.
50. Calder, *Impact of Intervention*, pp. 22–3.
51. Daugherty, *Counterinsurgency*, p. 99.
52. Juárez, 'US Withdrawal from Santo Domingo', pp. 157–8.
53. Grieb, 'Harding and the Dominican Republic', pp. 428–40.
54. Jonas, *US and Germany*, p. 148.

55. Dorn, 'American Occupation Policy', p. 486.
56. Buhite, *Decisions at Yalta*, pp. 21–2 and p. 30.
57. Lewkowicz, *The German Question*, p. 20.
58. Beschloss, *The Conquerors*, p. 169.
59. Madsen, 'Becoming a State-in-the-World', p. 167.
60. Dietrich, *The Morgenthau Plan*, p. 5.
61. 'The Potsdam Conference', *US Office of the Historian*.
62. Gimbel, *American Occupation of Germany*, pp. 14–16.
63. Boehling, *A Question of Priorities*, p. 3.
64. Miller, 'A bibliographic essay', pp. 751–9, notes that the decade-long occupation often exists only as an afterword to the war itself. Though this is certainly true, within what literature there is on the period of the Allied occupation, there are more works on US-occupied Germany than any of the other three zones of occupation. As Boehling, *A Question of Priorities*, p. 9, points out, this is partly due to the availability of documents relating to the US Zone, and partly due to the US hegemony in western Europe at the time.
65. Madsen, 'Becoming a State-in-the-World', p. 164.
66. Peterson, *American Occupation of Germany*, pp. 59–60.
67. Boehling, 'The Role of Culture', pp. 58–9.
68. For in-depth thematic chapters on US policy in occupied Germany, see: Diefendorf, Frohn and Rupieper, *American Policy and the Reconstruction of West Germany*.
69. Shibata, *Japan and Germany*, p. 108.
70. Byrnes, 'Restatement of Policy on Germany'.
71. Fulbrook, *History of Germany*, p. 139.
72. Jonas, *US and Germany*, p. 292.
73. Iriye, *Power and Culture*, pp. 122–3.
74. Iokibe, 'Diplomacy in Occupied Japan', pp. 25–6.
75. Koikari, *Pedagogy of Democracy*, pp. 2–3. Koikari also notes that, as well as a sense of racial hierarchy driving US policy, the US 'liberators' saw Japanese women as the long-term victims of Japanese male chauvinistic policies, and thus likely to benefit even more from 'western salvation and emancipation'.
76. Iokibe, 'Diplomacy in Occupied Japan', p. 29.
77. Shibata, *Japan and Germany*, p. 109. For details of the British attempts to restrict, at least partially, US unilateralism in Japan, see also: Buckley, *Occupation Diplomacy*, Chapter 5.
78. Iokibe, 'Diplomacy in Occupied Japan', pp. 30–6. For the final text of the constitution see: Japanese Constitution.
79. Schonberger, *Aftermath of War*, p. 60.
80. Williams, 'American Democratization Policy', pp. 179–202.
81. Takemae, *Allied Occupation of Japan*, p. xxvi.

82. Schonberger, *Aftermath of War*, pp. 61–3. The author notes that MacArthur's task in this arena became far easier after he lost his bid to become the 1948 Republican nominee for the US presidency.
83. Schwartzberg, 'Soft Peace Boys', p. 194.
84. Azuma, 'Brokering Race, Culture, and Citizenship', pp. 191–4.
85. Koikari, 'Rethinking gender and power', p. 314. However, as Koikari argues, to see the US occupation as the imposed liberation of women is far too one-dimensional, and instead she points to a far more complex interplay of gender, nationalism and imperialism in the formation of post-war Japan.
86. Dower, *Embracing Defeat*, pp. 203–6.
87. Sarantakes, 'Continuity through Change', pp. 41–2.
88. Braibanti, 'Ryukyu Islands', pp. 973–82.
89. Fifield, 'In Okinawa'.
90. McCurry, 'China lays claim to Okinawa'.
91. See: Gewertz, 'Looking at Germany'.

CHAPTER 8

Continuing Imperialism (1940–2013)

In the course of the twentieth century, the United States' empire certainly evolved and adapted to changing domestic and global situations. However, ideas about formally taking control of distant places or simply maintaining a military presence in those places on an indefinite basis have persisted. In the Pacific, the US continued to expand its formal empire after annexing Guam in 1898, formally taking control of the Northern Mariana Islands in the 1970s. The Cold War period also saw a huge increase in the number of US overseas military bases, a form of strategic and semi-formal territorial acquisition that has continued apace to the present. Finally, the Cold War competition between the US and USSR/Russia continues to see a form of preclusive competition for control of the Arctic that the fall of the Soviet Union has done little to impede.

Guam and the Pacific Trust Territories

The Pacific region of Micronesia comprises four main island groups: the Marianas, the Carolines, the Marshalls and the Gilberts. Prior to the late nineteenth century, Spain had ruled over the Marianas and Carolines, along with the Philippines, as the Spanish East Indies. The remaining Micronesian Islands were annexed by other European powers: the Marshalls by Germany in 1885, and the Gilberts by Britain, as a protectorate in 1892 and a colony from 1916.[1] The largest of the Mariana Islands, Guam, was annexed by the United States in the aftermath of the Spanish-American War, along with the Philippines (see Chapters 4 and 5). Although the US did not annex the remaining islands of the Marianas when it took on Guam, by the 1940s the United States was in control of almost all of Micronesia.

The main reason behind the United States not annexing the rest of the Spanish East Indies in 1898 was the existence of a secret treaty between the Spanish and Germans signed just two weeks after fighting in the Spanish-American War had ceased. Germany had coveted these Spanish islands since at least a decade earlier, seeing them as a natural extension to the existing German possessions of Kaiser-Wilhelmsland and the Bismarck Archipelago. This treaty allowed for Germany to purchase several of the Caroline Islands, and soon afterwards the German government proceeded to buy the remaining Carolines and Marianas, eradicating the Spanish presence in the region. The US, though sceptical about the Spanish sale of the islands to Germany for an estimated $4.2 million, did not object, despite some in the Navy Department suggesting that the islands would provide support for a future naval base in Guam.[2] Thus, between 1898 and 1914, these Micronesian islands formed part of the German Empire that surrounded the US possession of Guam until the outbreak of the First World War.[3]

In 1898 Guam, the largest of the Mariana Islands, was a Spanish colony that was home to a majority Chamorro Micronesian population. The US had a tentative history of interest in Guam dating back to the 1840s and 1850s, when whaling ships used the islands as a stopover point. However, the Spanish-American War brought Guam's potential as a military and strategic asset to the fore, particularly because of its geographical location between the more significant US possessions of the Philippines and Hawaii. On 21 June 1898 the US flag was raised on Guam above the captured Fort Santa Cruz and the 'Star Spangled Banner' played before a 21-gun salute aboard the USS *Charleston*. By the end of the year, with the US Navy Department recommending the establishment of a naval station on the island, President William McKinley formally placed the island under control of that department with a remit to establish authority and a government there. The first naval governor of Guam, Captain R. P. Leary, arrived on the island on 7 August 1899, and from that time until 1950, the island remained under the control of the US Navy.[4] In the following years the island gained a navy yard (1899), a Marine barracks (1901), a coaling station (1905) and gun emplacements (from 1909).[5]

As the United States had remained neutral at the outbreak of World War One, the chance to capitalise on any German imperial losses in the Pacific remained small, especially given President

Wilson's well-sounding anti-imperialist rhetoric. Rather than the US, Japan took control of German Micronesia with a pace that, according to historian Robert Rogers, alarmed both the Americans and the British, and left the northern Pacific divided precariously between the US and Japan. Guam itself played only a marginal role in the conflict. US naval strategists believed that roughly 8,500 marines would be required to defend it if the situation eventually arose. The US Congress was not willing to countenance any such force, agreeing in 1914 to boost numbers to only 200. After the US joined the conflict in 1917, the most significant action was the Germans' scuttling of their ship *Cormoran* in Guam's Apra Harbour shortly after the declaration of war.[6]

With the end of the First World War, the victorious powers passed the former German Micronesian islands formally to Japan, to govern as a mandate of the League of Nations, just as the British took control of German Samoa (see Chapter 6). The Japanese possessions in the Pacific formed a 'Class C mandate'. This category of mandates was seen, in contrast to Class A mandates like Iraq at this time, as the least prepared for self-government and independence, and were usually ruled as parts of the respective mandatory power's existing imperial territory. For example, German South West Africa (Namibia) became a mandate of neighbouring South Africa. However, Japan proved a most unwelcome neighbour for Guam and the US grew suspicious that the Japanese Empire was seeking to fortify its mandates in breach of League protocol. The Japanese mandate was not simply near US possessions, it divided sea communications between Guam and Hawaii and, as such, posed a real threat to the security of both.[7]

In 1933, Japan left the League of Nations and continued to fortify its Pacific possessions as it geared up for imperial expansion in Asia. In contrast, Guam was relatively poorly defended, and in 1938 the US Congress decided that further militarisation of the island would simply provoke the Japanese. Instead the US placed Guam in naval defence Category F, effectively indefensible.[8] On 7 December 1941 the Japanese attacked Pearl Harbor in Hawaii, on 8 December the US declared war on the Empire of Japan, and on the morning of 10 December 1941, Guam's military governor surrendered to the Japanese. Following their occupation of the British Gilbert and Ellice Islands in 1942, the Japanese controlled all of Micronesia, a situation that would last until nearly the end of the war. It was the only period in history during which one ruler united the entire island group.[9] Guam and other islands of Micronesia were destined thereafter to play an important role in the Pacific theatre of the war, leading some Americans to call for their annexation in the aftermath of US victory.[10]

In 1945, the newly formed United Nations (UN) set up a system similar to the League of Nations' mandate system before it. Established under Chapter XII of the UN Charter, the International Trusteeship System placed a variety of former mandates and 'detached' enemy territories under the supervision of victorious nations, with the general understanding that this status was a form of protectorate on the road to future self-government.[11] The United States now undertook an expanded protectorate in the region that it had missed out on in 1898. As well as regaining control of Guam as an 'unincorporated territory', like Puerto Rico, the US now took control of the bulk of Micronesia. This excluded the Gilbert and Ellice Islands, which reverted to British control as before the war.[12] The US decision to agree to the trusteeship was motivated directly by military security, rather than economic or humanitarian concerns, and this was made evident by the fact it was the only Trust Territory specifically designated by the UN as 'strategic' and allowed to be used for military purposes.[13] The US administered the new territory as the Trust Territory of the Pacific Islands (TTPI) from 1947 onwards, though the diverse parts of the scattered island group were to take a number of different routes towards self-government. At the same time the United States was able to increase its military-strategic presence in the region and afford favourable trade deals for US firms.[14]

Having officially taken on the new Trust Territories in 1947, the United States turned its attention once again to its otherwise neglected possession of Guam. In 1949, President Harry Truman issued Executive Order 10077, which transferred Guam to the Department of the Interior, effective the following summer. The island finally ceased being an overtly military possession of the United States, and the following year the US provided Guam with its own Organic Act, just as it had for Puerto Rico and the Philippines four decades earlier.[15] The residents of Guam became US citizens for the first time, albeit still of an 'unincorporated territory', and their civil rights were set out in a Bill of Rights presented in the act. In addition to this, the 1950 Act set out a new governmental system for the island, with an executive headed by a governor who was appointed by the US president, a popularly-elected unicameral legislature and a district court. This political relationship between the United States and Guam has remained largely unchanged ever since.

As for the TTPI, throughout the 1950s the islands remained largely undeveloped and there is little evidence that the US pursued any policy there at all.[16] The one exception to this neglect was the attention of the US military, which utilised Bikini Atoll in the Marshall Islands to test their hydrogen bomb in 1954.[17] The US gradually removed the islands from naval control to that of the Department of the Interior after 1951, a project completed in 1962 by President John F. Kennedy. During the 1960s, when European colonial powers were granting independence to most other UN Trust Territories, pressure grew on the United States to make some progress in moving the TTPI towards self-government and independence. Kennedy kick-started development in the islands as a result of a critical UN report into the state to the Trust Territories, and in 1964 a legislative body for the TTPI was created: the Congress of Micronesia.[18] In 1966, the US dispatched Peace Corps workers in an effort to speed up the improvement of the islands.[19] However, the sudden boom in US interest after such a long period of neglect led UN inspectors to question US motivations, with some feeling that the US government was motivated primarily by a desire to maintain control after a plebiscite to be held by the end of the decade.[20] Eventually, the Congress of Micronesia set up a commission to consider four options for the TTPI's future: free association, independence, integration and a continuation of the status quo. The commission recommended the first option in 1969, echoing an agreement made between the Cook Islands and New Zealand, but the United States had other ideas.[21]

In 1970, the United States offered 'Commonwealth' status to the TTPI rather than free association, to put the Trust Territory on the same footing as Puerto Rico.[22] This was the first time that a UN trustee power had officially moved to annex part of its Trust Territory, and the offer divided the Micronesian islanders.[23] The US subdivided the TTPI into six districts: Marianas, Marshalls, Palau, Yap, Truk and Ponape, the latter three of which later formed the Federated States of Micronesia. After the Micronesians' rejection of Commonwealth status as a collective, the US renegotiated with the six, then four, separate districts. The Northern Mariana Islands, the geographical group to which Guam belongs, agreed to form a 'Commonwealth' of the United States through a Covenant between the two parties, formed in 1975 and approved by the US Congress the following year. This came after proposals to adjoin the Marianas to either Guam or Hawaii failed, and in spite of resistance from Caroline minorities in the islands to the territorial split in the first place.[24] Guy Dempsey, a legal commentator writing in 1976, described the outcome as in 'the primary interests of all concerned': allowing separate status for the people of the Northern Marianas Islands and allowing the US to construct military bases in the islands on fully sovereign territory. With the signing of the covenant, the US took formal control of the Northern Mariana Islands and added the final piece to its Pacific Empire.

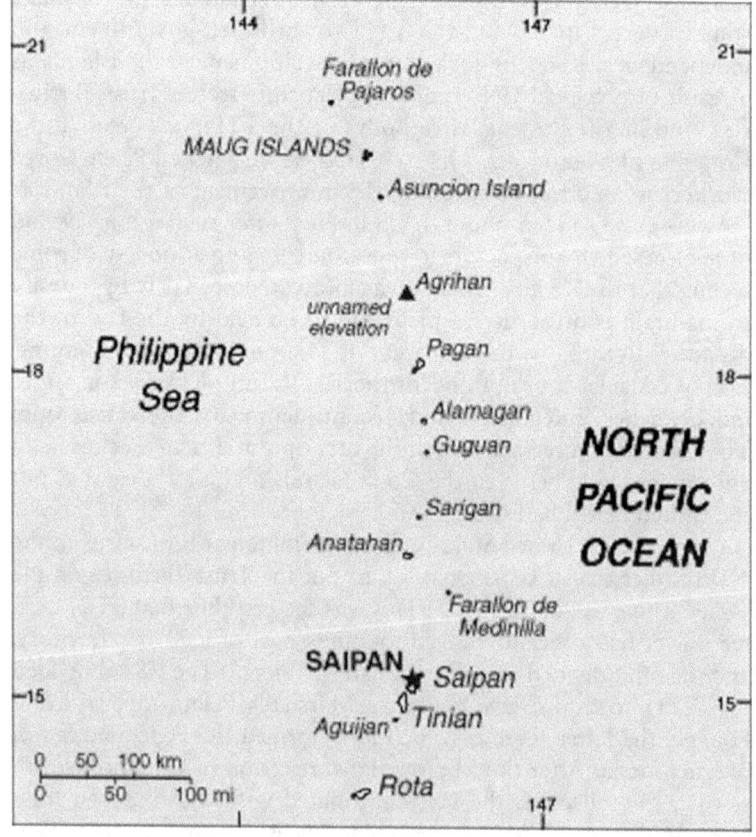

Figure 8.1 Northern Mariana Islands

Following the secession of the Northern Marianas from the TTPI, the remaining three groups took paths towards independence, forming the sovereign states of: the Marshall Islands (1986), the Federated States of Micronesia (1986) and Palau (1994). However, all three states also opted to negotiate a Free Association Agreement (FAA) with the US that would maintain some level of imperial bond after their independence. The FAAs are a form of pseudo-protectorate, according to which the United States offers economic support to the three states in return for the ability to intervene in their foreign and military affairs. Indeed, this is the sort of agreement that many of the UK dominions had with Britain prior to the 1931 Statute of Westminster, when Canada, Australia and the other dominions finally gained sovereignty over their foreign affairs, having already gained almost-complete domestic autonomy. Thus, today the US maintains two 'unincorporated territories' in Micronesia and has three FAAs with sovereign states. This is substantially more than the US had before the First World War, meaning that the Spanish-American War was certainly not the final word in Pacific imperial expansion.

Guantanamo Bay and Overseas Bases

Guantanamo Bay looms large in the present day anti-imperialist lexicon, a lasting sign of US imperialism in Latin America that has risen to international notoriety following the events of 11 September 2001. Although now primarily known worldwide as a holding camp for suspected terrorists, the naval base itself is over a century old. Indeed, the value of the base was not only clear to the Spanish, who ruled over Cuba for many centuries, but to the British and the early United States as well (see previous sections on Cuba). The British in the mid-eighteenth century were only too aware that the nation that held Cuba 'would command the trade and traffic not only of the Atlantic seaboard and North American continent, but of the Western Hemisphere itself'.[25] British naval officer Edward Vernon saw Guantanamo Bay in the 1740s as exceptional not only from a military standpoint, with access to Santiago and an enormous natural harbour better sheltered from storms than others, but also for its navigable rivers, fertile plains and rolling hills. Vernon lent his name to the home of George Washington, whose half-brother served under Vernon during the War of Jenkins' Ear in the 1740s, a connection that reveals how Guantanamo truly was part of US history from its beginning.[26]

Aside from early interests in Cuba in general, as explored in Chapter 3, the successful claim to Cuba, and with it Guantanamo Bay, came in 1898. The war was certainly not all about the bay itself, but even then there were those who recognised it as the potential prize of the war for 'Cuban liberation'. At the end of May 1898 US Captain Charles Sigsbee, formerly of the ill-fated *Maine*, urged the US to seize and occupy the bay because 'the land thereabouts is much lower than elsewhere, and therefore does not offer the usual facilities of the region for a plunging fire on vessels and troops from surrounding hills'. By the end of June the US had secured the bay, which served as a valuable anchorage for the remainder of the war.[27] However, after the war, when Cuba was temporarily ruled over by the United States, the fate of Guantanamo Bay began to separate from the rest of the island.

By the early 1900s there was a 'New Empire' group, headed by figures such as Theodore Roosevelt and Alfred Thayer Mahan, which advocated a strong US naval presence in the world but without the cumbersome annexation of distant lands, such as those maintained by the British.[28] Such figures were adamantly opposed to giving up a prize possession such as Guantanamo Bay, especially following the assassination of William McKinley in 1901, which sped Theodore Roosevelt, a champion of US naval power, to the White House. For the embryonic Cuban government negotiating with the United States, it was nigh on impossible to deny the United States some form of permanent naval base on the island. Indeed, it seems likely that the Cuban government sacrificed Guantanamo Bay to save Havana, so that at least this US base would not be at the heart of the Cuban capital.[29]

The Platt Amendment provided the key piece of legislation in regard to the formation of the Guantanamo Bay US Naval Base (GTMO).[30] Article VII of the Platt Amendment reads:

> That to enable the United States to maintain the independence of Cuba, and to protect the people thereof, as well as for its own defense, the government of Cuba will sell or lease to the United States lands necessary for coaling or naval stations at certain specified points to be agreed upon with the President of the United States.[31]

The Platt Amendment did not expressly name Guantanamo Bay, but the area had been touted as a highly desirable location for a coaling base and strategic US asset for some time. Discussions within the US regarding the building of a trans-isthmian canal lent even greater weight to the argument that a substantial Caribbean base such as GTMO was necessary. The curious wording of the Platt Amendment suggests that such a base should be established, at least partially, to maintain the independence of Cuba. However, for Cuba to become independent in the first place, it had to accept this cessation of territory to US control. In 1903 the US and Cuba signed a treaty giving some more ambiguous details of the lease on GTMO and the western base of Bahia Honda. The latter base, however, was never really developed and in 1912 it was returned to Cuba in exchange for an expansion of GTMO.[32] The third article in the 1903 treaty, written in very vague legal terminology, allowed for US occupation of the GTMO site to the present:

> While on the one hand the United States recognizes the continuance of the ultimate sovereignty of the Republic of Cuba over the above described areas of land and water, on the other hand the Republic of Cuba consents that during the period of the occupation by the United States. ... the United States shall exercise complete jurisdiction and control over and within said areas ...

In return for this exceptionally valuable base the United States paid Cuba $2,000 per year in gold (a figure scaled up to $3,403 in 1959).[33] The key question remaining related to how Cuba could hold 'ultimate sovereignty' over the base yet cede 'complete jurisdiction and control' over the site to the United States. In 1933 a new government in Cuba repealed the Platt Amendment and the question of the precise nature of US control of GTMO came into sharp relief.

Although the Guantanamo naval base now houses a military detention site, throughout the twentieth century it was far more of a military base than a holding pen. Indeed, GTMO provided the launch pad for US interventions in the Caribbean, such as those discussed in Chapter 7, throughout the early twentieth century.[34] Yet between 1933 and 1934 the final major change to the relationship between the US and GTMO arose, with a change in the Cuban political situation forcing the reassertion of US rights over the base.

Following the Fulgencio Batista-led 'Sergeants' Revolt' of 1933, the new civilian leader, Ramón Grau San Martín, unilaterally abrogated the Platt Amendment, which had remained the basis of US claims on GTMO for the previous thirty years.[35] Though the US conceded the end of the hated Enmienda Platt (see Chapter 5), in 1934 President Franklin D. Roosevelt signed a second treaty regarding GTMO with the Cubans. The 1934 treaty reiterated the 1903 agreement, but also stated that the base should remain in US hands until 'the two contracting parties agree to the modification or abrogation of the stipulations'.[36] Put simply, under the new treaty the United States could keep possession of GTMO until it decided otherwise.

Historian Amy Kaplan describes GTMO as, if not a formal colony, a social space that 'has long resembled a colonial outpost', a 'Little America' that has altered little since the Cuban Revolution except in the replacing of Cuban labourers with those from elsewhere.[37] In 1960 President Dwight Eisenhower announced there would be no change in the US lease of GTMO: 'because of its importance to the defense of the entire hemisphere, particularly in the light of the intimate relations which now exist between the present government of Cuba and the Sino-Soviet bloc'.[38] The Cuban Revolution seemed certain to put the GTMO site under pressure, and the US military feared revolutionaries would attack the base's Achilles' heel: its water supply.[39] Such a circumstance arose in 1964, when Fidel Castro cut the supply following the US seizure of four Cuban fishing vessels.[40] However, as Castro stated on a number of occasions in the 1960s and early 1970s, Cuba would not consider any measures to take possession of the base beyond the diplomatic. Following the US-backed Bay of Pigs invasion in 1961, Cuba was only too aware that the United States would not need to look too far for an excuse to remove the Castro regime. During the period running up to the Cuban Missile Crisis, GTMO was under close scrutiny from Cuban intelligence-gatherers seeking to ascertain US intentions.[41] In the midst of the crisis itself, those who sought a diplomatic solution, such as the US Ambassador to the United Nations, Adlai Stevenson, considered withdrawal from GTMO in return for Soviet dismantling of their missile sites.[42]

As the Cold War progressed, naval experts began to question the purpose of continuing the lease of GTMO, especially as the Puerto Rican base of Roosevelt Roads seemed to have duplicated GTMO's merits.[43] Nevertheless, as one military expert noted in 1966, during the Cold War the base's 'political and psychological' value far outweighed its military value, existing as a 'symbol of U.S. power and prestige'.[44] In 1996, the issue of negotiating the cessation of GTMO was inserted as one of a number of measures aimed at persuading Cuba to move towards a more democratic form of government in the Helms-Burton Act, a measure primarily designed to strengthen US sanctions against the island.[45] Despite a great deal of national and international attention focused on GTMO in the years since 9/11, even President Barack Obama's executive order of January 2009 – which aimed to close the detention facilities down – proved difficult to realise, largely due to Congressional opposition and the issue of where to relocate the remaining detainees.

Despite all the political and media attention focused on GTMO, it is not the only controversial or long-term US base. At least in part due to growing interest in GTMO, a number of scholars have, in recent years, begun to reconsider the proliferation of US bases overseas and their role in exerting and supporting a visible US imperial presence across the globe. As Alexander Cooley notes: 'Not surprisingly, some commentators refer to this vast overseas network of bases and troop deployments as the U.S. Empire and compare it to the peripheral holdings of previous imperial powers.'[46] The remainder of this section explores the growth in these overseas bases and this dimension of American imperialism.

Scholars such as Catherine Lutz and David Vine date the US culture of base formation on foreign soil back to the forts that sprang up along the western frontier in the 1780s.[47] However, such early bases were designed to be temporary, and the explosion of US extraterritorial bases only really began in 1940. It was in September of that year that President Franklin Roosevelt struck the 'Destroyers for Bases' deal. The agreement was part of a US-UK arrangement that saw the officially neutral US transfer fifty 'vintage' destroyers to the beleaguered UK after the fall of France. However, this was not quite the open embrace of UK-US unity and aid that Prime Minister Winston Churchill publicly hailed it to be. In return for some obsolescent destroyers, the United States was given a relative jackpot of ninety-nine-year leases to key military bases across UK imperial possessions, particularly those in the Caribbean.

The resultant US bases were, in the words of historian Thomas Howard, 'colonies within colonies – American bases, air strips, and service facilities constructed on British colonial soil, all with vast potential for discord and the spread of American influence'.[48] For Howard, Franklin Roosevelt did not simply lend Britain a symbolic hand in its war with Nazi Germany; he also secured useful strategic bases and planted the seeds of anti-British colonial sentiment. Roosevelt himself described the deal as the 'most important action in the reinforcement of our national defense that has been taken since the Louisiana Purchase'.[49] For historian Steven High, Roosevelt's most pressing concern was this defensive asset, which, he notes, US public opinion supported. With Nazi Germany seemingly unstoppable in Europe, a Gallup poll in June 1940 showed that 81 per cent of respondents favoured not only overseas bases, but also annexations.[50]

Anthropologist David Vine argues that most US citizens rarely consider these overseas military bases and that, with the exception of intermittent anti-base protests, they are largely accepted as being for the general good of the United States.[51] However, the growth of US military bases overseas has been a one-sided affair, with no freestanding foreign bases on US soil, in comparison with around 800 US bases on foreign soil (according to Vine's figure, or 686 according to the Pentagon). Despite the end of formal US occupation of the defeated Axis nations (see Chapter 7), in 2015 the US still maintained 174 base sites in Germany and 113 in Japan.[52] Some 190,000 troops and 115,000 civilian employees inhabit these current overseas bases, generally governed by Status of Forces Agreements (SOFAs) 'to specify what the military could do' in particular regions.[53] Moreover, unlike bases prior to 1940, these later bases have lasted far longer and some, such as the Ramstein Air Base in Germany, have become city-sized 'Little Americas' with schools, hospitals and power plants, while others are 'lily pads' that house drones or weapons.[54] In one particular instance, the construction of the US base of Diego Garcia in British Indian Ocean Territory led to the expulsion of the island's existing population, a controversial forced relocation that the former inhabitants still challenge today.[55] Far from retreating from this policy after World War Two, or even the Cold War, the post-9/11 War on Terror has led to even further expansion of US bases overseas.[56] Clearly this is at least one area where the expansion of US territorial control overseas has yet to hit a clear peak and is a form of US imperialism that is more evident across the world today than any other.

The Polar Frontier

This final example of American imperialism in a modern context involves the northern polar frontier. The Arctic is a vast frozen region at the top of our planet that drops down into several nations' territories and was initially deemed a distant irrelevance to the United States.[57] However, since the annexation of Alaska in the nineteenth century, the United States has possessed an Arctic frontier to its north. Over the course of the twentieth and early twenty-first centuries, the Arctic beyond the Alaskan border has become an area over which several nations (most notably the US, Canada and Russia) have increasingly sought to assert territorial rights for numerous reasons, and the United States has certainly made its voice heard among them.

In the nineteenth century, the most valuable Arctic resources included whales, fins, furs and the ivory tusks of narwhals and walruses, and increasingly coal, iron, lead, zinc, oil, gas, diamonds and other minerals over the course of the twentieth century and beyond. As global temperatures have risen, the fabled Northwest Passage (a route connecting the Pacific and Atlantic Oceans via the Arctic Ocean) has started to become a reality and, in conjunction with the Northern Sea Route, offers the United States and Canada certain strategic and commercial benefits from a transcontinental transport route.[58] Most recently, two pressing issues led the United States to assert its rights: defence, and Alaska's mineral wealth. The latter is strongly linked to the former in terms of the potential for the 'energy independence', or self-sufficiency, that Arctic resources could potentially offer.

The first real US claims to the northern Arctic came after they became an Arctic power following the Alaska Purchase of 1867. In the late nineteenth century a series of international Arctic explorations began, though Canada, rather than the United States, showed the greatest interest in the frozen north.[59] There were, nevertheless, some expressions of US interest in the Arctic at the turn of the century: in the De Long and Peary Arctic expeditions. In 1879 the American Arctic Expedition, under the command of Lieutenant George De Long of the US Navy, set out aboard the *Jeannette* to explore the northern extent of United States territory. The expedition ran into trouble after passing through the Bering Strait and discovering some previously uncharted islands off the coast of

Figure 8.2 Arctic Region

northern Russia. A number of the party died, including De Long himself, but eventually a few managed to return to the United States after finding salvation in native settlements in northern Siberia.[60] Following this disappointing start, Robert Peary's expedition of 1909 claimed to turn these fortunes around, to achieve what, in Peary's words, was: 'the last of the great earth stories, the story the world has been waiting to hear for three hundred years – the story of the discovery of the north pole'.[61] But the achievement, even at the time, was cast into doubt as Peary's claim competed with that of another American, Frederick Cook, who claimed to have reached the Pole in 1908.[62] In the same year an American citizen claimed to have planted the country's flag at the Pole, Canada began planting the British flag in its furthest northern territories, and pressing claims that its territory ran from the US border all the way to the North Pole (a claim that dated back to 1878).[63] Despite these early flag-planting escapades, it was not really until the outbreak of World War Two that the US began to rethink the strategic importance of the Arctic in a new world order.

From the Second World War onwards, the Arctic moved from being an afterthought for the United States to being one of its foremost strategic concerns by 1940, when Denmark (the imperial ruler of Greenland) fell to the Nazis. After this, the United States began to move into the region, establishing military bases in Greenland and essentially taking control of the island in the name of the Danish government in exile.[64] Thereafter the Cold War really increased the strategic value of the Arctic. In 1947 Secretary of State George C. Marshall pressed to maintain US control of its bases in Greenland for 'legitimate hemispheric defense purposes'. The *Washington Post* noted wryly that there was not the remotest chance that the US might send Americanised Danes to seize the 'reins of the Danish government' or 'provoke a revolt in Greenland' to ensure that the deal was done.[65] Another news article of the period noted that ever since World War One the US had touted the idea that Greenland lay within the aegis of the Monroe Doctrine and speculated that the United States might buy Greenland from Denmark in a reprise of its 1917 Virgin Islands purchase.[66] Although such speculation came to nothing, the island remained the most important strategic part of the Arctic for the United States as the shortest straight-line route between the industrial centres of the USA and USSR.[67] Following the 1951 Defense of Greenland Agreement, the US rapidly expanded its military presence at its Thule Air Base in Greenland as part of a wider 'military colonization' of the island.[68] The Arctic proved a fitting venue for the Cold War in more than name alone.

Greenland was not the only focal point of US military expansion in the Arctic; the Polar seas were equally under consideration.

Both the US and the Soviets maintained an underwater presence in the Arctic during the Cold War, dating back to the successful voyage of the USS *Nautilus* to the North Pole in 1958.[69] Between 1960 and the end of the Cold War, US submarines routinely traversed Canadian waters, an issue that did pose diplomatic questions but not, as a recent study by Adam Lajeunesse notes, truly in terms of defence. Lajeunesse successfully challenges traditional views that Canadian sovereignty was tested by US submarine activity and instead asserts that it was 'a fully cooperative venture', a fact that was glossed over by the 'bluster and nationalist rhetoric' of Canadian politicians.[70] However, as Carolyn James and Patrick James note, the 1985 voyage of the US *Polar Sea* icebreaker from Greenland to Alaska, through 'Canadian waters', nevertheless tested the position of the broadly pro-American prime minister Brian Mulroney. James and James illustrate well the difficulty Canadian prime ministers had, and still have, balancing Canadian public opinion and the undeniable power asymmetry between themselves and the United States.[71]

Present-day claims to the Arctic come from eight defined 'Arctic Nations' which, with the Ottawa Declaration of 1996, agreed to form the Arctic Council. This body came into being in 1998, comprising Canada, Denmark, Finland, Iceland, Norway, Russia, Sweden and the United States. The two stated aims of the council are to protect the environment in the region, and to explore sustainable development there. The council also gives a non-voting voice to native peoples across the Arctic Nations, as 'permanent participants' in the council. According to one US legal advisor, Canada initiated the formation of the Council, with the United States a more reluctant party to proceedings. As a result of US concerns, the council was formed *not* as a legally defined 'international organization', but rather as an 'informal cooperative structure'.[72] Even following the formation of the Arctic Council, the region has remained in relative flux and many of the nations involved have felt pressure to assert their sovereignty there. The Arctic might well prove to be the final frontier of US continental expansion, and it is a frontier that is still an ongoing concern.[73]

A 2009 Bush administration report on US interests in the Arctic noted the 'broad and fundamental' National Security and Homeland Security interests of the US in the region. The report suggested that the Arctic was key to US missile defence, early warning systems, strategic deterrence and particularly maritime security. It also noted how recent increases in human activity meant the United States needed to 'assert a more active and influential national presence' in line with its sovereign claims within the region, the sea, and to the continental shelf.[74] In 2013 the Obama administration issued a statement outlining a similar set of interests in the Arctic, citing defence as the top priority and, within the wider remit of defence, protecting energy security.[75] Indeed, though much US interest in the Arctic in the mid-twentieth century was military in perspective, by the mid-1960s the focus was beginning to encompass the potential of the Arctic as an area that would help provide security through energy independence. The region offered much in terms of oil, if it could be economically transported either by pipeline or by transportation via the Northwest Passage. This led to a protracted diplomatic joust between the United States and the then Canadian prime minster, Pierre Trudeau, over whether the Northwest Passage should be considered internal Canadian waters or an international asset. Consequently, Canada pursued an arguably superficial 'environmental stewardship' strategy to impose a unilaterally declared twelve-mile extent to its territorial waters. Trudeau's actions projected Canadian sovereignty in the face of the 'ever-expanding global reach of the United States in the post-1945 period'.[76]

Where Canada has been perhaps the most outspoken in its claims to North American territory stretching all the way to the Pole, the United States has taken almost the opposite view. From the US standpoint, the idea of claiming the Arctic Ocean and seabed initially seemed somewhat outlandish. This view was evident in the US reaction to the 2007 Russian claim to the Arctic symbolised by the planting of a Russian flag on the seabed at the North Pole.[77] Yet not long afterwards, the 2009 US report on the Arctic urged the Senate to accede to the UN Convention on the Law of the Sea not only to aid military defence of the area, but also to advance claims over marine areas in the Arctic and the 'valuable natural resources they claim'.[78] The report also focused on the issue of defining US claims to the Arctic seabed and subsoil in which it 'may exercise its sovereign rights over natural resources such as oil, natural gas, methane hydrates, minerals, and living marine species [which] is critical to our national interests in energy security, resource management, and environmental protection'.[79] A 2013 report built upon these foundations, highlighting changing climate conditions which were making the Arctic increasingly open to mineral exploitation:

> Scientific estimates of technically recoverable conventional oil and gas resources north of the Arctic Circle total approximately 13 percent of the world's undiscovered oil and 30 percent of the world's undiscovered gas deposits, as well as vast quantities of mineral resources, including rare earth elements, iron ore, and nickel. These estimates have inspired fresh ideas for commercial initiatives and infrastructure development in the region. As portions of the Arctic Ocean become more navigable, there is increasing interest in the viability of the Northern Sea Route and other potential routes, including the Northwest Passage, as well as in development of Arctic resources.[80]

Whatever the future holds for US claims to the Arctic, it is hard to dismiss the region, even if it primarily lies beneath water and ice, as a potential final frontier for United States imperialism in North America. Perhaps those who mocked Seward for his purchase of Alaska in 1867 were more mistaken in their estimation of the great frozen North's value than even our present generation has yet fully realised.

Notes

1. Beardsley, *Guam*, p. 194.
2. See especially Hezel, *Strangers in Their Own Land*, pp. 94–5.
3. Beardsley, *Guam*, p. 194.
4. McGrath, 'American Naval Period on Guam', pp. 42–3. See McGrath also for a detailed record of the naval administration's records concerning Guam.
5. Rottman, *Guam 1941 and 1944*, p. 13.
6. Rogers, *Destiny's Landfall*, pp. 135–40.
7. Burns, 'Inspection of Mandates', p. 445; Johnson, 'Trust Territory of the Pacific Islands', p. 233.
8. Hinz, *Pacific Island Battlegrounds*, p. 85; Rogers, *Destiny's Landfall*, p. 157.
9. Kiste, 'Termination of the US Trusteeship', p. 127.
10. Dempsey, 'Self-Determination and Security', p. 279.

11. 'International Trusteeship System', *United Nations*.
12. The Gilbert and Ellice Islands went on to gain independence from the UK separately as Kiribati (1979) and Tuvalu (1978) respectively.
13. Johnson, 'Trust Territory of the Pacific Islands', p. 234.
14. Dempsey, 'Self-Determination and Security', p. 282.
15. For in-depth coverage of the Guam Organic Act, see Rogers, *Destiny's Landfall*, pp. 224–44.
16. Kiste, 'Termination of the US Trusteeship', p. 128.
17. Dempsey, 'Self-Determination and Security', p. 283.
18. Ibid. pp. 283–5; 'Executive Order 11021', *US National Archives*.
19. Johnson, 'Trust Territory of the Pacific Islands', p. 237.
20. Kiste, 'Termination of the US Trusteeship', p. 129; Johnson, 'Trust Territory of the Pacific Islands', p. 238.
21. Kiste, 'Termination of the US Trusteeship', pp. 129–31.
22. Alkire, 'The Carolinians of Saipan', p. 270.
23. Dempsey, 'Self-Determination and Security', p. 278.
24. Alkire, 'The Carolinians of Saipan', pp. 270–5. The bulk of the population in the Northern Marianas was Chamorro, but there was a sizeable Carolinian population who feared domination when separated from the rest of the Caroline Islands. As Johnson, 'Trust Territory of the Pacific Islands', p. 235, notes, the administrative regions had some ethnic logic to them but were largely those previously used by the Germans and Japanese.
25. Hansen, *Guantánamo*, p. 26.
26. Ibid. p. 32.
27. Sigsbee quoted in Trask, *War with Spain*, p. 140.
28. Kaplan, 'Where is Guantánamo?', p. 837.
29. Lipman, *Guantánamo*, p. 24.
30. As Ellis, 'Problem of Guantánamo', p. 108, notes, the US naval base occupies only a small portion of the enormous natural bay on Cuba's south-eastern coast. Although a number of abbreviations are used for the US Naval Base at Guantanamo Bay, GTMO is the most common, and is favoured by the US military.
31. Platt Amendment, *Our Documents*.
32. Strauss, *Territorial Leasing*, p. 151.
33. Paterson, *Contesting Castro*, p. 61. The lease over GTMO itself is explored in: Strauss, *Leasing of Guantanamo Bay*.
34. Kaplan, 'Where is Guantánamo?', p. 837; Paterson, *Contesting Castro*, p. 62.
35. Lipman, *Guantánamo*, p. 27.
36. 'Treaty Between the United States of America and Cuba', *Avalon Project*. The treaty also notes that the area of GTMO remained as it stood in 1934 (given that it had expanded in 1912).

37. Kaplan, 'Where is Guantánamo?', p. 838.
38. Eisenhower, 1 November 1960, cited in L. Bender, 'Guantánamo', pp. 80–1.
39. Paterson, *Contesting Castro*, p. 62.
40. Bender, 'Guantánamo', p. 81.
41. Blight and Welch, *Intelligence and the Cuban Missile Crisis*, p. 165.
42. Strauss, *Leasing of Guantanamo Bay*, p. 109.
43. Bender, 'Guantánamo', p. 83.
44. Hanson Baldwin, former military editor of the *New York Times*, cited in ibid. p. 83.
45. Strauss, *Leasing of Guantanamo Bay*, p. 112.
46. Cooley, *Base Politics*, p. 5.
47. Vine, *Base Nation*; Lutz, 'Bases, Empire, and Global Response', pp. 1–46.
48. Howard, 'Franklin D. Roosevelt', p. 159.
49. Cited in High, *Base Colonies*, p. 18.
50. Ibid. p. 21, p. 9.
51. Vine, *Base Nation*, p. 2.
52. Ibid. pp. 2–3.
53. Lutz, 'Bases, Empire, and Global Response', p. 1, p. 6.
54. Vine, *Base Nation*, pp. 4–5.
55. For full coverage of Diego Garcia, see Vine, *Island of Shame*.
56. Lutz, 'Bases, Empire, and Global Response', p. 36.
57. If one takes the Arctic Circle as the imperfect guide, then much of Alaska falls inside the Arctic, as do the vast majority of Canada's northern islands and almost all of Greenland.
58. Grant, *Polar Imperative*, p. 10.
59. Doel et al., 'Strategic Arctic science', p. 68.
60. 'Loss of the Jeanette', *Washington Post*, p. 2.
61. Peary, 'How Peary Reached the North Pole'.
62. Henderson, 'Who Discovered the North Pole?'.
63. 'Canada's Farthest North', *New York Times*, p. 8.
64. Doel et al., 'Strategic Arctic science', p. 68.
65. 'Greenland Bases', *Washington Post*, p. 14.
66. 'Greenland's Future', *Washington Post*, p. 10.
67. Martin-Nielsen, 'The Other Cold War', p. 70.
68. Ibid. p. 71. As the author notes, Thule was the largest air base outside of the United States mainland.
69. Weir, 'Virtual War in the Ice Jungle', p. 413.
70. Lajeunesse, 'A Very Practical Requirement', p. 508.
71. James and James, 'Canada, the US and Arctic Sovereignty', p. 194.
72. Bloom, 'Establishment of the Arctic Council', p. 721.

73. For an excellent overview of recent literature on the future of the Arctic and international friction in the region see: Young, 'The Future of the Arctic', pp. 185–93.
74. Memorandum on US Arctic Region Policy, *Federation of American Scientists*, pp. 2–3.
75. 'National Strategy for the Arctic Region', *White House*, p. 9.
76. Meren and Plumptre, 'Rights of Passage', p. 172, p. 184.
77. Gerhardt et al., 'Contested Sovereignty', pp. 996–7.
78. Memorandum on US Arctic Region Policy, *Federation of American Scientists*, pp. 4–5.
79. Ibid.
80. 'National Strategy for the Arctic Region', *White House*, p. 6.

Conclusion

'American imperialism' remains a contested term and, though the weight of evidence presented here suggests that it is a viable one, even the relatively narrow usage within this book is bound to vex some. The American 'empire' has certainly evolved since its beginnings in the wake of the American Revolution, from continental to overseas and thence into a variety of different, and sometimes more abstruse, forms. From examining the subjugation of Native Americans and contrasting this to a not dissimilar picture in the Philippines, or considering the development of military occupations from the early-twentieth-century Caribbean to post-World War Two Germany and Japan, this book helps to encourage readers to appreciate important, if contestable, parallels in American imperial history. Indeed, by looking at the subject in the round, it is easier to see continuities as well as examples of where the experience of imperialism has been built upon and adapted in later manifestations.

Just as the nature of imperialist policy has altered, so have the debates over US imperialism in a multiplicity of geopolitical contexts. Judgements on whether, or how, to impose US sovereignty beyond its extant borders – permanently or temporarily – have punctuated US history from the beginning and are, almost always, accompanied by an element of hand-wringing over whether such extensions were (and are) in keeping with the ideals of the nation. Decisions over whether or not the US should be an empire resulted from (or perhaps more accurately, encouraged) large-scale conflicts, such as the Mexican-American and Spanish-American Wars. On other occasions such debates led to far less bloody resolutions, such as in Alaska, the US Virgin Islands or the Mariana Islands.

This book offers an accessible introduction to the subject of American imperialism, narrowly defined as territorial but broadly exemplified.[1] In addition, this volume provides an added level of context to its examination of American imperialism by exploring examples that never quite came to be, such as in Canada or Liberia.

Some readers might question certain inclusions, while others will probe what is missing, yet what is included provides the necessary coverage for students and enthusiasts of American history to form the starting point for their own investigations and research. The contested nature of the topics explored in this volume are certainly of continued significance, and while there is still a genuine debate about American imperialism in the world today there remains a need for the sort of discussion and analysis provided here.

This book strongly concurs with Niall Ferguson's contention that the United States has always been an empire.[2] By exploring the great variety of US imperial endeavours over the course of more than two centuries, the idea of the United States as anything other than an empire seems somewhat nonsensical. Indeed, from the very birth of the United States, founding father Thomas Jefferson envisaged the new nation as an 'Empire of Liberty', one which would need to acquire land to progress and prosper. The course of US history has certainly lived up to Jefferson's vision: there is scarcely a decade in which the discussion or realisation of imperial expansion has not taken place. Just as Jefferson's vision of an 'Empire of *Liberty*' was fraught with paradoxes – such as his 1820s advocacy of the diffusion of slavery throughout the Louisiana Purchase territories – so the United States has grappled throughout its history to come to terms with being a nation born of a rejection of empire, yet being one itself.[3] 'American imperialism' is not simply a catchphrase for those who seek to critique or demonise the United States, it is a phrase with deep roots and – though undoubtedly complex – it is a valid description of US expansionism throughout its history.

Notes

1. In line with the examples of American imperialism that MacDonald in 'Those who forget historiography', p. 50) sees as both straightforward (annexations) and more difficult to place (military occupations and overseas bases).
2. Ferguson, *Colossus*, pp. 2–6. Unlike Ferguson, though, this book does not take a political stance that advocates the embrace and expansion of American imperialism in the twenty-first century. Also, this book exemplifies American imperialism over a greater chronological span than Ferguson's more twentieth-century-focused work.
3. Jefferson, 'Letter to John Holmes', *Founders Online*.

Bibliography

Recommended Online Archives and Collections for Scholars

(* marks those which require a paid subscription, but many universities have this)

America: History and Life*
<https://www.ebscohost.com/academic/america-history-and-life>
A bibliographic resource and a great starting point for any research into the history of the United States.

American Memory, Library of Congress
<http://memory.loc.gov/ammem/index.html>
Provides access to primary resources in thematic sections.

The American Presidency Project, University of California, Santa Barbara
<http://www.presidency.ucsb.edu>
Contains a huge array of documents related to the presidency, including State of the Union addresses, public papers and executive orders, among a huge variety of primary documents.

The Avalon Project, Documents in Law, History and Diplomacy, Yale Law School <http://avalon.law.yale.edu>
A great source of official historical documents, especially the full text of treaties.

The Canadian Encyclopedia
<http://www.thecanadianencyclopedia.ca/en/>
An excellent, free online encyclopaedia of Canadian history.

Chronicling America: Historic American Newspapers, Library of Congress
<http://chroniclingamerica.loc.gov>
A huge array of digitised and searchable newspapers, with coverage from 1836–1922 at the time of writing.

Digital History, University of Houston
<http://www.digitalhistory.uh.edu>
An online archive of historical overviews and documents.

Google Scholar and Google Books
<https://scholar.google.co.uk>

<https://books.google.co.uk>
Increasingly a go-to for those searching for works on a particular subject that can later be accessed via online journal archives or university libraries.
JSTOR*
<http://www.jstor.org>
A digital library primarily comprising academic journal articles.
JUSTIA, US Supreme Court
<https://supreme.justia.com>
Online access to US Supreme Court decisions.
Library of Congress
<https://www.congress.gov/>
Searchable repository of US legislative bills.
Maps, Library of Congress
<https://www.loc.gov/maps/collections/>
A fantastic collection of digitised historical maps of the US.
Milestones in the History of US Foreign Relations, US Department of State, Office of the Historian
<https://history.state.gov/milestones>
Excellent short overviews of American foreign affairs.
The Miller Center, University of Virginia
<http://millercenter.org/president>
A detailed and accessible overview of every president, including details of specific administrations.
Our Documents, National Archives
<http://www.ourdocuments.gov/index.php?flash=true&>
Online access to photographed original documents from US history and their transcripts.
Perry-Castañeda Library Map Collection, University of Texas at Austin
<http://www.lib.utexas.edu/maps/>
An impressive archive of historical maps, most of which are not subject to copyright restrictions.
Political Graveyard
<http://politicalgraveyard.com>
A fantastic way to discover the identity of the more obscure congressmen in US history.
Project MUSE*
<http://muse.jhu.edu>
A great accompaniment to JSTOR as an archive of scholarly journal articles.
Proquest Historical Newspapers*
<http://www.proquest.com/libraries/schools/news-newspapers/>
Online, searchable access to many US and UK historical newspapers.

Newspaper Articles

'A Venture in Guano' (1898), *Washington Post*, 2 January, p. 6.
'Article 7 – No Title' (1866), *New York Times*, 20 July, p. 4.
'Bitter in Canada: Alaska Award Leads to Talk of Independence' (1903), *Washington Post*, 23 October, p. 1.
'Canada's Farthest North' (1909), *New York Times*, 7 October, p. 8.
'Danish West Indies' (1867), *New York Times*, 16 December, p. 1.
Glen, Francis Wayland (1900), 'The Danish West Indies', *New York Times*, 4 January, p. 8.
'Great Danger: Samoa Revolution May Lead to War' (1899), *Los Angeles Times*, 20 January, p. 1.
'Greenland Bases' (1947), *Washington Post*, 4 June, p. 14.
'Greenland's Future' (1947), *Washington Post*, 7 October, p. 10.
'Hay and Varilla Sign Canal Treaty' (1903), *Los Angeles Times*, 20 November, p. 1.
Jefferson, Thomas (1820), 'Letter to John Holmes', 22 April, *Founders Online*, <http://founders.archives.gov/documents/Jefferson/98-01-02-1234> (last accessed 18 July 2016).
'Loco Foco Motto' (1848), *Jeffersonian Republican* [Stroudsburg, PA], 15 June, p. 2.
'Lonely Midway Islands' (1904), *New York Times*, 6 March, p. 4.
'Loss of the Jeanette' (1882), *Washington Post*, 7 April, p. 2.
'Midway is Ready as Pacific Airport' (1935), *New York Times*, 7 June, p. 2.
Nevins, Peter J. (1902), 'Danish West Indies Question', *New York Times*, 7 September, p. 38.
'Our New Possessions on the Pacific Coast – Peaceable Annexation' (1867), *New York Times*, 22 September, p. 4.
'Our Samoan Relations' (1889), *New York Times*, 20 February, p. 3.
Paine, Elijah (1839), 'Colonization', *Vermont Phoenix*, 1 February, p. 1.
Peary, Robert E. (1909), 'How Peary Reached the North Pole', *New York Times*, 12 September, p. SM1.
'Quincy Adams Upon Genesis' (1846), *The Examiner* [eds Hunt, Fonblanque and Forster], 14 March, p. 162.
'Sale Planned Twice Before' (1916), *New York Times* 'Special', 21 February, p. 01.
'The Americans and the Guano Islands' (1852), *The Observer* [Manchester, UK], 22 August, p. 3.
'The Control of Samoa' (1889), *Washington Post*, 15 June, p. 1.
'The London Papers and the Oregon Question' (1846), *The Observer* [Manchester, UK], 9 March, p. 6.
'Treaty Signed for Danish West Indies' (1902), *Washington Post*, 25 January, p. 2.

Twain, Mark (1900), excerpt from the New York *Herald*, 15 October, reproduced at 'The World of 1898: The Spanish-American War', Library of Congress, <http://www.loc.gov/rr/hispanic/1898/twain.html> (last accessed 31 August 2016).

Government Documents and Political Speeches

'1844 Democratic Party Platform: May 27, 1844' (1844), *American Presidency Project*, <http://www.presidency.ucsb.edu/ws/?pid=29573> (last accessed 31 August 2016).

'Agreement Between the United States and Cuba for the Lease of Lands for Coaling and Naval Stations; February 23, 1903' (1903), *Avalon Project*, <http://avalon.law.yale.edu/20th_century/dip_cuba002.asp> (last accessed 31 August 2016).

'Articles of Confederation: March 1, 1781' (1781), *Avalon Project*, <http://avalon.law.yale.edu/18th_century/artconf.asp> (last accessed 31 August 2016).

Byrnes, James F. (1946), 'Restatement of Policy on Germany', speech, *US Diplomatic Mission to Germany*, <http://usa.usembassy.de/etexts/ga4-460906.htm> (last accessed 31 August 2016).

'Convention between the United States and Denmark' (1917), *US Department of the Interior*, <http://www.doi.gov/oia/about/upload/vitreaty.pdf> (last accessed 31 August 2016).

'Executive Order 11021– Administration of the Trust Territory of the Pacific Islands by the Secretary of the Interior' (1962), *US National Archives*, <http://www.archives.gov/federal-register/codification/executive-order/11021.html> (last accessed 31 August 2016).

Guano Island Act (1856), *American Memory*, <http://memory.loc.gov/cgi-bin/ampage?collId=llsl&fileName=011/llsl011.db&recNum=140> (last accessed 31 August 2016).

Helms-Burton Act (1996), *Library of Congress*, <https://www.congress.gov/bill/104th-congress/house-bill/927/text/enr> (last accessed 31 August 2016).

'International Trusteeship System' (n.d.), *United Nations*, <http://www.un.org/en/decolonization/its.shtml> (last accessed 31 August 2016).

Japanese Constitution (1947), *Prime Minister of Japan and His Cabinet*, <http://japan.kantei.go.jp/constitution_and_government_of_japan/constitution_e.html> (last accessed 31 August 2016).

Johnson, Andrew (1868), 'Fourth Annual Message: December 9, 1868', *American Presidency Project*, <http://www.presidency.ucsb.edu/ws/?pid=29509> (last accessed 31 August 2016).

'Joint Resolution of the Congress of the United States, March 1, 1845' (1845), Avalon Project, <http://avalon.law.yale.edu/19th_century/texan01.asp> (last accessed 31 August 2016).

Madison, James (1810), 'Proclamation 16: Taking Possession of Part of Louisiana: October 27, 1810', *American Presidency Project*, <http://www.presidency.ucsb.edu/ws/?pid=65912> (last accessed 31 August 2016).

Memorandum on US Arctic Region Policy (2009), *Federation of American Scientists Intelligence Resource Program*, <https://fas.org/irp/offdocs/nspd/nspd-66.pdf> (last accessed 31 August 2016).

'National Strategy for the Arctic Region: May 2013' (2013), *White House*, <https://www.whitehouse.gov/sites/default/files/docs/nat_arctic_strategy.pdf> (last accessed 31 August 2016).

Ostend Manifesto (1854), *American History Leaflets*, University of Virginia, <http://xroads.virginia.edu/~HYPER/HNS/Ostend/ostend.html> (last accessed 31 August 2016).

Platt Amendment (1903), *Our Documents*, <http://www.ourdocuments.gov/doc.php?flash=true&doc=55> (last accessed 31 August 2016).

'Preliminary Emancipation Proclamation, September 22, 1862' (1862), *US National Archives*, <http://www.archives.gov/exhibits/american_originals_iv/sections/transcript_preliminary_emancipation.html> (last accessed 31 August 2016).

'Republican Party Platform of 1900: June 19, 1900' (1900), *American Presidency Project*, <http://www.presidency.ucsb.edu/ws/?pid=29630> (last accessed 31 August 2016).

Roosevelt, Theodore (1903), 'Third Annual Message: December 7, 1903', *American Presidency Project*, <http://www.presidency.ucsb.edu/ws/?pid=29544> (last accessed 31 August 2016).

Roosevelt, Theodore (1904), 'Fourth Annual Message: December 6, 1904', *American Presidency Project*, <http://www.presidency.ucsb.edu/ws/?pid=29545> (last accessed 31 August 2016).

Teller Amendment (1898), *History of Cuba*, <http://www.historyofcuba.com/history/teller.htm> (last accessed 31 August 2016).

'The Alaska Boundary Case (Great Britain, United States)' (1903), *United Nations Office of Legal Affairs*, <http://legal.un.org/riaa/cases/vol_XV/481-540.pdf> (last accessed 31 August 2016).

Treaty Between the United States of America and Cuba: May 29, 1934 (1934), *Avalon Project*, <http://avalon.law.yale.edu/20th_century/dip_cuba001.asp> (last accessed 31 August 2016).

Treaty of Paris, 1783 (1783), *Avalon Project*, <http://avalon.law.yale.edu/18th_century/paris.asp> (last accessed 31 August 2016).

Treaty of Paris, 1898 (1898), *Avalon Project*, <http://avalon.law.yale.edu/19th_century/sp1898.asp> (last accessed 31 August 2016).

'US Insular Areas: Application of the US Constitution' (1997), *US Government Accountability Office*, <http://www.gao.gov/archive/1998/og98005.pdf> (last accessed 31 August 2016).

Books and Articles

'A Brief History of the Danish Virgin Islands' (n.d.), *Danish National Archives*, <http://www.virgin-islands-history.dk/eng/vi_hist.asp> (last accessed 31 August 2016).

Aguilar, Luis E. (1993), 'Cuba c. 1860 – c.1930', in L. Bethell (ed.), *Cuba: A Short History*, Cambridge: Cambridge University Press, pp. 21–56.

Alkire, William H. (1984), 'The Carolinians of Saipan and the Commonwealth of the Northern Mariana Islands', *Pacific Affairs*, 57: 2, 270–83.

Ambacher, Bruce (1973), 'George M. Dallas, Cuba, and the Election of 1856', *Pennsylvania Magazine of History and Biography*, 97: 3, 318–32.

Associated Press (2015), 'People from American Samoa don't have right to US citizenship, court rules', *The Guardian*, 5 June, <http://www.theguardian.com/travel/2015/jun/05/appeals-court-american-samoa-us-citizenship> (last accessed 31 August 2016).

Atkins, G. Pope, and Lamar C. Wilson (1988), *The Dominican Republic and the United States: From Imperialism to Transnationalism*, Athens: University of Georgia Press.

Azuma, Eiichiro (2009), 'Brokering Race, Culture, and Citizenship: Japanese Americans in Occupied Japan and Postwar National Inclusion', *Journal of American-East Asian Relations*, 16: 3, 183–211.

Bagley, Will (2010), *So Rugged and Mountainous: Blazing the Trails to Oregon and California, 1812–1848: Volume I*, Norman: University of Oklahoma Press.

Bank of Commerce (1917), *The Virgin Islands: A Description of the Commercial Value of the Danish West Indies*, New York: National Bank of Commerce, available at <http://www.archive.org/stream/virginislandsadoonewgoog/virginislandsadoonewgoog_djvu.txt> (last accessed 31 August 2016).

Baker, George W., Jr. (1966), 'The Wilson Administration and Nicaragua, 1913–1921', *The Americas*, 22: 4, 339–76.

Barker, Eugene C. (1946), 'The Annexation of Texas', *Southwestern Historical Quarterly*, 50: 1, 49–74.

Beardsley, Charles (1964), *Guam: Past and Present*, Rutland, VT: Tuttle Publishing.

Beisner, Robert L. (1968), *Twelve against Empire: The Anti-Imperialists, 1898–1900*, New York: McGraw-Hill.

Beisner, Robert L. (1982), 'Book Review: Thomas J. Osborne, "Empire Can Wait": American Opposition to Hawaiian Annexation, 1893–1898', *American Historical Review*, 87: 5, 1475–6.

Bellesiles, Michael A. (1987), 'The Establishment of Legal Structures on the Frontier: The Case of Revolutionary Vermont', *Journal of American History*, 73: 4, 895–915.

Bemis, Samuel Flagg (1936), *A Diplomatic History of the United States*, New York: Henry Holt.
Bender, Lynn D. (1973), 'Guantánamo: Its Political, Military and Legal Status', *Caribbean Quarterly*, 19: 1, 80–6.
Bender, P. (1883), 'A Canadian View of Annexation', *North American Review*, 136: 317, 326–37.
Bender, P. (1884), 'The Annexation of Canada', *North American Review*, 139: 332, 42–51.
Benjamin, Jules R. (1977), *The United States and Cuba: Hegemony and Dependent Development*, Pittsburgh, PA: Pittsburgh University Press.
Bennett, David (2014), *A Few Lawless Vagabonds: Ethan Allen, the Republic of Vermont, and the American Revolution*, Havertown, PA: Casemate.
Bergeron, Paul H. (ed.) (1998), *The Papers of Andrew Johnson: Volume 15*, Knoxville: University of Tennessee Press.
Beschloss, Michael (2002), *The Conquerors: Roosevelt, Truman and the Destruction of Hitler's Germany, 1941–1945*, New York: Simon & Schuster.
Black, Jeremy (2011), *Fighting for America: The Struggle for Mastery in North America, 1519–1871*, Bloomington: Indiana University Press.
Black, Lydia T. (2004), *Russians in Alaska, 1732–1867*, Fairbanks: University of Alaska Press.
Blight, James G., Bruce J. Allyn and David A. Welch (2002), *Cuba on the Brink: Castro, the Missile Crisis, and the Soviet Collapse*, Boston: Rowman & Littlefield.
Blight, James G., and David A. Welch (eds) (2003), *Intelligence and the Cuban Missile Crisis*, Abingdon: Frank Cass.
Bloom, Evan T. (1999), 'Establishment of the Arctic Council', *American Journal of International Law*, 93: 3, 712–22.
Blyden, Nemata Amelia (2004), '"Back to Africa": The Migration of New World Blacks to Sierra Leone and Liberia', *OAH Magazine of History*, 18: 3, 23–5.
Boehling, Rebecca L. (1996), *A Question of Priorities: Democratic Reforms and Economic Recovery in Postwar Germany*, Providence, RI: Berghahn Books.
Boehling, Rebecca L. (1999), 'The Role of Culture in American Relations with Europe: The Case of the United States' Occupation of Germany', *Diplomatic History* 23: 1, 57–69.
Borneman, Walter R. (2004), *1812: The War that Forged a Nation*, New York: HarperCollins.
Bosque-Pérez, Ramón (2006), 'Political Persecution against Puerto Rican Anti-Colonial Activists in the Twentieth Century', in R. Bosque-Pérez and J. J. Colón Morera (eds), *Puerto Rico Under Colonial Rule:*

Political Persecution and the Quest for Human Rights, Albany: State University of New York Press, pp. 13–48.

Boyd, Willis Dolmond (1956), 'Negro Colonization in the Reconstruction Era 1865–1870', *Georgia Historical Quarterly*, 40: 4, 360–82.

Braibanti, Ralph (1954), 'The Ryukyu Islands: Pawn of the Pacific', *American Political Science Review*, 48: 4, 972–98.

Brands, H. W. (1992), *Bound to Empire: The United States and the Philippines*, Oxford: Oxford University Press.

Brown, Dee (1971), *Bury My Heart at Wounded Knee: An Indian History of the American West*, London: Barrie & Jenkins.

Buchenau, Jürgen (1993), 'Counter-intervention against Uncle Sam: Mexico's Support for Nicaraguan Nationalism, 1903–1910', *The Americas* 50: 2, 207–32.

Buckley, Roger (1982), *Occupation Diplomacy: Britain, the United States and Japan, 1945–1952*, Cambridge: Cambridge University Press.

Buhite, Russell D. (1986), *Decisions at Yalta: An Appraisal of Summit Diplomacy*, Lanham, MD: SR Books.

Burnett, Christina D. (2005), 'The Edges of Empire and the Limits of Sovereignty: American Guano Islands', *American Quarterly*, 57: 3, 779–803.

Burnett, Christina Duffy, and Burke Marshall (2001), 'Between the Foreign and the Domestic: The Doctrine of Territorial Incorporation, Invented and Reinvented', in C. Duffy Burnett and B. Marshall (eds), *Foreign in a Domestic Sense: Puerto Rico, American Expansion and the Constitution*, Durham, NC: Duke University Press, pp. 1–38.

Burns, Adam (2010), 'An Imperial Vision: William Howard Taft and the Philippines, 1900–1921', unpublished PhD dissertation (University of Edinburgh), <https://www.era.lib.ed.ac.uk/handle/1842/4506> (last accessed 31 August 2016).

Burns, Adam (2010), 'Without Due Process: Albert E. Pillsbury and the Hoar Anti-Lynching Bill', *American Nineteenth Century History*, 11: 2, 233–52.

Burns, Adam (2011), 'Winning "Hearts and Minds": American Imperial Designs of the Early Twentieth and Twenty-First Centuries', *History & Policy*, 1 October, <http://www.historyandpolicy.org/papers/policy-paper-123.html> (last accessed 31 August 2016).

Burns, Adam (2013), 'Adapting to Empire: William H. Taft, Theodore Roosevelt, and the Philippines, 1900–1908', *Comparative American Studies*, 11: 4, 418–33.

Burns, Adam (2013), 'Retentionist in Chief: William Howard Taft and the Question of Philippine Independence, 1912–1916', *Philippine Studies: Historical and Ethnographic Viewpoints*, 61: 2, 163–92.

Burns, Adam (2015), 'William Howard Taft', in C. Magoc and D. Bernstein (eds), *Imperialism and Expansionism in American History: A Social,*

Political, and Cultural Encyclopedia and Document Collection, Volume 3, Santa Barbara, CA: ABC-CLIO, pp. 850–1.
Burns, Richard Dean (1968), 'Inspection of the Mandates, 1919–1941', *Pacific Historical Review*, 37: 4, 445–62.
Bush, Robert D. (2014), *The Louisiana Purchase: A Global Context*, New York: Routledge.
Byrd, Brandon R. (2015), 'Black Republicans, Black Republic: African-Americans, Haiti, and the Promise of Reconstruction', *Slavery & Abolition*, 36: 4, 545–67.
Calder, Bruce J. (1984), *The Impact of Intervention: The Dominican Republic During the U.S. Occupation of 1916–1924*, Austin: University of Texas Press.
Campbell, W. E. (2013), *The Aroostook War of 1839*, Fredericton, NB: Goose Lane Editions.
Caron, James E. (2008), 'The Blessings of Civilization: Mark Twain's Anti-Imperialism and the Annexation of the Hawai'ian Islands', *Mark Twain Annual*, 6: 1, 51–63.
Chaffin, Tom (2003), *Fatal Glory: Narciso López and the First Clandestine U.S. War Against Cuba*, Baton Rouge: Louisiana State University Press.
Chambers, Frank Taylor (1905), 'American Samoa', *Bulletin of the American Geographical Society*, 37: 11, 641–7.
Chock, Jennifer M. L. (1995), 'One Hundred Years of Illegitimacy: International Legal Analysis of the Illegal Overthrow of the Hawaiian Monarchy, Hawai'i's Annexation, and Possible Reparations', *University of Hawai'i Law Review*, 17, 463–512.
Churchill, Ward (1997), *A Little Matter of Genocide: Holocaust and Denial in the Americas 1492 to the Present*, San Francisco: City Lights Books.
Cleaver, Nick (2014), *Grover Cleveland's New Foreign Policy: Arbitration, Neutrality, and the Dawn of American Empire*, London: Palgrave Macmillan.
Cogliano, Francis D. (2014), *Emperor of Liberty: Thomas Jefferson's Foreign Policy*, New Haven, CT: Yale University Press.
Coletta, Paolo E. (1957), 'Bryan, McKinley, and the Treaty of Paris', *Pacific Historical Review*, 26: 2, 131–46.
Coletta, Paolo E. (1961), 'McKinley, the Peace Negotiations, and the Acquisition of the Philippines', *Pacific Historical Review*, 30: 4, 341–50.
Cooke, Adam (2010), '"An Unpardonable Bit of Folly and Impertinence": Charles Francis Adams Jr., American Anti-Imperialists, and the Philippines', *New England Quarterly*, 83: 2, 313–38.
Cooley, Alexander (2008), *Base Politics: Democratic Change and the U.S. Military Overseas*, Ithaca, NY: Cornell University Press.
Crapol, Edward P. (2000), *James G. Blaine: Architect of Empire*, Wilmington, DE: Scholarly Resources.

Cullinane, Michael Patrick (2012), *Liberty and American Anti-Imperialism, 1898–1909*, London: Palgrave Macmillan.
Currie, David P. (2000), 'Rumors of Wars: Presidential and Congressional War Powers, 1809–1829', *University of Chicago Law Review*, 67: 1, 1–40.
Dalton, Kathleen (2002), *Theodore Roosevelt: A Strenuous Life*, New York: Vintage.
Dando-Collins, Stephen (2008), *Tycoon's War: How Cornelius Vanderbilt Invaded a Country to Overthrow America's Most Famous Military Adventurer*, Cambridge, MA: Da Capo Press.
Daugherty, Leo J. III (2015), *Counterinsurgency and the United States Marine Corps: Volume 1, The First Counterinsurgency Era, 1899–1945*, Jefferson, NC: McFarland & Co.
Davis, Janet M. (2002), *The Circus Age: Culture and Society Under the American Big Top*, Chapel Hill: University of North Carolina Press.
Davis, William C. (2013), 'The History of the Short-Lived Independent Republic of Florida', *Smithsonian Magazine*, May, <http://www.smithsonianmag.com/history/the-history-of-the-short-lived-independent-republic-of-florida-28056078/?no-ist> (last accessed 31 August 2016).
De Santis, Hugh (1981), 'The Imperialist Impulse and American Innocence, 1865–1900', in G. K. Haines and J. S. Walker (eds), *American Foreign Relations: A Historiographical Review*, Westport, CT: Greenwood Press, pp. 64–90.
DeLay, Brian (2015), 'Indian Polities, Empire, and the History of American Foreign Relations', *Diplomatic History*, 39: 5, 927–42.
Dempsey, Guy (1976), 'Self-Determination and Security in the Pacific: A Study of the Covenant between the United States and the Northern Mariana Islands', *NYUJ International Law and Politics*, 9, 277.
Devine, Michael J. (1977), 'John W. Foster and the Struggle for the Annexation of Hawaii', *Pacific Historical Review*, 46: 1, 29–50.
Dickerson, Donna L. (2003), *The Reconstruction Era: Primary Documents on Events from 1865–1877*, Westport, CT: Greenwood Press.
Diefendorf, Jeffry M., Axel Frohn and Hermann-Josef Rupieper (eds) (1994), *American Policy and the Reconstruction of West Germany, 1945–1955*, Cambridge: Cambridge University Press.
Dietrich, John (2013), *The Morgenthau Plan: Soviet Influence on American Postwar Policy*, New York: Agora Publishing.
Dietz, James L (1986), *Economic History of Puerto Rico: Institutional Change and Capitalist Development*, Princeton, NJ: Princeton University Press.
Dinwoodie, David H. (1970), 'Dollar Diplomacy in the Light of the Guatemalan Loan Project, 1909–1913', *The Americas*, 26: 3, 237–53.

Dodd, Douglas W. (2002), 'Oregon Country', in J. Rodriguez (ed.), *Louisiana Purchase: A Historical and Geographical Encyclopedia*, Santa Barbara, CA: ABC-CLIO, pp. 263–5.

Doel, Ronald E., Robert M. Friedman, Julia Lajus, Sverker Sörlin and Urban Wråkberg (2014), 'Strategic Arctic science: national interests in building natural knowledge – interwar era through the Cold War', *Journal of Historical Geography*, 44, 60–80.

Dohnal, Cheri (2003), *Columbia River Gorge: Natural Treasure on the Old Oregon Trail*, Charleston, SC: Arcadia Publishing.

Dookhan, Isaac (2002), *A History of the Virgin Islands of the United States*, Kingston, Jamaica: Canoe Press.

Dorn, Walter L. (1957), 'The Debate over American Occupation Policy in Germany in 1944–1945', *Political Science Quarterly*, 72: 4, 481–501.

Dower, John W. (1999), *Embracing Defeat: Japan in the Wake of World War II*, London: Allen Lane.

Drez, Ronald J. (2014), *The War of 1812, Conflict and Deception: The British Attempt to Seize New Orleans and Nullify the Louisiana Purchase*, Baton Rouge: Louisiana State University Press.

Drinnon, Richard (1980), *Facing West: the Metaphysics of Indian Hating and Empire-Building*, Minneapolis: University of Minnesota Press.

Duignan, Peter, and L. H. Gann (1987), *The United States and Africa: A History*, Cambridge: Cambridge University Press.

Dulles, Foster Rhea (1963), *America's Rise to World Power, 1898–1954*, New York: Harper Torchbooks.

Ealy, Lawrence (1958), 'The Development of an Anglo-American System of Law in the Panama Canal Zone', *American Journal of Legal History*, 2: 4, 283–303.

Ellis, Richard J. (2010), '"I know for certain . . . that these are bad people": The Intractable Problem of Guantánamo', *Comparative American Studies*, 8: 3,169–84.

Elman, Colin (2004), 'Extending Offensive Realism: The Louisiana Purchase and America's Rise to Regional Hegemony', *American Political Science Review*, 98: 4, 563–76.

Emmerich, Alexander (2013), *John Jacob Astor and the First Great American Fortune*, Jefferson, NC: McFarland & Co.

Falkner, Roland P. (1910), 'The United States and Liberia', *American Journal of International Law*, 4: 3, 529–45.

Fellow, Anthony R. (2013), *American Media History*, 3rd edition, Boston: Wadsworth.

Ferguson, Niall (2005), *Colossus: The Rise and Fall of the American Empire*, London: Penguin.

Ferrer, Ada (1999), *Insurgent Cuba: Race, Nation, and Revolution, 1868–1898*, Chapel Hill: University of North Carolina Press.

Fifield, Anna (2016), 'In Okinawa, protesters dig in as work proceeds to relocate U.S. Marine base', *Washington Post*, 7 February, <https://www.washingtonpost.com/world/asia_pacific/in-okinawa-protesters-dig-in-as-work-proceeds-to-relocate-us-marine-base/2016/02/06/82d05264-c481-11e5-b933-31c93021392a_story.html> (last accessed 31 August 2016).
Fitzgibbon, Russell H. (1964), *Cuba and the United States, 1900–1935*, New York: Russell & Russell.
Foner, Eric (2010), *The Fiery Trial: Abraham Lincoln and American Slavery*, New York: W. W. Norton.
Foner, Philip S. (1972), *The Spanish-Cuban-American War and the Birth of American Imperialism, 1895–1902: Volume I*, New York: Monthly Review Press.
Font-Guzmán, Jacqueline N. (2015), *Experiencing Puerto Rican Citizenship and Cultural Nationalism*, Basingstoke: Palgrave Macmillan.
Foster, Charles I. (1953), 'The Colonization of Free Negroes, in Liberia, 1816–1835', *Journal of Negro History*, 38: 1, 41–66.
Freehling, William W. (1991), *The Road to Disunion: Secessionists at Bay, 1776–1854*, Oxford: Oxford University Press.
Friedlander, Robert A. (1961), 'A Reassessment of Roosevelt's Role in the Panamanian Revolution of 1903', *Western Political Quarterly*, 14: 2, 535–43.
Fry, Joseph A. (1979), 'William McKinley and the Coming of the Spanish-American War: A Study of the Besmirching and Redemption of an Historical Image', *Diplomatic History*, 3: 1, 77–98.
Fulbrook, Mary (2009), *A History of Germany, 1918–2008: The Divided Nation*, Malden, MA: Wiley-Blackwell.
Gates, John M. (1973), *Schoolbooks and Krags: The United States Army and the Philippines, 1898–1902*, Westport, CT: Greenwood Press.
Gates, John M. (1977), 'Philippine Guerrillas, American Anti-Imperialists, and the Election of 1900', *Pacific Historical Review*, 46: 1, 51–64.
Gatewood, Willard B., Jr. (1972), 'Black Americans and the Quest for Empire, 1898–1903', *Journal of Southern History*, 38: 4, 545–66.
Gerhardt, H., P. E. Steinberg, J. Tasch, S. J. Fabiano and R. Shields (2010), 'Contested sovereignty in a changing Arctic', *Annals of the Association of American Geographers*, 100: 4, 992–1002.
Gewertz, Ken (2004), 'Looking at Germany, Japan, Iraq: A tale of three occupations', *Harvard Gazette*, 18 March, <http://news.harvard.edu/gazette/2004/03.18/13-democratization.html> (last accessed 1 April 2016).
Gilliam, Angela, and Lenora Foerstel (1992), 'Margaret Mead's Contradictory Legacy', in L. Foerstel and A. Gilliam (eds), *Confronting the Margaret Mead Legacy: Scholarship, Empire, and the South Pacific*, Philadelphia: Temple University Press, pp. 101–58.

Gimbel, John (1968), *The American Occupation of Germany: Politics and the Military, 1945–1949*, Stanford: Stanford University Press.

Gleeck, Lewis E., Jr. (1984), *The American Half-Century, 1898–1946*, Quezon City: Historical Conservation Society.

Go, Julian (2008), *American Empire and the Politics of Meaning: Elite Political Cultures in the Philippines and Puerto Rico during U.S. Colonialism*, Durham, NC: Duke University Press.

Gobat, Michel (2005), *Confronting the American Dream: Nicaragua under U.S. Imperial Rule*, Durham, NC: Duke University Press.

Golay, Frank H. (1997), *Face of Empire: United States-Philippine Relations, 1898–1946*, Quezon City: Ateneo de Manila University Press.

Goldfrank, David M. (2013), *The Origins of the Crimean War*, Abingdon: Routledge.

Goldstein, Alyosha (2014), 'Towards a Genealogy of U.S. Colonial Present', in A. Goldstein (ed.), *Formations of United States Colonialism*, Durham, NC: Duke University Press, pp. 1–32.

Gott, Richard (2005), *Cuba: A New History*, New Haven, CT: Yale Nota Bene.

Gould, Lewis L. (1982), *The Spanish-American War and President McKinley*, Lawrence: University Press of Kansas.

Grant, Shelagh D. (2010), *Polar Imperative: A History of Arctic Sovereignty in North America*, Vancouver: Douglas & McIntyre.

Grieb, Kenneth J. (1969), 'Warren G. Harding and the Dominican Republic U.S. Withdrawal, 1921–1923', *Journal of Inter-American Studies*, 11: 3, 425–40.

Griswold del Castillo, Richard (1990), *The Treaty of Guadalupe Hidalgo: A Legacy of Conflict*, Norman: University of Oklahoma Press.

Guyatt, Nicholas (2011), 'America's Conservatory: Race, Reconstruction, and the Santo Domingo Debate', *Journal of American History*, 97: 4, 974–1000.

Haglund, David G., and Tudor Onea (2008), 'Victory without Triumph: Theodore Roosevelt, Honour, and the Alaska Panhandle Boundary Dispute', *Diplomacy & Statecraft*, 19: 1, 20–41.

Hämäläinen, Pekka (2008), *The Comanche Empire*, New Haven, CT: Yale University Press.

Hamilton, Richard F. (2006), *President McKinley, War and Empire: Volume 1 – President McKinley and the Coming of War, 1898*, Piscataway, NJ: Transaction Publishers.

Hansen, Jonathan M. (2011), *Guantánamo: An American History*, New York: Hill & Wang.

Harrington, Peter (2011), 'Photography (Spanish-American War)', in M. J. Manning and C. R. Wyatt (eds), *Encyclopedia of Media and Propaganda in Wartime America, Volume 1*, Santa Barbara: ABC-CLIO, pp. 419–20.

Harrison, Benjamin (1995), 'The United States and the 1909 Nicaragua Revolution', *Caribbean Quarterly*, 41: 3–4, 45–63.
Harrison, Benjamin (2005), 'Woodrow Wilson and Nicaragua', *Caribbean Quarterly*, 51: 1, 25–36.
Haycox, Stephen W., and Mary Childers Mangusso (eds) (1996), *An Alaska Anthology: Interpreting the Past*, Seattle: University of Washington Press.
Healy, David (1970), *US Expansionism: The Imperialist Urge in the 1890s*, Madison: Wisconsin University Press.
Henderson, Bruce (2009), 'Who Discovered the North Pole?' *Smithsonian Magazine*, April, <http://www.smithsonianmag.com/history/who-discovered-the-north-pole-116633746/?no-ist> (last accessed 31 August 2016).
Hendrickson, Kenneth E., Jr. (1967), 'Reluctant Expansionist: Jacob Gould Schurman and the Philippine Question', *Pacific Historical Review*, 36: 4, 405–21.
Hendrickson, Kenneth E., Jr. (2003), *The Spanish-American War*, Westport, CT: Greenwood Press.
Hernández, José M. (1993), *Cuba and the United States: Intervention and Militarism, 1868–1933*, Austin: University of Texas Press.
Herring, George C. (2008), *From Colony to Superpower: U.S. Foreign Relations since 1776*, Oxford: Oxford University Press.
Hezel, Francis X. (2003), *Strangers in Their Own Land: A Century of Colonial Rule in the Caroline and Marshall Islands*, Honolulu: Hawaii University Press.
Hickey, Donald (2012), *The War of 1812: A Forgotten Conflict*, Champaign: Illinois University Press.
High, Steven (2009), *Base Colonies in the Western Hemisphere, 1940–1967*, New York: Palgrave Macmillan.
Hilfrich, Fabian (2012), *Debating American Exceptionalism: Empire and Democracy in the Wake of the Spanish-American War*, London: Palgrave Macmillan.
Hinckley, Ted C. (1973), 'Alaska as an American Botany Bay', *Pacific Historical Review*, 42: 10, 1–19.
Hinz, Earl (1995), *Pacific Island Battlegrounds of World War II: Then and Now*, Honolulu: Bess Press.
Hitchman, James H. (1967), 'The Platt Amendment Revisited: A Bibliographical Survey', *The Americas*, 23: 4, 343–69.
Hogan, J. Michael (1986), *The Panama Canal in American Politics: Domestic Advocacy and the Evolution of Policy*, Carbondale: Southern Illinois University Press.
Hoganson, Kristin L. (1998), *Fighting for American Manhood: How Gender Politics Provoked the Spanish-American and Philippine-American Wars*, New Haven, CT: Yale University Press.

Holmes, James R. (2006), *Theodore Roosevelt and World Order: Police Power in International Relations*, Dulles, VA: Potomac Books.
Holt, Michael F. (2003), *The Rise and Fall of the American Whig Party: Jacksonian Politics and the Onset of the Civil War*, Oxford: Oxford University Press.
Howard, Thomas C. (2003), 'Franklin D. Roosevelt, the Caribbean, and the Postcolonial World', in T. C. Howard and W. D. Pederson (eds), *Franklin D. Roosevelt and the Formation of the Modern World*, Armonk, NY: M. E. Sharpe, pp. 157–68.
Howe, Daniel Walker (1979), *The Political Culture of the American Whigs*, Chicago: University of Chicago Press.
Hunt, Michael H. (1987), *Ideology and U.S. Foreign Policy*, New Haven, CT: Yale University Press.
Immerman, Richard H. (2010), *Empire for Liberty: A History of American Imperialism from Benjamin Franklin to Paul Wolfowitz*, Princeton, NJ: Princeton University Press.
Immerwahr, Daniel (2016), 'The Greater United States: Territory and Empire in US History', *Diplomatic History*, 40: 3, 373–91.
Iokibe, Makoto (2011), 'Diplomacy in occupied Japan: Japanese diplomacy in the 1940s', in M. Iokibe (ed.) and R. Eldridge (trans.), *The Diplomatic History of Postwar Japan*, London: Routledge, pp. 17–49.
Iriye, Akira (1981), *Power and Culture: The Japanese-American War, 1941–1945*, Cambridge, MA: Harvard University Press.
Jackson, C. Ian (1967), 'The Stikine Territory Lease and Its Relevance to the Alaska Purchase', *Pacific Historical Review*, 36: 3, 289–306.
James, Carolyn C., and Patrick James (2014), 'Canada, the United States and Arctic Sovereignty: Architecture without Building?' *American Review of Canadian Studies*, 44: 2: 187–204.
Jenks, Leland Hamilton (1928), *Our Cuban Colony: A Study in Sugar*, New York: Vanguard Press.
Johnson, Donald (1970), 'The Trust Territory of the Pacific Islands', *Current History*, 58: 344, 233–9.
Jonas, Manfred (1984), *The United States and Germany: A Diplomatic History*, Ithaca, NY: Cornell University Press.
Jones, Howard (2009), *Crucible of Power: A History of American Foreign Relations to 1913*, Lanham, MD: Rowman & Littlefield.
Jones, Maldwyn Allen (1995), *The Limits of Liberty: American History, 1607–1992*, Oxford: Oxford University Press.
Juárez, Joseph R. (1962), 'United States Withdrawal from Santo Domingo', *Hispanic American Historical Review*, 42: 2, 152–90.
Kaplan, Amy (2005), 'Where is Guantánamo?' *American Quarterly*, 57: 3, 831–58.

Kaplan, Lawrence S. (1999), *Thomas Jefferson: Westward the Course of Empire*, Wilmington, DE: Scholarly Resources.
Karnow, Stanley (1990), *In Our Image: America's Empire in the Philippines*, London: Century.
Kashay, Jennifer Fish (2007), 'Agents of Imperialism: Missionaries and Merchants in Early-Nineteenth-Century Hawaii', *New England Quarterly*, 80: 2, 280–98.
Kennedy, Charles Stuart (1990), *The American Consul: A History of the United States Consular Service, 1776–1914*, New York: Greenwood Press.
Kennedy, Robert C. (n.d.), 'On this Day, June 19, 1886: Our Next Haul', *New York Times*, <http://www.nytimes.com/learning/general/onthisday/harp/0619.html> (last accessed 31 August 2016).
Kidwell, Clara Sue (2008), *The Chocktaws in Oklahoma: From Tribe to Nation, 1855–1970*, Norman: University of Oklahoma Press.
Kiste, Robert C. (1986), 'Termination of the U.S. Trusteeship in Micronesia', *Journal of Pacific History*, 21: 3, 127–38.
Kiste, Robert C. (1994), 'United States', in K. Howe, R. Kiste and B. Lal (eds), *Tides of History: The Pacific Islands in the Twentieth Century*, Honolulu: University of Hawaii Press, pp. 227–57.
Koikari, Mire (1999), 'Rethinking gender and power in the US occupation of Japan, 1945–1952', *Gender & History*, 11: 2, 313–35.
Koikari, Mire (2008), *Pedagogy of Democracy: Feminism and the Cold War in the U.S. Occupation of Japan*, Philadelphia: Temple University Press.
Kotlowski, Dean (2010), 'Independence or Not? Paul V. McNutt, Manuel L. Quezon, and the Re-examination of Philippine Independence, 1937–9', *International History Review*, 32: 3, 501–31.
Kramer, Paul (2006), *The Blood of Government: Race, Empire, the United States and the Philippines*, Chapel Hill: University of North Carolina Press.
La Croix, Sumner J., and Christopher Grandy (1997), 'The Political Instability of Reciprocal Trade and the Overthrow of the Hawaiian Kingdom', *Journal of Economic History*, 57: 1, 161–89.
LaFeber, Walter (1963), *The New Empire: An Interpretation of American Expansion, 1860–1898*, Ithaca, NY: Cornell University Press.
LaFeber, Walter (1994), *The American Age: U.S. Foreign Policy at Home and Abroad, 1750 to the Present*, New York: W. W. Norton.
Lajeunesse, A. (2013), 'A very practical requirement: under-ice operations in the Canadian Arctic, 1960–1986', *Cold War History*, 13: 4, 507–24.
Langley, Lester D. (1983), *The Banana Wars: An Inner History of the American Empire, 1900–1934*, Lexington: University Press of Kentucky.

Lasch, Christopher (1958), 'The Anti-Imperialists, the Philippines, and the Inequality of Man', *Journal of Southern History*, 24: 3, 319–31.
Laughlin, Stanley K., Jr. (1982), 'United States Government Policy and Social Stratification in American Samoa', *Oceania*, 53: 1, 29–38.
Lawson, Gary, and Guy Seidman (2004), *The Constitution of Empire: Territorial Expansion and American Legal History*, New Haven, CT: Yale University Press.
Leonard, Thomas M. (2001), *James K. Polk: A Clear and Unquestionable Destiny*, Wilmington, DE: Scholarly Resources.
Leonard, Thomas M. (2004), *Encyclopedia of Cuban-United States Relations*, Jefferson, NC: McFarland & Co.
Lepore, Jill (1998), *The Name of War: King Philip's War and the Origins of American Identity*, New York: Alfred A. Knopf.
Lewkowicz, Nicolas (2008), *The German Question and the Origins of the Cold War*, Milan: IPOC.
Linn, Brian McAllister (2000), *The Philippine War, 1899–1902*, Lawrence: University Press of Kansas.
Lipman, Jana K. (2009), *Guantánamo: A Working-Class History between Empire and Revolution*, Berkeley: University of California Press.
Lutz, Catherine (2009), 'Introduction: Bases, Empire, and Global Response', in C. Lutz (ed.), *The Bases of Empire: The Global Struggle Against U.S. Military Posts*, New York: New York University Press, pp. 1–46.
Maass, Richard W. (2015), '"Difficult to Relinquish Territory Which Had Been Conquered": Expansionism and the War of 1812', *Diplomatic History*, 39: 1, 70–97.
McAfee, Ward (1980), 'A Reconsideration of the Origins of the Mexican-American War', *Southern California Quarterly*, 62: 1, 49–65.
McCallum, Jack Edward (2006), *Leonard Wood: Rough Rider, Surgeon, Architect of American Imperialism*, New York: New York University Press.
McCoy, Alfred W., Francisco A. Scarano and Courtney Johnson (2009), 'On the Tropic of Cancer: Transitions and Transformations in the U.S. Imperial State', in A. McCoy and F. Scarano (eds), *Colonial Crucible: Empire in the Making of the Modern American State*, Madison: Wisconsin University Press, pp. 3–33.
McCulloch, Tony (2011), 'Theodore Roosevelt and Canada: Alaska, the "Big Stick" and the North Atlantic Triangle, 1901–1909', in S. Ricard (ed.), *A Companion to Theodore Roosevelt*, Malden, MA: Wiley-Blackwell, pp. 293–313.
McCurry, Justin (2013), 'China lays claim to Okinawa as territory dispute with Japan escalates', *Guardian*, 15 May, <http://www.theguardian.com/world/2013/may/15/china-okinawa-dispute-japan-ryukyu> (last accessed 31 August 2016).

MacDonald, Paul K. (2009), 'Those who forget historiography are doomed to republish it: empire, imperialism and contemporary debates about American power', *Review of International Studies*, 35: 1, 45–67.
McGrath, Thomas B. (1981), 'Records of the American Naval Period on Guam 1898–1950', *Journal of Pacific History*, 16: 1, 42–53.
Mackin, Anne (2006), *Americans and their Land: The House Built on Abundance*, Ann Arbor: University of Michigan Press.
McLaughlin, Shaun J. (2013), *The Patriot War Along the Michigan-Canada Border: Raiders and Rebels*, Charleston, SC: The History Press.
McMichael, F. Andrew (2008), *Americans in Spanish West Florida, 1785–1810*, Athens: University of Georgia Press.
McPherson, Alan (2004), 'Courts of World Opinion: Trying the Panama Flag Riots of 1964', *Diplomatic History*, 28: 1, 83–112.
McPherson, Alan (2012), 'The Irony of Legal Pluralism in U.S. Occupations', *American Historical Review*, 117: 4, 1149–72.
McPherson, Alan (2014), 'Herbert Hoover, Occupation Withdrawal, and the Good Neighbor Policy', *Presidential Studies Quarterly*, 44: 4, 623–39.
Madsen, Grant (2012), 'Becoming a State-in-the-World: Lessons Learned from the American Occupation of Germany', *Studies in American Political Development*, 26, 163–79.
Magness, Phillip W., and Sebastian N. Page (2011), *Colonization after Emancipation: Lincoln and the Movement for Black Resettlement*, Columbia: University of Missouri Press.
Mahan, Alfred Thayer (1890), *The Influence of Sea Power upon History, 1660–1783*, Boston: Little, Brown & Co.
Manela, Erez (2007), *The Wilsonian Moment: Self-Determination and the International Origins of Anticolonial Nationalism*, Oxford: Oxford University Press.
Marks, Frederick W. III (1979), *Velvet on Iron: The Diplomacy of Theodore Roosevelt*, Lincoln: University of Nebraska Press.
Martin, Susan F. (2011), *A Nation of Immigrants*, Cambridge: Cambridge University Press.
Martínez, Rubén Berríos (1997), 'Puerto Rico's Decolonization', *Foreign Affairs*, 76: 6, 100–14.
Martin-Nielsen, J. (2012), 'The other cold war: The United States and Greenland's ice sheet environment, 1948–1966', *Journal of Historical Geography*, 38: 1, 69–80.
Massachusetts Colonization Society (1831), *American Colonization Society, and the Colony at Liberia*, Boston: Pierce & Parker.
Maurer, Noel, and Carlos Yu (2010), *The Big Ditch: How America Took, Built, Ran, and Ultimately Gave Away the Panama Canal*, Princeton: Princeton University Press.

May, Ernest R. (1973), *Imperial Democracy: The Emergence of America as a Great Power*, New York: Harper Torchbooks.

May, Robert E. (2002), *Manifest Destiny's Underworld: Filibustering in Antebellum America*, Chapel Hill: University of North Carolina Press.

Meiser, Jeffrey W. (2015), *Power and Restraint: The Rise of the United States, 1898–1941*, Washington, DC: Georgetown University Press.

Meleisea, Malama, and Penelope Schoeffel Meleisea (1987), *Lagaga: A Short History of Western Samoa*, Suva: South Pacific University Press.

Meren, David, and Bora Plumptre (2013), 'Rights of Passage: The Intersecting of Environmentalism, Arctic Sovereignty, and the Law of the Sea, 1968–82', *Journal of Canadian Studies*, 47: 1, 167–96.

Merk, Frederick (1995), *Manifest Destiny and Mission in American History*, Cambridge, MA: Harvard University Press.

Miller, Jake C. (1974), 'The Virgin Islands and the United States: Definition of a Relationship', *World Affairs*, 136: 4, 297–305.

Miller, Paul D. (2013), 'A bibliographic essay on the Allied occupation and reconstruction of West Germany, 1945–1955', *Small Wars and Insurgencies*, 24: 4, 751–9.

Miller, Stuart Creighton (1982), *'Benevolent Assimilation': The American Conquest of the Philippines, 1899–1903*, New Haven, CT: Yale University Press.

Miranda, Rafael Cancel (2000), 'Powers Held by the United States over Puerto Rico', *Social Justice*, 27: 4, 152–3.

Mommsen, Wolfgang (1982), *Theories of Imperialism*, Chicago: University of Chicago Press.

Monet, Jacques (2013), 'Annexation Association', *Canadian Encyclopedia*, <http://www.thecanadianencyclopedia.ca/en/article/annexation-association/> (last accessed 31 August 2016).

Monge, José Trías (1999), *Puerto Rico: The Trials of the Oldest Colony in the World*, New Haven, CT: Yale University Press.

Moore, J. Preston (1955), 'Pierre Soulé: Southern Expansionist and Promoter', *Journal of Southern History*, 21: 2, 203–23.

Morgan, James G. (2014), *Into New Territory: American Historians and the Concept of US Imperialism*, Madison: University of Wisconsin Press.

Morgan, William Michael (2011), *Pacific Gibraltar: U.S.-Japanese Rivalry over the Annexation of Hawai'i, 1885–1898*, Annapolis, MD: Naval Institute Press.

Morison, Samuel L., Henry S. Commager and William E. Leuchtenburg (1969), *The Growth of the American Republic, Volume I, 6th Edition*, New York: Oxford University Press.

Morris, Edmund (2001), *The Rise of Theodore Roosevelt*, New York: Modern Library.

Morrison, Michael A. (1990), 'Westward the Curse of Empire: Texas Annexation and the American Whig Party', *Journal of the Early Republic*, 10: 2, 221–49.
Morrison, Michael A. (1995), 'Martin Van Buren, the Democracy, and the Partisan Politics of Texas Annexation', *Journal of Southern History*, 61: 4, 695–724.
Mower, J. H. (1947), 'The Republic of Liberia', *Journal of Negro History*, 32: 3, 265–306.
Munro, Dana G. (1958), 'Dollar Diplomacy in Nicaragua, 1909–1913', *Hispanic American Historical Review*, 38: 2, 209–34.
Munro, Dana G. (1969), 'The American Withdrawal from Haiti, 1929–1934', *Hispanic American Historical Review*, 49: 1, 1–26.
Murphy, Erin L. (2009), 'Women's Anti-Imperialism, "The White Man's Burden", and the Philippine-American War: Theorizing Masculinist Ambivalence', *Protest, Gender and Society*, 23: 2, 244–70.
Neuman, Gerald L., and Tomiko Brown-Nagin (2015), *Reconsidering the Insular Cases: The Past and Future of the American Empire*, Cambridge, MA: Harvard University Press.
Neunherz, Richard E. (1996), '"Hemmed In": Reactions in British Columbia to the Purchase of Russian America', in S. Haycox and M. Mangusso (eds), *An Alaska Anthology: Interpreting the Past*, Seattle: University of Washington Press, pp. 118–33.
Nichols, Christopher McKnight (2011), *Promise and Peril: America at the Dawn of a Global Age*, Cambridge, MA: Harvard University Press.
Nivison, Kenneth (2010), 'Purposes Just and Pacific: Franklin Pierce and the American Empire', *Diplomacy & Statecraft*, 21: 1, 1–19.
Nolan, Cathal J. (2006), 'Learning to Lead: Theodore Roosevelt, Woodrow Wilson, and the Emergence of the United States as a World Power', in W. Tilchin and C. Neu (eds), *Artists of Power: Theodore Roosevelt, Woodrow Wilson, and Their Enduring Impact on U.S. Foreign Policy*, Westport, CT: Praeger, pp. 139–62.
Nugent, Walter (2008), *Habits of Empire: A History of American Expansion*, New York: Alfred A. Knopf.
O'Connell, Dan (1993), 'The Pacific Guano Islands: The Stirring of American Empire in the Pacific Ocean', *Pacific Studies*, 16: 1, 43–66.
Offner, John L. (1992), *An Unwanted War: The Diplomacy of the United States and Spain over Cuba, 1895–1898*, Chapel Hill: University of North Carolina Press.
Onuf, Peter (2000), *Jefferson's Empire: The Language of American Nationhood*, Charlottesville: Virginia University Press.
Orent, Beatrice, and Pauline Reinsch (1941), 'Sovereignty over Islands in the Pacific', *American Journal of International Law*, 35: 3, 443–61.

Ortega, Carlos F. (2003), 'Gadsten Purchase', in L. Stacey (ed.), *Mexico and the United States*, Tarrytown, NY: Marshall Cavendish, p. 361.
Osborne, Thomas J. (1970), 'The Main Reason for Hawaiian Annexation in July, 1898', *Oregon Historical Quarterly*, 71: 2, 161–78.
Osborne, Thomas J. (1981), 'Trade or War? America's Annexation of Hawaii Reconsidered', *Pacific Historical Review*, 50: 3, 285–307.
Ostler, Jeffrey (2004), *The Plains Sioux and US Colonialism from Lewis and Clark to Wounded Knee*, Cambridge: Cambridge University Press.
Owens, Robert M. (2007), *Mr. Jefferson's Hammer: William Henry Harrison and the Origins of American Indian Policy*, Norman: University of Oklahoma Press.
Oyebade, Adebayo, and Toyin Falola (2008), 'West Africa and the United States in Historical perspective', in A. Jalloh and T. Falola (eds), *The United States and West Africa: Interactions and Relations*, Rochester, NY: University of Rochester Press, pp. 17–37.
Pamphile, Leon D (1985), 'America's Policy-Making in Haitian Education, 1915–1934', *Journal of Negro Education*, 54: 1, 99–108.
Paterson, Thomas G. (1994), *Contesting Castro: The United States and the Triumph of the Cuban Revolution*, Oxford: Oxford University Press.
Pérez, Louis A., Jr. (1978), *Intervention, Revolution, and Politics in Cuba, 1913–1921*, Pittsburgh: Pittsburgh University Press.
Pérez, Louis A., Jr. (1986), *Cuba under the Platt Amendment, 1902–1934*, Pittsburgh: Pittsburgh University Press.
Pérez, Louis A., Jr. (1997), *Cuba and the United States: Ties of Singular Intimacy, Second Edition*, Athens: University of Georgia Press.
Pérez, Louis A., Jr. (1998), *The War of 1898: The United States and Cuba in History and Historiography*, Chapel Hill: University of North Carolina Press.
Pérez, Louis A., Jr. (2008), *Cuba in the American Imagination: Metaphor and the Imperial Ethos*, Chapel Hill: University of North Carolina Press.
Pérez y González, María (2000), *Puerto Ricans in the United States*, Westport, CT: Greenwood Press.
Peterson, Edward N. (1977), *The American Occupation of Germany: Retreat to Victory*, Detroit: Wayne State University Press.
Pinheiro, John C. (2007), *Manifest Ambition: James K. Polk and Civil-Military Relations During the Mexican War*, Westport, CT: Praeger.
Pike, Fredrick B. (1995), *FDR's Good Neighbor Policy: Sixty Years of Generally Gentle Chaos*, Austin: University of Texas Press.
Pletcher, David M. (2001), *The Diplomacy of Involvement: American Economic Expansion Across the Pacific, 1784–1900*, Columbia: University of Missouri Press.
Plummer, Brenda Gayle (1982), 'The Afro-American Response to the Occupation of Haiti, 1915–1934', *Phylon*, 43: 2, 125–43.

Plummer, Brenda Gayle (1992), *Haiti and the United States: The Psychological Moment*, Athens: University of Georgia Press.
Poyo, Gerald E. (1979), 'Key West and the Cuban Ten Years War', *Florida Historical Quarterly*, 57: 3, 289–307.
Pratt, Julius W. (1932), 'The "Large Policy" of 1898', *Mississippi Valley Historical Review*, 19: 2, 219–42.
Rauchway, Eric (2001), 'The Global Emergence of the United States, 1867–1900', in W. Barney (ed.), *A Companion to 19th-Century America*, Malden, MA: Blackwell, pp. 104–20.
Reding, Andrew (1996), 'Exorcising Haiti's Ghosts', *World Policy Journal*, 13: 1, 15–26.
Renda, Mary A. (2001), *Taking Haiti: Military Occupation and the Culture of U.S. Imperialism, 1915–1940*, Chapel Hill: University of North Carolina Press.
Ricard, Serge (2006), 'The Roosevelt Corollary', *Presidential Studies Quarterly*, 36: 1, 17–26.
Riccards, Michael P. (1995), *The Ferocious Engine of Democracy: A History of the American Presidency, Volume 1*, Lanham, MD: Madison Books.
Robinson, Edgar E., and Victor J. West (1917), *Foreign Policy of Woodrow Wilson, 1913–1917*, New York: Macmillan.
Rodriguez, Junius P. (2002), 'West Florida', in J. Rodriguez (ed.), *Louisiana Purchase: A Historical and Geographical Encyclopedia*, Santa Barbara: ABC-CLIO, p. 350.
Rogers, Robert F. (1995), *Destiny's Landfall: A History of Guam*, Honolulu: Hawaii University Press.
Roorda, Eric P. (1998), *The Dictator Next Door: The Good Neighbor Policy and the Trujilo Regime in the Dominican Republic, 1930–1945*, Durham, NC: Duke University Press.
Roosevelt, Theodore (1882), *The Naval War of 1812*, New York: G. P. Putnam's Sons.
Ropp, Steve C. (1979), 'Ratification of the Panama Canal Treaties: The Muted Debate', *World Affairs*, 141: 4, 283–92.
Ross, Rodney J. (2011), 'New York Journal', in M. Manning and C. Wyatt (eds), *Encyclopedia of Media and Propaganda in Wartime America, Volume 1*, Santa Barbara: ABC-CLIO, 2011, pp. 417–19.
Rottman, G. (2004), *Guam 1941 and 1944: Loss and Reconquest*, Oxford: Osprey Publishing.
Ruttan, Stephen (2010), 'The Pig War', Greater Victoria Public Library, <https://gvpl.ca/using-the-library/our-collection/local-history/tales-from-the-vault/the-pig-war> (last accessed 31 August 2016).
Salamanca, Bonifacio S. (1984), *The Filipino Reaction to American Rule, 1901–1913*, Quezon City: New Day Publishers.

Sanchez, Michael (2004), 'Philander C. Knox', in E. Mihalkanin (ed.), *American Statesmen: Secretaries of State from John Jay to Colin Powell*, Westport, CT: Greenwood Press, pp. 307–13.

Sarantakes, Nicholas Evan (1994), 'Continuity through Change: The Return of Okinawa and Iwo Jima, 1967–1972', *Journal of American-East Asian Relations*, 3: 1, 35–53.

Schellinger, Paul E., and Robert M. Salkin (eds) (1996), *International Dictionary of Historic Places: Volume 5*, London: Routledge.

Schirmer, Daniel B. (1972), *Republic or Empire: American Resistance to the Philippine War*, Cambridge, MA: Schenkman Publishing.

Schirmer, Daniel B. (1974), 'On the Anti-Imperialist Movement: A Rejoinder', *Science & Society*, 38: 1, 85–9.

Schlesinger, Arthur M., Jr. (1999), *The Cycles of American History*, Boston: Mariner Books.

Schmidt, Hans (1995), *The United States Occupation of Haiti, 1915–1934*, New Brunswick, NJ: Rutgers University Press.

Scholes, Walter V., and Marie V. Scholes (1970), *The Foreign Policies of the Taft Administration*, Columbia: University of Missouri Press.

Schonberger, Howard B. (1989), *Aftermath of War: Americans and the Remaking of Japan, 1945–1952*, Kent, OH: Kent State University Press.

Schoultz, Lars (1998), *Beneath the United States: A History of U. S. Policy Toward Latin America*, Cambridge, MA: Harvard University Press.

Schoultz, Lars (2009), *That Infernal Little Cuban Republic: the United States and the Cuban Revolution*, Chapel Hill: University of North Carolina Press.

Schumacher, Frank (2002), 'The American Way of Empire: National Tradition and Transatlantic Adaptation in America's Search for Imperial Identity, 1898–1910', *Bulletin of the German Historical Institute*, 31, 35–50.

Schwartzberg, Steven (1993), 'The "Soft Peace Boys": Presurrender Planning and Japanese Land Reform', *Journal of American-East Asian Relations*, 2: 2, 185–216.

Schwenkbeck, Rahima (2015), 'Bear Flag Revolt', in C. Magoc and D. Bernstein (eds), *Imperialism and Expansionism in American History: A Social, Political, and Cultural Encyclopedia and Document Collection, Volume 3*, Santa Barbara: ABC-CLIO, pp. 850–1.

Shay, Martha J. (1976), 'The Panama Canal Zone: In Search of a Juridical Identity', *NYUJ International Law & Politics*, 9, 15–60.

Shibata, Masako (2005), *Japan and Germany under the U.S. Occupation: A Comparative Analysis of Post-War Education Reform*, Lanham, MD: Lexington Books.

Silbey, David J. (1997), *A War of Frontier and Empire: The Philippine-American War, 1899–1902*, New York: Hill & Wang.
Silverstone, Scott A. (2004), *Divided Union: The Politics of War in the Early American Republic*, Ithaca, NY: Cornell University Press.
Singletary, Otis A. (1962), *The Mexican War*, Chicago: University of Chicago Press.
Skaggs, Jimmy M. (1994), *The Great Guano Rush: Entrepreneurs and American Overseas Expansion*, New York: St. Martin's Griffin.
Smith, Angel, and Emma Dávila-Cox (eds) (1999), *The Crisis of 1898: Colonial Redistribution and Nationalist Mobilization*, London: Macmillan.
Smith, Ephraim K. (1993), 'William McKinley's Enduring Legacy: The Historiographical Debate on the Taking of the Philippine Islands', in J. Bradford (ed.), *Crucible of War: The Spanish-American War and Its Aftermath*, Annapolis, MD: Naval Institute Press, pp. 205–49.
Smith, Goldwin (1891), *Canada and the Canadian Question*. London: Macmillan.
Smith, Joseph (2011), 'The Assistant Secretary of the Navy and the Spanish-American War Hero', in S. Ricard (ed.), *A Companion to Theodore Roosevelt*, Malden, MA: Wiley-Blackwell, pp. 45–58.
Smith, Robert Freeman (1969), 'A Note on the Bryan-Chamorro Treaty and German Interest in a Nicaraguan Canal, 1914', *Caribbean Studies*, 9: 1, 63–6.
Sonneborn, Liz (2009), *The Acquisition of Florida: America's Twenty-seventh State*, New York: Chelsea House.
Sparrow, Bartholomew H. (2006), *The Insular Cases and the Emergence of American Empire*, Lawrence: University Press of Kansas.
Stanley, Peter W. (1974), *A Nation in the Making: The Philippines and the United States, 1899–1921*, Cambridge, MA: Harvard University Press.
Statham, E. Robert, Jr. (2002), *Colonial Constitutionalism: The Tyranny of United States' Offshore Territorial Policy and Relations*, Lanham, MD: Lexington Books.
Steinmetz, George (2007), *The Devil's Handwriting: Precoloniality and the German Colonial State in Qingdao, Samoa, and Southwest Africa*, Chicago: University of Chicago Press.
Strauss, Michael J. (2009), *The Leasing of Guantanamo Bay*, Westport, CT: Praeger.
Strauss, Michael J. (2015), *Territorial Leasing in Diplomacy and International Law*, Leiden: Brill Nijhoff.
Strong, Robert A. (1991), 'Jimmy Carter and the Panama Canal Treaties', *Presidential Studies Quarterly*, 21: 2, 269–86.
Stuart, Peter C. (2007), *Planting the American Flag: Twelve Men Who Expanded the United States Overseas*, Jefferson, NC: McFarland & Co.

Takemae, Eiji (2002), *The Allied Occupation of Japan*, New York: Continuum.
Tate, Merze (1962), 'Great Britain and the Sovereignty of Hawaii', *Pacific Historical Review*, 31: 4, 327–48.
Taylor, Alan (2010), *The Civil War of 1812: American Citizens, British Subjects, Irish Rebels, and Indian Allies*, New York: Alfred A. Knopf.
'The Potsdam Conference, 1945' (n.d.), *US Office of the Historian*, <https://history.state.gov/milestones/1937-1945/potsdam-conf> (last accessed 31 August 2016).
Thompson, John H., and Stephen J. Randall (2008), *Canada and the United States: Ambivalent Allies*, Athens: University of Georgia Press.
Tindall, George B., and David E. Shi (2007), *America: A Narrative History*, 7th Edition, New York: W. W. Norton.
Tompkins, E. Berkeley (1967), 'Scylla and Charybdis: The Anti-Imperialist Dilemma in the Election of 1900', *Pacific Historical Review*, 36: 2, 143–61.
Tone, John Lawrence (2006), *War and Genocide in Cuba, 1895–1898*, Chapel Hill: University of North Carolina Press.
Trask, David F. (1996), *The War with Spain in 1898*, Lincoln: University of Nebraska Press.
Turner, Frederick Jackson [1893] (1947), 'The Significance of the Frontier in American History', in Frederick Jackson Turner, *The Frontier in American History*, New York: Henry Holt, pp. 1–38.
Turpie, David (2009), '"Howling Upon the Scent of Another Victim": Senator Edward W. Carmack, the Philippine Issue, and Southern Opposition to Imperialism', *Tennessee Historical Quarterly*, 68: 4, 411–32.
Tyrell, Ian (2007), *Transnational History: United States History in Global Perspective Since 1789*, London: Palgrave Macmillan.
Venator-Santiago, Charles R. (2015), *Puerto Rico and the Origins of the US Global Empire: The Disembodied Shade*, Abingdon: Routledge.
Vine, David (2011), *Island of Shame: The Secret History of the U.S. Military Base on Diego Garcia*, Princeton: Princeton University Press.
Vine, David (2015), *Base Nation: How U.S. Military Bases Abroad Harm America and the World*, New York: Metropolitan Books.
Vinkovetsky, Ilya (2011), *Russian America: An Overseas Colony of a Continental Empire, 1804–1867*, Oxford: Oxford University Press.
Vouri, Mike (n.d.), 'The Pig War', National Park Service, <http://www.nps.gov/sajh/historyculture/the-pig-war.htm> (last accessed 31 August 2016).
Vouri, Mike (2013), *The Pig War: Standoff at Griffin Bay*, Seattle, WA: Discover Your Northwest.
Walther, Eric H. (2004), *The Shattering of the Union: America in the 1850s*, Oxford: SR Books.

Waugh, Alec (1964), *A Family of Islands: A History of the West Indies from 1492 to 1898*, London: Weidenfeld & Nicolson.

Weber, David J. (ed.) (2003), *Foreigners in Their Native Land: Historical Roots of the Mexican Americans*, Albuquerque: University of New Mexico Press.

Weeks, William E. (1992), *John Quincy Adams and American Global Empire*, Lexington: University Press of Kentucky.

Weinberg, Albert K. (1958), *Manifest Destiny: A Study of Nationalist Expansionism in American History*, Gloucester, MA: Peter Smith.

Weir, G.E. (2005), 'Virtual War in the Ice Jungle: "We don't know how to do this"', *Journal of Strategic Studies*, 28: 2, 411–27.

Welch, Richard E., Jr. (1979), *Response to Imperialism: The United States and the Philippine-American War, 1899–1902*, Chapel Hill: University of North Carolina Press.

Welch, Richard E., Jr. (1996), 'American Public Opinion and the Purchase of Russian America', in S. Haycox and M. Mangusso (eds), *An Alaska Anthology: Interpreting the Past*, Seattle: University of Washington Press, pp. 102–17.

Whitehead, John (1992), 'Hawaii: The First and Last Far West?' *Western Historical Quarterly*, 23: 2, 153–77.

Whittaker, William George (1969), 'Samuel Gompers, Anti-Imperialist', *Pacific Historical Review*, 38: 4, 429–45.

Williams, Justin, Sr. (1988), 'American Democratization Policy for Occupied Japan: Correcting the Revisionist Version', *Pacific Historical Review*, 57: 2, 179–202.

Williams, Walter L. (1980), 'United States Indian Policy and the Debate over Philippine Annexation: Implications for the Origins of American Imperialism', *Journal of American History*, 66: 4, 810–31.

Williams, William Appleman [1969] (1972), *The Tragedy of American Diplomacy*, 2nd Edition, New York: Dell Publishing.

Wolff, Leon (1961), *Little Brown Brother: America's Forgotten Bid for Empire Which Cost 250,000 Lives*, London: Longman.

Wood, Gordon S. (2009), *Empire of Liberty: a History of the Early Republic, 1789–1815*, Oxford: Oxford University Press.

Wooster, Robert (1988), *The Military and United States Indian Policy, 1865–1903*, New Haven, CT: Yale University Press.

Wrobel, David M. (1993), *The End of American Exceptionalism: Frontier Anxiety from the Old West to the New Deal*, Lawrence: University Press of Kansas.

Yarema, Allan E. (2006), *American Colonization Society: An Avenue to Freedom?* Lanham, MD: University Press of America.

Young, Oran R. (2011), 'The future of the Arctic: cauldron of conflict or zone of peace?' *International Affairs*, 87: 1, 185–93.

Young, Raymond A. (1963), 'Pinckney's Treaty – A New Perspective', *Hispanic American Historical Review*, 43: 4, 526–35.

Zeihan, Peter (2014), *The Accidental Superpower: The Next Generation of American Preeminence and the Coming Global Disaster*, New York: Grand Central Publishing.

Zimmerman, James A. (1977), 'Who Were the Anti-Imperialists and the Expansionists of 1898 and 1899? A Chicago Perspective', *Pacific Historical Review*, 46: 4, 589–601.

Index

Numbers in *italic* refer to illustrations.

aberration thesis, 3, 27n, 76, 109
Abyssinia, 55
Adams, John Quincy, 15, 16, 40, 60, 66
Adams-Onís Treaty, 15–16, 48n
Admission of States and Territorial Acquisitions, *21*
African Americans, 31, 50–2, 53, 54, 86, 143
Aguinaldo, Emilio, 102, 104, *105*
air bases *see* bases overseas
Alabama, 24
Alamo, Battle of the, 16
Alaska, 35, 42–7, 76, 171, 178n
Alaska boundary dispute, 45–6
Alaska Purchase, 43–4, 171
Albizu Campos, Pedro, 101
Allen, Ethan, 11
Allied Control Council (ACC), 147, 148
Alta California, 20
Alverstone, Lord, 45
Ambacher, Bruce, 64–5
American Anti-Imperialist League (AIL), 84–5
American Artic Expedition, 171–2
American Board of Commissioners for Foreign Mission, 71
American Colonization Society (ACS), 50, 51–3, 54
American exceptionalism, 82
American Guano Company, 56

American imperialism
 literature, 2–4
 working definition, 1
American Revolution, 36; *see also* Revolutionary War
American Samoa, 59, 113, 114–19, *117*
Americo-Liberians, 55
Anglo-Russian Convention 1825, 45
Annexation Association, 34
Annexation Bill, 35
Anti-Imperialist leagues, 82–3
anti-imperialists, 76, 80–7
Apia, 116, *118*, 119
Appalachia (French Louisiana), 8, 10, 11–13
Arctic, 171–6
Arctic Circle, 178n
Arctic Council, 174
Arctic expeditions, 171–3
Arctic Nations, 174
Arctic Region, *172*
Arias, Desiderio, 145
Arizona, 26
Army Appropriations Bill, 95, 96
Aroostook War, 33–4
Articles of Confederation, 30–1
Astor, John Jacob, 37
attraction, policy of, 106, 107
Austria, 146
Aves Island, 56
Azuma, Eiichiro, 152

Bacon, Augustus, 83
Báez, Buenaventure, 145
Bahia Honda, 167
Balboa High School, 126
Banana Republics, 137
Banana Wars, 137
Banks, Nathaniel, 35
bases overseas, 169–70, 173, 178n
  Guantanamo Bay, 165–9
Batista, Fulgencio, 168
Baton Rouge, 14
Battle of Gonzales, 16
Battle of Little Bighorn, 26
Battle of Manila Bay, 104
Battle of the Alamo, 16
Battle of the Thames, 24
Battle of the Windmill, 33
Bayonet Constitution, 73
Beach, Moses, 62
Bear Flag Revolt, 20, 29n
Beisner, Robert, 82
Bemis, Samuel Flagg, 3, 76
Bender, Prosper, 35–6
Bering, Vitus, 42
Berlin, 147
Berlin Blockade, 150
Beschloss, Michael, 148
Big Stick diplomacy, 140, 155n
Bikini Atoll, 163
Bingham, Hiram, 119
Bismarck, Herbert, 73
Bismarck, Otto von, 113, 114, 115
Black, Lydia, 42
Black Warrior, 63
Blaine, James, 73, 74, 142
Blount, James, 75
Boehling, Rebecca, 148
Boer Wars, 121
Bonaparte, Napoleon, 11–13, 32, 59–60
Bonin Islands, 153–4
Borah, William, 141
Bosque-Pérez, Ramón, 99

Britain *see* Great Britain
British Columbia, 41
British Empire, 8, 16, 30, 50–1, 58; *see also* Great Britain
British Honduras, 54
British North America, 30–6, 43, 44–5, 51; *see also* Canada
British press, 39–40
British Sierra Leone, 51, 52, 53
Brooke, John, 93, 95
Brown, Henry Billings, 101
Bryan, William Jennings, 108
  anti-imperialism, 82, 87
  Haiti, 142
  Nicaragua, 140, 141
  Puerto Rico, 99
  Treaty of Paris 1898, 83
Bryan-Chamorro Treaty, 141
Buchanan, James, 41, 62, 65
buffaloes, 25
Bunau-Varilla, Philippe, 121–2, 123
Bush (George W.) administration, 174
Byrnes, James, 149

California, 22, 29n, 72
California Republic, 29n
Californian rebellion, 20
Campos, Arsenio Martínez, 77
Canada, 30–6
  Alaska boundary dispute, 45–7
  Arctic, 171, 173, 178n
  Hawaii, 73–4
  Northwest Passage, 175
  sovereignty, 174
  see also British North America
Cape Mesurado, 52
Caribbean Occupations, 136–9
  Dominican Republic, 142, 144–6
  Haiti, 142–4, 146
  Nicaragua, 139–41
Carmack, Edward Ward, 86
Carnegie, Andrew, 82, 84

INDEX

Caroline Islands, 159, 160, 164, 177n
Carter, Henry, 73
Carter, Jimmy, 126
Carter-Blaine Treaty, 73
Carter-Torrijos treaties, 126
Cass, Lewis, 62
Castro, Fidel, 168
Central America and the Caribbean, 61
Central American Court of Justice, 141
Central Polynesia Land and Commercial Company, 114
Céspedes, Carlos Manuel de, 65
Chaffee, Adna, 106
Chaffin, Tom, 63
Chamorro-Wietzel Treaty, 140–1
chartered companies, 50–1, 56
Cherokee, 24, 25
Chicksaw, 24
China
  Okinawa, 154
  relationship with Japan, 58, 108–9
  Russian interest in, 43
  US access to, 75, 84, 104
Chincha Islands, 55
Choctaw, 24
Christian IX, King of Denmark, 129
churches, 51–2
Churchill, Winston, 147, 169
citizenship
  American Samoans, 119
  Filipinos, 105
  Guam residents, 162
  Hawaiians, 72
  Mexicans, 20–1
  Northern Mariana Islanders, 134n
  overseas territories, 111n
  Puerto Ricans, 101, 133n
  unincorporated territories, 100–1
  US Virgin Islanders, 129, 132, 135n
Civil War, 25, 34, 39, 41, 54, 142, 144
Clay, Lucius D., 148–9
Clayton-Bulwer Treaty, 121
Cleveland, Grover, 74–5, 82, 84, 117, 118
Clipperton Island, 57–8
Coblenz, 146
Cogliano, Francis, 13
Cold War, 46, 146, 153, 168–9, 173, 174
Coletta, Paolo, 83, 104
Colombia, 122
Colonial North America, 9
Columbus, Christopher, 127
Comanche people, 24
Commonwealth of Liberia, 53
Commonwealth status, 101, 108, 163–4
communism, 146, 147, 148, 150
Compromise of 1850, 22
concentration camps, 77
Congress
  American Colonization Society (ACS), 52
  American Samoa, 119
  Cuba, 65, 80, 96
  Guam, 161
  guano islands, 58
  Hawaii, 76
  Panama Canal, 121, 122
  Puerto Rico, 99–100
  US Virgin Islands, 132
Congress of Micronesia, 163
constabulary *see* Gendarmerie
Continental Congress, 10
Convention of 1818, 37
Convention of the Law of the Sea, 175
Cook, Frederick, 173

Cook, James, 70
Cook Islands, 163
Cooley, Alexander, 169
Coolidge, Calvin, 141
Cooper Act, 107
Córdoba, Treaty of, 16
Corn Islands, 141, 155n
Côte d'Ivoire, 53
Creek, 24
Creek War, 24
Crimean War, 43
Criollos, 60
CSS *Alabama*, 35
Cuba, 59–67, 92–7, 109, 138
  Guantanamo Bay, 165–6, 167–9
Cuban Liberal Party, 138
Cuban Revolution, 76–8, 79, 168
Cuban Revolutionary Party, 77
Culebra, 99
Culebrita, 99
Cullinane, Michael P., 82
Curtis Act, 26
Custer, George, 26
Cutlar, Lyman, 41

Dalton, Kathleen, 120
Danish West Indies, 127, 128; see also US Virgin Islands; Virgin Islands
Davis, George W., 125
Davis, William C., 14
Dawes Act, 26
De Long, George, 171–2
Debs, Eugene, 112n
Declaration of Independence, 9
Democratic Party
  anti-imperialism, 82, 87
  Panama Canal Zone (PCZ), 125
  Puerto Rico, 102
  US election 1912, 107, 112n
  US election 1932, 108
democratisation, 148, 149, 151, 152, 153

Dempsey, Guy, 164
Denmark, 128–31, 173, 174
Destroyers for Bases deal, 169–70
Dewey, George, 79, 104
Díaz, Adolfo, 140
Dickerson, Donna, 44
Diego Garcia, 170
Dietz, James, 98
Diplomatic History of the United States, A (Bemis, 1936), 3
Dollar Diplomacy, 140, 155n
Dominican Republic, 142, 144–6
Douglas, Stephen, 62, 64
Dower, John, 152–3
Downes v. Bidwell (1901), 100, 101
Drinnon, Richard, 3
Du Bois, W.E.B., 143
Dulles, Foster Rhea, 76
Dulles, John Foster, 154

East Florida, 13, 15–16
economic intervention
  Cuba, 95
  Germany, 148, 149
  Japan, 152
  Philippines, 109
Egypt, 120
Eisenhower, Dwight D., 47, 168
elections
  Cuba, 96
  Philippines, 107
  US election 1896, 78
  US election 1900, 86, 87
  US election 1912, 107, 108, 112n
  US election 1920, 145
  US election 1932, 108
  US election 2012, 102
elites
  Cuba, 94, 95, 96
  Hawaii, 72–3, 74
  Philippines, 107
  Puerto Rico, 98

INDEX

Ellice Islands, 161, 162, 177n
emigration, 25, 31, 65; see also immigration
empire, 1, 9–10, 181
Empire for Liberty, 10
Empire of Liberty, 9, 10, 13, 181
energy independence, 171
Equal Rights Amendment, Japan, 152
Estrada, Juan, 140
Estrada Palma, Tomás, 97, 138
ethnic homeland, 23
exceptionalism, 82
Executive Order 9066, 152
Executive Order 10077, 162
expansion
 from the Atlantic, 8–16
 in the South-west, 16–22
 westward, 17

Fairbanks, 45
federal lands, 10
Federal Republic of Germany (FRG), 150
Federated States of Micronesia, 165
Ferguson, Niall, 3–4, 181
Filipinization, 107, 108
Filipinos, 85; see also Philippines
Fillmore, Millard, 22
Finland, 174
Finley, Robert, 52
First Seminole War, 15
First World War, 131, 132, 138, 145, 146, 160
Fish, Hamilton, 35
fishing rights, 35, 36, 48n
'Five Civilized Tribes', 24, 26, 29n
Florida, 13–16, 24
Foner, Eric, 54
Font-Guzmán, Jacqueline, 99
Foraker, Joseph, 95
Foraker Act, 99–100

Foraker Amendment, 95
forced emigration, 25
Ford, Gerald, 126
Fort Astoria, 37
Fort George, 37
Fort Santa Cruz, 160
Fort Wayne, Treaty of, 24
Foster, Charles, 51
Foster, John W., 74
France
 Hawaiian independence, 71
 occupation of Germany, 147, 149, 150
 'quasi' naval war with US, 31–2
 Republic of Texas, 18
 Revolutionary Wars, 12
 sale of Louisiana, 11–13, 32
 Treaty of San Ildefonso, 12
 US dependence on, 10
 US trade with, 32
 war with Britain, 32
Free Association Agreement (FAA), 165
Frémont, John, 20
French and Indian War, 8, 13
French Canada, 8
French Louisiana (Appalachia), 8, 10, 11–13
French settlers, 31, 42
Friedlander, Robert A., 123
Friendship, Treaty of, 71
fur trade, 37, 71

Gadsten, James, 22
Gadsten Purchase, 22
Garcia, Calixto, 93
Gendarmerie, 143, 144, 145
gender, 82, 90n
General Allotment Act, 26
George III, King of the United Kingdom, 8
Georgia, 24
German South West Africa, 161

Germany
  Colombia, 122
  First World War, 132
  imperialism, 113–14
  Marshall Islands, 159
  Micronesia, 160–1
  overseas empire, 133n
  Panama Canal, 120
  Philippines, 85
  Samoa, 114, 115–16, 117–18, 118–19
  US military bases in, 170
  US occupation, 146–50
  Virgin Islands, 131, 132
  World War I, 138
Ghana, 53
Ghent, Treaty of, 33, 37
Gilbert Islands, 159, 161, 162, 177n
Glen, Francis Wayland, 129–30
Gold Coast, 53
gold rush, 45, 47
Goldstein, Alyosha, 2
Golikov, Ivan, 42
Gonzales, Battle of, 16
Good Neighbor Policy (F. Roosevelt), 97, 141, 156n
good neighbour policy (W. Wilson), 140, 155n
Gott, Richard, 96
Grant, Ulysses S., 35, 66, 115, 145
Grau San Martín, Ramón, 168
Gravier, Charles, 10
Great Britain
  Alaska, 43
  Canada, 30
  chartered companies, 50–1
  Destroyers for Bases deal, 169–70
  East Florida, 15
  Florida territories, 13
  Guantanamo Bay, 165–6
  Hawaii, 71, 73
  occupation of Germany, 147, 149, 150
  Oregon, 37, 38–40
  Pacific islands, 159, 162
  Panama Canal, 120–1
  Republic of Texas, 18
  Samoa, 114, 116, 117, 118–19
  support for Native Americans, 24
  Texas, 16
  US trade with, 32
  war with France, 32
  see also British Empire
Green Mountain Boys, 11
Greenebaum, Bertold, 115–16
Greenland, 173, 178n
Grito de Yara, 65
Guadalupe Hidalgo, Treaty of, 20–1, 22, 60, 62
Gualberto Gómez, Juan, 97
Guam, 85, 100, 119, 159–65
Guano Island Act (GIA), 57–8, 66
guano islands, 55–9, 66
Guantanamo Bay, 109, 165–9
Guantanamo Bay US Naval Base (GTMO), 166–9
Gvozdev, Mikhail, 42

Haglund, David, 46
Haiti, 57, 130, 131, 142–4, 146
Haitian-American Convention (Treaty), 143, 156n
Haitianisation, 144, 156n
Hämäläinen, Pekka, 24
Harding, Warren G., 145–6
Harrison, Benjamin, 74, 82, 99, 117, 118
Harrison, William Henry, 24
Hawaii, 57, 59, 70–6, 82, 85, 101
Hay, John, 121
Hay-Bunau-Varilla Treaty, 123, 125
Haycox, Steven, 47

Hayes, Rutherford B., 121
Hay-Herrán Treaty, 122
Hay-Pauncefote Treaty, 121
Healy, David, 78
Hearst, William Randolph, 4, 79
Helms-Burton Act, 169
Hickey, Donald, 32
High, Steven, 170
Hilfrich, Fabian, 82, 105
Hirohito, Emperor, 151
historiography, 2–4
Hoar, George F., 76, 82, 87
Hobart, Garret, 84
Holmes, James, 120
Honolulu, 71, 74
Hoover, Herbert, 144, 156n
House of Representatives, 35, 44, 101–2, 108
Houston, Sam, 18
Howard, Thomas, 169–70
Hudson's Bay Company (HBC), 37, 38, 40–1, 42, 43
Hunt, Michael, 25
Hunter's Lodges, 33

Iceland, 174
Idaho, 41
Immerman, Richard, 9–10
Immerwahr, Daniel, 6n
immigration, 16, 31, 38, 65; see also emigration
independence see self-government
informal imperialism, 2
Insular Cases, 100, 105
International Trusteeship System, 162
Iraq, 161
Irish nationalists, 35
island territories
    Cuba, 59–67
    guano islands, 55–9
    Hawaii, 70–6
    present day, 59

isthmian canal see Panama Canal
Isthmian Canal Commission, 125
Ivory Coast, 53
Iwo Jima, 153

Jackson, Andrew, 15, 16, 18, 24–5
Jackson, Ian, 43
James, Carolyn, 174
James, Patrick, 174
Japan, 85, 107
    Hawaii, 75
    Micronesia, 161–2
    relationship with China, 58, 108–9
    Russian interest in, 43
    US military bases in, 170
    US occupation, 150–4
Japanese Americans, 152
Japanese Constitution 1946, 151
Jay's Treaty, 14, 28n
JCS 1067, 147–8, 149
Jefferson, Thomas
    anti-imperialism, 85
    Canada, 30
    Cuba, 59–60, 66
    Empire of Liberty, 9–10, 181
    Lewis and Clark expedition, 29n, 36
    Louisiana Purchase, 13, 32
    Native Americans, 23
    Nicaragua, 139
    resettlement of freed slaves, 51
    West Florida, 14
Jenkins' Ear, War of, 165
Jenks, Leland H., 97
Jiménez, Juan, 145
Johnson, Andrew, 35, 65, 66, 142
Johnson, Lyndon, 126, 144–5, 153
Johnston Islands, 57
Jones, William A., 108, 133n
Jones Act, 108, 111n
Jones-Shafroth Act, 101, 133n

Kalakaua, David, King of Hawaii, 72, 73–4
Kamehameha III, King of Hawaii, 72
Kansas-Nebraska Act, 64–5, 69n, 72, 88n
Kaplan, Amy, 168
Kennedy, John F., 163
Kingdom of Hawaii, 57, 70–5
Kiribati, 177n; *see also* Gilbert Islands
Klondike territory, 45
Knapp, Harry, 145
Knox, Philander C., 139, 140
Knox-Castillo Treaty, 140
Kodiak Island, 42
Korea, 146

LaFeber, Walter, 3, 80, 90n, 121
Lajeunesse, Adam, 174
land purchase
  Alaska, 43–4, 171
  American Samoa, 114
  Cuba, 62, 63–4, 66, 80
  Dominican Republic, 145
  Gadsten Purchase, 22
  Louisiana Purchase, 11–13, 14, 21, 24, 32
  Pacific islands, 160
  Panama, 123
  Philippines, 83, 105
  Puerto Rico, 99
  US Virgin Islands, 127
  Virgin Islands, 128–32
  West Africa, 52–3
Lansing, Robert, 131, 143
Lares Revolt, 98
large policy, 78, 89n, 104, 120
Laurier, Wilfred, 46
League of Nations, 133n, 145, 161
Leary, R. P., 160
Lee, Jason, 38
Lepore, Jill, 23

Lewis, Merriweather, 36
Lewis and Clark expedition, 24, 29n, 36
Liberia, 50–6, 66
Liliuokalani, Queen of Hawaii, 74
Lincoln, Abraham, 54, 129, 142
Linn, Brian McAllister, 105
literature, 2–4
Little Bighorn, Battle of, 26
Livingstone, David, 51
Lodge, Henry Cabot, 89n, 99, 104, 105, 113, 129
Long, John D., 79
López, Narciso, 62–3
Louisiana Purchase, 11–13, 14, 21, 24, 32
Louisiana sugar planters, 72
Lower Canada, 33
Lutz, Catherine, 169
Luzon, 104

Maass, Richard, 32–3
McAfee, Ward, 20
MacArthur, Arthur, 106
MacArthur, Douglas, 109, 150–1, 152, 153
MacDonald, Paul, 1
Mackenzie, William Lyon, 33
McKinley, William
  assassination, 166
  Cuba, 90n
  Guam, 160
  Hawaii, 75, 76
  Panama Canal, 121
  Philippines, 85, 102, 104–5, 106
  Spanish-American War, 80, 92
  US election 1896, 78
  US election 1900, 86
McKinley Tariff Act, 73, 74
McLaughlin, Shaun, 33
McNutt, Paul, 108
Madison, James, 14–15, 32, 59–60
Madriz, José, 140

Magness, Phillip, 54
Magoon, Charles E., 138
Mahan, Alfred Thayer, 166
Maine, 27n, 33–4
Malietoa Laupepa, 115, 116
Malietoa Tanumafili I, 118
Manela, Erez, 127
Mangusso, Mary C., 47
Manifest Destiny, 1, 6n, 19, 25, 26, 62, 71, 74
Manila, 106
Manila Bay, Battle of, 104
Manitoba, 38
Marcy, William, 63–4
Mariana Islands, 159, 160, 164; see also Northern Mariana Islands
Marks, Frederick, 122
Marshall, George C., 173
Marshall, John, 13
Marshall Islands, 159, 163, 165
Marshall Plan, 149–50
Martí, José, 77
Martínez, Rubén, 101
May, Ernest, 80
Mead, Margaret, 119
Meade, Richard W., 114–15
Merk, Frederick, 19
Methodist missionaries, 38
Mexican Empire, 16
Mexican Republic, 16
Mexican-American War, 19–21, 60, 63, 101
Mexico, 16, 18, 20–1, 137, 139
Micronesia, 159–65
Midway Atoll (Islands), 58–9, 67n
migration *see* emigration; immigration
military bases, 169–70, 178n
 Guantanamo Bay, 165–9
mineral resources, 171, 175
missionaries, 38, 71, 102
Mississippi, 24

Missouri Compromise, 21–2
Mobile, 63
Môle-Saint-Nicolas, 142
Monroe, James, 15, 52
Monroe Doctrine, 73, 85, 99, 131, 136–7
Monrovia, 52
Morgan, William, 75, 89n
Morgenthau, Henry, 147
Morgenthau Plan, 147, 148
Mulroney, Brian, 174
Murphy, Erin L., 90n

Namibia, 161
Napoleon Bonaparte *see* Bonaparte, Napoleon
National Association for the Advancement of Colored People (NAACP), 143
Native Alaskans, 42
Native Americans, 3, 14, 15, 23–7, 31, 42, 105
native people, Arctic, 174
Naval War College, 107
Navassa Island, 57, 59
Nebraska, 41; *see also* Kansas-Nebraska Act
Nevins, Peter J., 130
New Brunswick, 33
New Deal era, 58
New Empire group, 166
New England, 82, 84
New France, 8
New Granada, 122
New Hampshire Grants, 11
New Left (Wisconsin) school, 3, 6n
New Mexico, 20, 22, 26
New Orleans, 63
New Spain, 16
New York, 11, 82
New York Times, 35, 44–5, 58–9, 116, 129–30, 130–1

New Zealand, 163
newspapers, 4; *see also* British Press; US press
Nicaragua, 121, 139–41
Nichols, Christopher, 85
Nigeria, 50
Nisei, 152
Nixon, Richard, 126
Nolan, Cathal, 131
Nome, 45
North Pole, 173, 174, 175
North West Company of Montreal (NWC), 37, 42
Northern Mariana Islands, 134n, 163–4, 164, 177n
Northern Sea Route, 171
Northwest Ordinance, 10–11
Northwest Passage, 171, 175
Northwest Territory, 11
Norway, 174
Nova Scotia, 36, 51
Nugent, Walter, 3

Obama, Barack, 169
Obama administration, 175
O'Connell, Dan, 57
Okinawa, 154
Oklahoma, 25, 26
Onea, Tudor, 46
Onís, Don Luis de, 15
Ontario, 33
Orange Plan, 107
Oregon, 36–41
Oregon Treaty, 40
Osborne, Thomas, 75
Ostend Manifesto, 63–4
Ostler, Jeffrey, 24
O'Sullivan, John L., 6n, 19, 62
Otis, Ewell, 106
Ottawa Declaration, 174
overseas bases, 169–70, 178n
　Guantanamo Bay, 165–9

Pacific Fur Company, 37
Pacific islands, 55–9, 66
Pacific Trust Territories, 162–5
Page, Sebastian, 54
Pago Pago, 115, 116, 119
Paine, Elijah, 53
Palau, 165
Palmyra Atoll, 59
Panama, 113, 120–7, 124
Panama Canal, 120–2, 123, 125–6, 131, 139
Panama Canal Zone (PCZ), 123, 125, 126
Papineau, Louis-Joseph, 34
Paris, 1763 Treaty of, 8
Paris, 1783 Treaty of, 10, 27n, 34
Paris, 1898 Treaty of, 83–4, 86, 94, 105
Patriot War, 33, 34
Peace Corps, 163
Pearl Harbor, 59, 73, 75, 109, 161
Peary, Robert, 172–3
Peary Arctic expedition, 172–3
Peel, Sir Robert, 38–9
Pérez, Louis A., Jr., 94, 138
Perry, Matthew C., 153
Peru, 55–6
Phelps, John W., 54
Philippine Organic Act *see* Jones Act
Philippines, 102–9, *103*
　anti-imperialism, 87
　German claim to, 85
　independence, 127
　land purchase, 83
　self-government, 87, 119
　Spanish-American War, 79–80
　unincorporated territory, 100
　see also Filipinos
Pinckney's Treaty, 14
Pierce, Franklin, 22, 57, 63, 64–5, 72, 144
Pig War, 41
Pinheiro, John, 20

Platt, Orville, 96
Platt Amendment, 96–7, 138, 141, 166–7, 168
Platte City, Missouri, 38
Plummer, Brenda Gayle, 142
Poland, 149
Polar Frontier, 171–6
Polar seas, 173–4
policy of attraction, 106, 107
Polk, James, K., 18
  annexation of Cuba, 62
  Mexican-American War, 19, 20, 21
  Oregon, 38, 39
popular revolt, Cuba, 62–3
popular sovereignty, 22, 69n, 88n
Portland Canal, 45
Potsdam Conference, 148
Powell, Lewis, 129
preclusive imperialism, 113
public opinion, 104–5, 107, 145–6
Puerto Ricans, 2, 85, 133n
Puerto Rico, 83, 87, 98–102, 109, 119, 162, 163, 168
Pulitzer, Joseph, 4, 79
Puritans, 23

Quebec, 34
Quezon, Manuel, 108, 109
Quitman, John, 64

racial hierarchy, 91n, 101, 151
racial integration, 85–6
racism, 142, 143
railroads, 22, 25, 121
Ramstein Air Base, 170
Reagan, Ronald, 126
Realpolitik, 114
reconcentrados, 77
re-concentration tactics, 106
Red River Colony, 38
referendums, 102
Renda, Mary, 143

Republic of Canada, 33
Republic of Hawaii, 75, 89n
Republic of Liberia, 54–5
Republic of Texas, 18–19
Republic of West Florida, 14
Republican Party
  American Samoa, 117
  anti-imperialism, 82
  Civil War, 156n
  Philippines, 108
  Puerto Rico, 102
  US election 1896, 78
  US election 1900, 87
reservations, 25, 26
resettlement of freed slaves, 50–2, 53, 54
Revolutionary War, 8, 10, 11
Rhineland, 146
Ricard, Serge, 123
Rio Grande, 20
Robinson, Edgar, 131
Rogers, Robert, 161
Roosevelt, Franklin
  Destroyers for Bases deal, 169–70
  Executive Order 9066, 152
  Good Neighbor Policy, 97, 141, 155n
  guano islands, 58
  Guantanamo Bay US Naval Base (GTMO), 168
  Teheran Conference, 147
Roosevelt, Theodore
  Alaska Purchase, 46
  Big Stick diplomacy, 140, 155n
  Japan, 108
  large policy, 78, 89n
  New Empire group, 166
  Panama, 122–3
  Panama Canal, 120–1, 123, 125
  Philippines, 104, 106, 107
  Spanish-American War, 78–80
  US election 1912, 112n

Roosevelt Corollary to Monroe Doctrine, 136–7
Roosevelt Roads, 168
Root, Elihu, 95–6, 97, 139
Ropp, Steve C., 126
Russia, 42–4, 48n, 171, 174, 175; see also USSR
Russian-American Company (RAC), 42–3
Ryukyu Islands, 153–4

Sacasa, Juan, 141
St Croix, 127
St John, 127, 129
St Thomas, 127, 129, 130
Salisbury, Marquis of, 73
Samana Bay, 144
Samana Bay Company, 145
Samoa see American Samoa
Samoza, Anastasio, 141
San Francisco, Treaty of, 153
San Ildefonso, Treaty of, 12
San Juan Island, 40–1
San Lorenzo, Treaty of, 14
Sand Island, 58–9
Sandino, Augusto, 141
Sandwich Islands, 71; see also Hawaii
Santa Anna, Antonio López de, 16
Santo Domingo, 156n; see also Dominican Republic
Schurman, Jacob Gould, 106
Scott, Winfield, 41
Second Boer War, 121
Second War of Independence see War of 1812
Second World War, 47, 58, 170, 173
self-determination, 127, 142, 143
self-government
    Class C mandate (League of Nations), 161
    Cuba, 94

International Trusteeship System, 162
Liberia, 52
Philippines, 87, 106, 119
Puerto Rico, 87, 119
Trust Territory of the Pacific Islands (TTPI), 163
Seminole tribe, 15, 24
Senate
    Alaska, 44
    Arctic, 175
    Dominican Republic, 144, 145, 146
    Hawaii, 72, 74, 76
    Nicaragua, 140, 141
    Panama Canal, 121
    Texas, 18, 19
    Treaty of Paris 1898, 83, 83–4
    US Virgin Islands, 129
Sergeants' Revolt, 168
settlers
    Alaska, 42
    Alta California, 20
    British North America, 31
    guano islands, 58
    Louisiana, 24
    North America, 25
    Oregon, 38
    Sand Island, 58–9
    Texas, 16, 18
    West Florida, 15
Seward, William, 34, 43–4, 129, 142, 144
Shawnee people, 24
Shelekhov, Grigori, 42
Sierra Leone, 51, 52, 53
Sierra Leone Company, 51
'Significance of the Frontier in American History, The' (Turner, [1893] 1947), 23
Sigsbee, Charles, 166
Silbey, David, 105
Sinclair, James, 38

INDEX

Sino-Japanese relations, 58, 108–9
Sioux, 26
Skaggs, Jimmy, 55
Skagway, 45
slavery
  abolition of, 16, 65, 66
  Cuba, 60, 62, 66
  Danish West Indies, 128
  Haiti, 142
  Kansas-Nebraska Act, 69n, 88n
  Missouri Compromise, 21–2
  Oregon, 39
  resettlement of freed slaves,
    50–2, 53, 54
  Texas, 18
Slidell, John, 19–20
Smith, Ephraim, 80
Smith, Goldwin, 36
SMS *Cormoran*, 161
Soulé, Pierre, 63–4
South Africa, 161
Southern states, 86
Soviet Union *see* USSR
Spain
  colonies, 84, 87
  Cuba, 60, 62, 63–4, 65–6
  Louisiana Purchase, 13
  Oregon, 48n
  Philippines, 102, 104
  Puerto Rico, 83, 98, 99
  Spanish East Indies, 159, 160
  Ten Years' War, 65–6, 76
  Transcontinental Treaty, 15–16
  Treaty of San Ildefonso, 12
Spanish East Indies, 159, 160
Spanish Florida, 8, 14
Spanish-American War, 1, 76–80,
    87
  anti-imperialism, 82
  Cuba, 92–3
  Hawaii, 70, 75
  Philippines, 102, 104, 109
  Puerto Rico, 98

spoils of war, 11
Stalin, Joseph, 150
statehood, 11
Statham, E. Roberts, Jr., 101, 111n
Status of Forces Agreements
  (SOFAs), 170
Steinberger, Albert B., 115
Stevens, John, 74
Stevenson, Adlai, 168
Stikine Lease, 43
Stimson, Henry, 141
Stoeckl, Edouard de, 44
Strong, Robert, 126
Stuart, Peter, 115
Suez Canal, 120–1
sugar industry, 72–3, 74, 75, 128
Sugar Intervention, 138
Sumner, Charles, 129, 145
Supreme Court, 100, 105
Sweden, 174

Taft, William Howard
  Cuba, 138
  Dollar Diplomacy, 140, 155n
  Dominican Republic, 145
  Nicaragua, 140
  Philippines, 106, 107–8
  US election 1912, 112n
Taiwan, 146
Taylor, Zachary, 20
Tecumseh, 24
Teheran Conference, 147
Teller, Henry Moore, 93
Teller Amendment, 93, 94, 95, 96
Ten Years' War, 65–6, 76
territorial expansion *see* expansion
Territory of Washington, 41
Texas, 16, 18–19, 20, 21, 38, 39
Texas Revolution, 18
Thames, Battle of the, 24
Thirteenth Amendment, 65
Three Saints Bay, 42
Thule Air Base, 173, 178n

Tompkins, E. Berkeley, 86
Torrijos, Omar, 126–7
trade, 32, 37, 42–3, 71, 72–3, 75, 95
Trail of Tears, 25
Transcontinental Treaty (Adams-Onís Treaty), 15–16, 48n
Treaty of 1818, 37
Treaty of Córdoba, 16
Treaty of Fort Wayne, 24
Treaty of Friendship, 71
Treaty of Ghent, 33, 37
Treaty of Guadalupe Hidalgo, 20–1, 22, 60, 62
Treaty of Paris 1763, 8
Treaty of Paris 1783, 10, 27n, 34
Treaty of Paris 1898, 83–4, 86, 94, 105
Treaty of San Francisco, 153
Treaty of San Ildefonso, 12
Treaty of San Lorenzo, 14
Treaty of Washington, 35, 41
Trieste, 146
Trist, Nicholas, 20
Trizonia, 150
Trudeau, Pierre, 175
Truman, Harry, 119, 162
Truman Doctrine, 149–50
Trust Territory of the Pacific Islands (TTPI), 162–5
Turner, Frederick Jackson, 23
Turpie, David, 86
Tutuila, 115
Tuvalu, 177n; *see also* Ellice Islands
Twain, Mark, 72, 85
Tydings-McDuffie Act, 108
Tyler, John, 18, 19, 28n
Tyrell, Ian, 12, 23

unincorporated territories, 59, 100–1, 105, 132, 162, 165
United Nations (UN), 162, 163, 175
Upper Canada, 33
US and Outlying Areas, 1970, 81

US citizenship
 American Samoans, 119
 Filipinos, 105
 Guam residents, 162
 Hawaiians, 72
 Mexicans, 20–1
 Northern Mariana Islanders, 134n
 overseas territories, 111n
 Puerto Ricans, 101, 133n
 unincorporated territories, 100–1
 US Virgin Islanders, 129, 132, 135n
US Congress
 American Colonization Society (ACS), 52
 American Samoa, 119
 Cuba, 65, 80, 96
 Guam, 161
 guano islands, 58
 Hawaii, 76
 Panama Canal, 121, 122
 Puerto Rico, 99–100
 US Virgin Islands, 132
US House of Representatives, 35, 44, 101–2, 108
US imperialism *see* American imperialism
US press, 77
 New York Times, 35, 44–5, 58–9, 116, 129–30, 130–1
 Washington Post, 46, 57–8, 117–18, 130, 133n, 173
 see also yellow press
US Senate
 Alaska, 44
 Arctic, 175
 Dominican Republic, 144, 145, 146
 Hawaii, 72, 74, 76
 Nicaragua, 140, 141
 Panama Canal, 121
 Texas, 18, 19

INDEX 223

Treaty of Paris 1898, 83, 83–4
US Virgin Islands, 129
US Supreme Court, 100, 105
US Virgin Islands, 113, 127–32, 128, 135n
USCGC *Polar Sea*, 174
USS *Charleston*, 160
USS *Maine*, 79, 92
USS *Nautilus*, 174
USS *Philadelphia*, 118
USS *Trenton*, 116
USSR, 147, 149, 150
Utah, 22

Van Buren, Martin, 18, 34
Vancouver Island, 40, 41
Vanderbilt, Cornelius, 139
Venezuela, 56
Vermont Republic, 11
Vernon, Edward, 165
Vietnam War, 153
Vine, David, 169, 170
Virgin Islands, 99; *see also* US Virgin Islands

Wake Island, 58, 67n
Walker, William, 139
War of 1812, 24, 32–3, 37, 47
War of Jenkins' Ear, 165
Washington, George, 10, 23, 85, 165
Washington, Territory of, 41
Washington Post, 46, 57–8, 117–18, 130, 133n, 173
Washington Treaty, 35, 41
waterboarding, 106
Webb, William H., 114
Webster-Ashburton Treaty, 34
Weinberg, Albert, 19
Welch, Richard E., Jr., 44
Weltpolitik, 114
West, Victor, 131
West Africa *see* Liberia
West Florida, 13, 14–15

West Germany, 150
western frontier, 23
Westward Expansion, 17
Weyler y Nicolau, Valeriano, 77–8
whaling industry, 71, 160
Whig Party, 18, 28n, 63
white elite, 72–3, 74
Wilhelm I, German Kaiser, 41, 113
Wilhelm II, German Kaiser, 113–14
Willamette Valley, 38
Williams, Justin, 151
Williams, Walter L., 3, 26–7, 105
Williams, William Appleman, 3
Wilmot, David, 22
Wilson, James H., 95
Wilson, Woodrow
  Cuba, 138
  Dominican Republic, 145
  Haiti, 142
  Nicaragua, 140–1
  Panama Canal Zone (PCZ), 125
  self-determination, 127, 143
  US election 1912, 108, 112n
  Virgin Islands, 130–1, 132
Winant, John G., 147
Windmill, Battle of the, 33
Wisconsin school, 3, 6n
women, 90n, 152, 157n, 158n; *see also* gender
Wood, Leonard, 95, 96, 108
Wooster, Robert, 25, 29n
World War I, 131, 132, 138, 145, 146, 160
World War II, 47, 58, 170, 173
Wounded Knee Massacre, 26

Yalta Conference, 147
yellow press, 78–9, 92
Yorubaland, 50
Yucatán province, 21

Zelaya, José, 139, 140
Zimmerman, James A., 90n
Zimmermann Telegram, 132

Series Editors: Martin Halliwell, Professor of American Studies at the University of Leicester; and Emily West, Professor of American History at the University of Reading.

The British Association for American Studies (BAAS)

The British Association for American Studies was founded in 1955 to promote the study of the United States of America. It welcomes applications for membership from anyone interested in the history, society, government and politics, economics, geography, literature, creative arts, culture and thought of the USA.

The Association publishes a newsletter twice yearly, holds an annual national conference, supports regional branches and provides other membership services, including preferential subscription rates to the *Journal of American Studies*.

Membership enquiries may be addressed to the BAAS Secretary. For contact details visit our website: www.baas.ac.uk

EU representative:
Easy Access System Europe
Mustamäe tee 50, 10621 Tallinn, Estonia
Gpsr.requests@easproject.com

www.ingramcontent.com/pod-product-compliance
Lightning Source LLC
Chambersburg PA
CBHW051810230426
43672CB00012B/2676